THE ARCHAEOLOGY OF AMERICAN
Childhood and Adolescence

JANE EVA BAXTER

Foreword by Michael S. Nassaney

University Press of Florida
Gainesville · Tallahassee · Tampa · Boca Raton
Pensacola · Orlando · Miami · Jacksonville · Ft. Myers · Sarasota

Copyright 2019 by Jane Eva Baxter
All rights reserved

This book may be available in an electronic edition.

24 23 22 21 20 19   6 5 4 3 2 1

Library of Congress Cataloging-in-Publication Data
Names: Baxter, Jane Eva, 1971– author. | Nassaney, Michael S., author of foreword.
Title: The archaeology of American childhood and adolescence / Jane Eva Baxter ; foreword by Michael S. Nassaney.
Other titles: American experience in archaeological perspective.
Description: Gainesville : University Press of Florida, 2019. | Series: The American experience in archaeological perspective | Includes bibliographical references and index.
Identifiers: LCCN 2018018486 | ISBN 9780813056098 (cloth : alk. paper)
Subjects: LCSH: Children—United States—History. | Children—United States—Social life and customs. | Social archaeology—United States.
Classification: LCC HQ792.U5 B39 2018 | DDC 305.230973—dc23
LC record available at https://lccn.loc.gov_2018018486

The University Press of Florida is the scholarly publishing agency for the State University System of Florida, comprising Florida A&M University, Florida Atlantic University, Florida Gulf Coast University, Florida International University, Florida State University, New College of Florida, University of Central Florida, University of Florida, University of North Florida, University of South Florida, and University of West Florida.

University Press of Florida
2046 NE Waldo Road
Suite 2100
Gainesville, FL 32609
http://upress.ufl.edu

The Archaeology of American Childhood and Adolescence

The American Experience in Archaeological Perspective

UNIVERSITY PRESS OF FLORIDA

Florida A&M University, Tallahassee
Florida Atlantic University, Boca Raton
Florida Gulf Coast University, Ft. Myers
Florida International University, Miami
Florida State University, Tallahassee
New College of Florida, Sarasota
University of Central Florida, Orlando
University of Florida, Gainesville
University of North Florida, Jacksonville
University of South Florida, Tampa
University of West Florida, Pensacola

Hey, Hudson! Check it out—Auntie Jane wrote a book for you. Thanks for sharing your amazing twenty-first-century American childhood with me! I love you, buddy!

CONTENTS

List of Figures   ix

Series Foreword   xi

Acknowledgments   xv

1. Archaeologies of American Childhoods   1

2. Material and Social Histories of Childhood and Adolescence in the United States   22

3. Children in Their Living Spaces: Nineteenth- and Twentieth-Century Domestic Sites   67

4. Institutions for Children and Children at Institutions   95

5. Children's Bodies and Commemorations of Children   124

6. The Archaeology and Material Culture of Contemporary Childhood   152

References Cited   181

Index   201

FIGURES

2.1. *David, Joana, and Abigail Mason* by Freake-Gibbs painter   27
2.2. Baby whistle and teething stick   29
2.3. Two children circa 1755–1760   33
2.4. *The Artist and His Family* by James Peale, 1795   34
2.5. *Band of Captives Driven into Slavery*   37
2.6. "Elsie Leslie as Little Lord Fauntleroy circa 1888"   40
2.7. Mid-nineteenth-century mechanical toy carousel   53
2.8. Mid-nineteenth-century child's plate   54
2.9. *Leave It to Beaver*: The Cleaver family   57
2.10. Christmas advertising in the *Chicago Tribune*, December 13, 1896   62
2.11. Advertisement for Erector Set toy, 1952   63
2.12. Photo of the Mouseketeers   65
3.1. A "typical" assemblage of children's artifacts   68
3.2. The sod house of Martinus B. Olson circa 1886   72
3.3. Stevens School playground, Allentown, Pennsylvania, 1903   80
3.4. Children working, New York, 1912, by Lewis Wickes Hine   82
3.5. "Playground in Tenement Alley, Boston MA 1909" by Lewis Wickes Hine   83
4.1. Archaeological work at the Old Edgebrook Schoolhouse   109
4.2. Writing slate   111
4.3. An example of a nineteenth-century institution for children   117
5.1. A series of nineteenth-century headstones for individual children of the same family   125
5.2. Photo of deceased child, a common nineteenth-century practice   127
5.3. A particularly elaborate child's headstone   139
5.4. A small marble pillow reading "Our Darling Walter"   140

5.5. A lamb resting on top of a child's headstone   142

5.6. Promotional still from the 1944 film *Meet Me in St. Louis* by Metro-Goldwyn-Mayer   146

5.7. "The William Channing Memorial in Mt. Auburn Cemetery"   147

5.8. Marbles excavated at the Haymarket Martyrs' Memorial   148

6.1. The iconic character of Veruca Salt   159

6.2. Barbie doll mother and child   168

6.3. McDonald's restaurant with prominent kids' Playland   173

FOREWORD

As the archaeology of gender came of age in the twentieth century, childhood and adolescence began attracting increasing attention from social archaeologists. An examination of the materiality of youth illuminates the American experience, since children are implicated in archaeological remains by virtue of their agency, omnipresence, and relationship to adults. If social relations structure the material world, then childhood is central to the organization of social groups and consequently integral to all archaeological inquiry into our national patrimony.

Childhood first gained currency in archaeological circles as researchers began looking for and identifying markers that could be directly linked to children and their daily practices. More recent studies are taking a subtler approach to the study of children by locating them in all American contexts across time, space, ethnicities, and class divisions. Once considered relatively disempowered and archaeologically invisible, children and adolescents have emerged as active agents who have exerted an influence on family structure, institutions, and legislation for centuries. Many scholars now recognize that childhood experiences are of fundamental importance in the lives of all adults. Material messages, cultural values, and proper behaviors are transmitted during youth and even before birth when expectant parents, particularly mothers, embrace maternal care in anticipation of a healthy fetus, safe delivery, and contented baby.

Early childhood experiences typically involve engagement with the material world, some of which are formative if not determinative of adult aspirations. My mother often recounted an early play activity that occupied me as an 18-month-old at the home of my paternal grandmother. Because I was the first of her twenty-five grandchildren, she had few toys at her house for my amusement; instead she encouraged me to spend countless hours with a large jar filled with buttons of varying materials, colors, shapes, and sizes. Arguably my first foray into typology led me to organize these buttons into groups based on similar attributes. This playful practice stimulated my power of observation, attention to detail, and visual memory, and perhaps led to my fascination with material culture.

Suitable playthings and activities differed between boys and girls and socialized children into culturally prescribed gender roles throughout history. As a boy of eight or ten years old, I was allowed to wander to the local sandlot to play baseball and other seasonal sports, in contrast to my three younger sisters who were tethered closer to home. During my adolescence, I frequently escaped with a group of male friends to a wooded area adjacent to the local mill pond to build a clubhouse from recycled and pilfered lumber where we established a place to mimic adult behaviors away from the prying eyes of our elders. There were clear differences in the liberties that my parents allowed me compared to my siblings, that went beyond birth order, though this was also significant. These personal accounts suggest that childhood is marked by similarities and differences over time and space.

In *The Archaeology of American Childhood and Adolescence*, Jane Baxter highlights some of the patterns that archaeologists and historians have observed in the materiality afforded to and by children. She has been among the most vocal proponents of the significance of childhood as a subject of archaeological inquiry and a social construction—a relational category—that cannot be conceived apart from parenting. Moreover, she recognizes that material culture is integral to the process of contesting and negotiating identity. Thus, not only is childhood amenable to archaeological investigation, but it is incumbent upon archaeologists to interrogate the material world with childhood in mind because every category of evidence implicates children, not merely toys, games, and other amusements.

Children have been and continue to be everywhere in historic and contemporary America and are important cultural agents. Furthermore, everyone was once a child. In her historical overview, Baxter rightly notes that the ways in which American childhood is constructed, idealized, transformed, and "lost" left an indelible mark on the American landscape and psyche, and material culture played a significant role in all of these practices, underscoring the potency and potential of archaeology to illuminate childhood and adolescence in the American experience.

Baxter discusses important changes in the ways in which childhood has been defined over the past few centuries, with the emergence of adolescence in the early twentieth century, yet she avoids a strictly chronological approach to the subject and features youngsters in domestic settings (rural, urban, and industrial), institutions, and death. In each of these contexts, she provides relevant case studies to illuminate what archaeology can tell us about the activities of children that went unrecorded. What emerges is a mosaic of action that delineates the efforts of adults to construct literal and conceptual spaces for children and how children enacted their own strategies to assert themselves and their material desires. The "pestering power of children" is but one example that illustrates how children at a very young age can insert themselves into the wider arena of the marketplace, even in the absence of disposable income.

The richness of Baxter's theoretical insights and revelations causes us to ponder why children had been underappreciated for so long. She reasons that sites with children's objects are underreported due to the prevalence of compliance-driven archaeology and the avoidance of "small finds" in favor of more frequently encountered artifacts. The occasional clay marble, miniature tea cup fragment, and lead whizzer provide limited data for meaningful analyses of youth culture and reduce children to their play. As Baxter notes, the "tyranny of toys" represents very large populations of people through a very small proportion of the artifacts they encountered and engaged with in their daily lives. Nevertheless, episodic events associated with limited finds may be quite expressive, as in archaeological evidence of highly fragmented doll heads that had been brutally and intentionally smashed in clear acts of violence. Clearly, toys are but one dimension of the lives of children who created imaginative worlds in their own backyards, sought play areas away from grown-ups, and simultaneously required surveillance by adults. For example, nineteenth-century middle-class homes included nurseries in proximity to women's work spaces such as the kitchen, providing testimony to the role of women in children's lives and the regard mothers placed on their offspring.

Baxter also points to the complexity of the relationships between children, gender, and associated cultural values regarding the ways identity should be expressed and inculcated and at what age. For example, while toys, as but one case, were often gendered (e.g., dolls and soldiers), dress and hairstyle have been much more androgynous at times in the past. My sisters and I recall with some hilarity a formal studio photograph taken in about 1926 of my father (two years old) and his slightly older brother (four years old) donning what appeared to be very feminine-looking bob haircuts and frilly frocks. Baxter explains that clothing and hairstyles were meant to hide sexual expressions among children in the late nineteenth and, apparently, into the early twentieth century. This stands in stark contrast with the pervasive pink and blue color signification later in the century that marked the identities of girls and boys respectively, especially among infants and toddlers.

In the latter half of the twentieth century, young middle-class children were furnished materially by their parents, family, and friends at baby showers, birthday parties, and other gift-giving events. However, school-age children soon desired trendy goods advertised in the media and reinforced during encounters with a peer culture that valued and prized some objects and styles over others. Conversely, they also determined which products to eschew. I learned this lesson when my son came home from preschool vowing to never wear a purple shirt and pants outfit that he liked so much; he had been admonished by his four-year-old peers for choosing clothing of an unacceptable color!

In the final chapter of the book, Baxter turns her attention to contemporary archaeology, noting that contemporary childhood must be appreciated in its own right and understandings derived from it cannot be extended into the past. To employ a hackneyed phrase, understanding context is essential. Baxter observes several trends in the twenty-first century: children have replaced fathers as the central focus of families; parents are extremely indulgent with their children; and adolescence often extends well beyond one's twenty-fifth birthday. Parents allow children greater independence and yet are increasingly concerned with their safety. Finally, children have become one of the most significant consumer forces in America, responsible for literally billions of dollars in sales, much of it in electronic and digital forms. While some lament that the dematerializing of children's worlds into the digital domain will doom the archaeology of childhood and adolescence to the dustbins of history, suffice it to say that children's impact on contemporary society is unlikely to wane. Witness the recent movement for gun reform (#ENOUGH!) as an example of the power of the people. In America, almost anything is possible, and children have proven to form enduring love affairs with a wide array of distractions and attractions from Barbie and G. I. Joe to Easy-Bake Ovens, Rubik's Cubes, video games, and other activities that make the twenty-first century the age of the indoor child. Whatever the future may hold for unborn generations, rest assured that archaeological insight will be welcome as present and future archaeologists continue to decipher the role of childhood and adolescence in the American experience.

Michael S. Nassaney
Series Editor

ACKNOWLEDGMENTS

It's been over a decade since Michael Nassaney first asked me to write a book on childhood and adolescence for his series on the archaeology of the American experience. When he first asked, I had just completed my first book on the archaeology of childhood and I told him I'd love to do the project, but only once I felt I had something new and worthwhile to say. That time has most certainly come, and the field of archaeology has expanded and embraced childhood studies in a variety of creative and unexpected ways. Historical archaeology is not at the forefront of many of these changes, but studies of children and childhood have emerged and are developing in the field, making this book a timely contribution. I am grateful to Michael for the opportunity to write this book and for his patience in allowing it to be penned at a time that made sense in the intellectual context of our discipline rather than a time that suited the production goals of the series. His encouragement and guidance were so very important as I crafted this manuscript.

I am also grateful to the many authors whose work I share in the pages of this book for their thoughtful and useful contributions to archaeology and to the study of childhood in the past. I also owe a debt of gratitude to the other authors in this series. I was greatly nourished by the contributions that these authors have made toward an archaeological exploration of the American past, and delving into this book series was essential to how I formulated my approach to this project. I also want to thank Meredith Babb for being such a patient, trusting, and encouraging editor. Teresa Krauss at Springer deserves a shout-out for all of the advice on publishing she's given me over the past several years. Finally, in terms of editorial thanks, I am very lucky that one of my dearest friends is also an incredibly experienced and talented editor (now retired)—so, thank you, Mitch Allen, for being a constant source of wisdom, humor, and encouragement in my life and behind this project.

Being among the first to write about something in a field offers an incredible opportunity but can also be incredibly isolating. I am so fortunate that my work on the archaeology of childhood has brought me into a community of incredibly engaged, thoughtful, and creative scholars. As we are all watching our scholarship become increasingly embraced and accepted in our disciplines as important and significant work, we are all also aware of the scholarly community we have created that offers so much mutual support and encouragement—often across continents and disciplinary boundaries. So, many thanks to my fellow scholars on childhood in the past for all of your encouragement and for the many opportunities you have brought to my career. I owe thanks to so many of you, but want to particularly thank Kathy Kamp, Jo Sofaer, Meredith Ellis, Shauna Vey, Grete Lillehammer, Sally Crawford, Dawn Hadley, Sían Halcrow, Eileen Murphy, Marga Sanchez-Romero, Leslie Van Gelder, and especially Traci Ardren, for all you have done to help further my interests and thinking about childhood in the past.

My archaeological community is so very large, and I cannot possibly thank all of the colleagues who support my career in so many ways. I owe a debt of gratitude to everyone who has been an ally and supporter throughout my career—thank you. I am so lucky that so many of my archaeology colleagues are people I count among my friends. Thank you to Gordon Rakita, Caryn Berg, John Douglass, Steven Silliman, Uzma Rizvi, Yorke Rowan, Sunday Eiselt, Shannon Dawdy, Deb Rotman, Rebecca Graff, Mary Jane Berman, Perry Gniveki, April Kamp-Whittaker, John Norder, April Beisaw, Alice Yao, Zoe Crossland, Brian Boyd, Sonya Atalay, Natasha Lyons, and Kisha Supernant—all of whom have been important sounding boards, cheerleaders, and mentors to me at different times in my career and throughout this project. I also want to thank several women who have taken the time to offer me support and encouragement at several important junctures in my career. Thank you Meg Conkey, Lynne Goldstein, Patricia McAnany, Joyce Marcus, and Carla Sinopoli. Thank you also to Tobi Brimsek, executive director of the SAA, who has mentored me in my career since I was a graduate student. To all my #archaeotwitter peeps—I love you guys so much! Thanks for being such an amazingly supportive and fun community in the social media world and at our real world meet-ups. To my DePaul colleagues, Morag Kersel, Marcia Good, John Mazzeo (and Ruth and the boys!), and Chris Milan—thank you for all the balance you bring into the workplace and the friendship you bring into my world.

Maintaining a work-life balance is essential for me and I am grateful to the many friends I have outside of my profession who have enriched my life and offered many pleasant distractions as I produced this work. Many thanks to Astrid Fingerhut, Paul Belloni, John White, David Schultz, Betty Stephenson, Blaine Parks, Debbie Robes, Diane Richards, Debbie Slayton, Aaron Hunt, John Quintero, Morgan Krause, Arlene Nash Ferguson, Silbert Ferguson, Karen Millett, Kimberly Leger, Michael Leger, Cindy Manson, Sharona Jacobs, Jody Nardone, Alex Mack, Liz Theran, Lauren Bigelow, and Barbara Tresback, for your ongoing friendship and support. Thanks to my guitar teacher, Josh, my ceramics instructor, Dee Smith, and my tattoo artist, Dawn Grace (and Brennan!), for cultivating my interests beyond academia and putting up with my hectic schedule.

I also have a handful of friends who are like family, and they deserve a very special acknowledgment for their many, many years of devoted friendship. Thank you, Amanda Sprochi, Megan Perry, April Nowell, Jen Meizels, and Melissa Hall-Devine. A very special acknowledgment must be made to my brother Jay and my two closest friends who are indeed my chosen family: Carole McGranahan and John Burton. The three of you have been on the front lines of all the ups and downs, triumphs and failures, and joys and sorrows that make up a life—my life. You are always there whenever I need you, and you give me the strength and courage to be myself even when the world would make it far easier to do otherwise. I love you all so dearly, and am so grateful for the happiness, support, and love you bring to my world.

Finally, thanks to my family. My parents, John and Sheila Jalutkewicz supported my decision to become an archaeologist beginning at age 15, and invested a great deal of financial and emotional capital to make my career dreams come true. They still read everything I write, even though they generally claim not to know what I am writing about. Thanks to my sister-in-law Ginny and my nephew Hudson, to whom this book is dedicated, for being such fun companions in all kinds of family adventures. Samantha Aislynn Dourney and James I. Dourney—you have come into my life and brought me so many things I didn't even know were missing. I love you both. And to Jim—my best friend, life partner, and the very best thing that has ever happened to me in this wonderful and rich life. Thank you for being so incredibly supportive in big and little ways, and for being the best adventure partner a girl could ask for. You are my everything—I love you, babe!

1

Archaeologies of American Childhoods

Writing a book on the American experience from any angle is a daunting task. The very term "America" is a protean concept that is heartily debated and contested at any given moment of the nation's history, and has shifted profoundly with the growth and development of the nation. The diversity of the American population rests at the core of this mythological, singular identity as a "melting pot," and the multiplicity of human experiences that can be reasonably termed "American" makes any concise summation a challenge. As Stacey Camp (2013) illustrates in her book on the archaeology of citizenship, ideas about identity on a national scale are most visible archaeologically at broader levels of institutions, communities, and social movements rather than at more intimate scales such as the internal dynamics of family life. While ideas of childhood and adolescence are germane at these broader scales, the lives of children and adolescents are quite often defined and understood in more intimate, interpersonal terms and are perhaps most often archaeologically visible at domestic sites and in moments of individual commemoration and loss. In her recent book on American childhood, historian Paula Fass (2016) addresses explicitly this tension of bridging scales between the personal world of the family and broad sweeping ideas of America. She notes that, despite the difficulties inherent in such an endeavor, there is a deep and abiding relationship between the two arenas that demands historical attention.

Archaeological work on the American past suggests archaeologists share this sentiment. The idea of "becoming American" has been an enduring theme in historical archaeology, where broad ideas of identity, worldview, and membership have been connected to the fragmentary remains of daily lives and the mundane objects that structure the material world (Deetz 1977; Loren and Beaudry 2006). The idea of becoming and the idea of America have been invoked together in archaeological studies of early contact, the formation of the republic, and later experiences of immigrants throughout the nineteenth and twentieth centuries. Loren and Beaudry (2006: 255) have actively critiqued this idea in saying, "The words 'becoming American' evoke a process by which people in early America created (using material culture, of course) identities that could be described as *American*." This idea of moving toward a singular sense of identity is erroneous, as people are often negotiating multiple, often conflicting identities simultaneously, and the diversity of how America is understood as part of this negotiated, often political process is a much more realistic understanding of life in the past than any singular notion of "Americanness."

Contemporary childhood is also commonly understood as a time of becoming as well as of being, creating a poignant parallel between these concepts. Childhood, like America, is a social construction that is historically, culturally, and socially variable, and the meaning of childhood is negotiated both in public discourse and in interpersonal relationships (Mintz 2004). The definition and maintenance of the social category of childhood depends on multiple types of discourse. There are adult discourses about childhood produced primarily for adults, and others produced by adults for children. Children also actively negotiate their categorical identity among themselves and with adults. Material culture is integral to all of these types of discourse, as these contested and negotiated identities are embodied and performed in the material world as integral aspects of people's daily lives.

Childhood is a category that is both relational and ideological. It is primarily defined by its opposition to the category of adulthood, and can be internally expanded and contracted to include multiple stages and phases of nonadulthood, including the concept of adolescence. Childhood is also a set of meanings that are informed by an ideology, which "serves to rationalize, to sustain, or to challenge existing relationships of power between adults and children, and indeed between adults themselves" (Buckingham 2000: 11). Given these understandings of the interrelationships that create childhood in a historical moment, the archaeology of childhood is perhaps best understood as the archaeology of everyone undertaken from a vantage point that offers unique and potent ways of exploring shared experiences of family, community, and nation.

Writing about the archaeology of childhood in the American experience is an exercise in capturing a moving target, and normalizing categories of identity that are characterized by diversity and contestation at any given moment in time. Accomplishing this task requires a great deal of selectivity in case material and a multidisciplinary arsenal of sources. This chapter sets the stage by delving into the works of historians and others who have already attempted diachronic studies of American childhood, as well as exploring the disciplinary basis for studying children archaeologically. Resulting from these summations are a series of strategies for defining a broad and complex topic, and themes that transcend historical changes, site types, and categories of material culture when thinking about childhoods and adolescences that are particularly American.

What Is an American Childhood? A Historical and Thematic Approach

The landscape is becoming crowded with historical considerations of what constitutes an "American" childhood. Beginning in the 1980s, edited volumes addressing aspects of American childhoods emerged on the scholarly landscape (e.g., Hawes and Hiner 1985; Hiner and Hawes 1985) and became quite influential, as did historical monographs focusing on American childhoods in particular regions, time periods, and topical perspectives (e.g., Ashby 1997; Berrol 1995; Calvert 1992; Clement 1997; Graff 1997; West 1989). The twenty-first century has seen historians tackle America as a concept for understanding childhood in relationship to particular topics such as play (Chudacoff 2007) and nature (Riney-Kehrberg 2014), and for examining the diversity of childhood through different populations including slaves, pioneers, farmers, and urban laborers (Fass 2016; Mintz 2004). Authors of these works have each developed their own unique approach to handling time and change when telling the American story. Most often, the issue of change takes on a tone of marked declension, with American childhood being increasingly lost to interventionist parents and concerns for risk, health, and safety (Buckingham 2000; Chudacoff 2007). Historians are situated in the present contemplating contemporary childhoods through a historical lens, and are seeking causal connections to explain how we got here. Archaeologists are, too, making it a useful endeavor to start an archaeological study of American childhood with a thematic review of the works of these historians.

For some historians (e.g., Chudacoff 2007; Riney-Kehrberg 2014), writing a history of American childhood is an endeavor that seeks to understand childhood experiences within the geographical and social confines of America along a timeline of American history. The "Americanness" of these childhoods is not particularly problematized as being different from contemporaneous childhoods elsewhere, only that the specificity of the narrative can be understood as springing from a particular set of historical circumstances that is American. Other authors, particularly Mintz (2004) and Fass (2016), attempt to complicate the "American" in "American childhood" by suggesting ways in which childhood was uniquely constructed in specifically American contexts.

Regardless of the particular trajectory of the work, there is a narrative thread that runs through all of these histories. The works begin with the colonial period of the seventeenth century or at the dawn of the eighteenth and continue into the late nineteenth century, describing childhoods that, while highly variable, are generally filled with opportunity, freedom, and possibility. Beginning in the late nineteenth century, reform movements and new scientific ideas about optimizing childhood enter into the discourse and, as a result, American childhood enters into a period of decline. This decline accelerates in the later twentieth century until it reaches its current woeful state of the present day. While some authors fully embrace this declension model for American childhood (e.g., Chudacoff 2007), others engage more critically with the notion of the loss of childhood but engage it because it is part of the rhetoric that permeates the primary documentary record (Buckingham 2000; Fass 2016; Mintz 2004; Riney-Kehrberg 2014). This common narrative strain is not only important because it offers a causal historical model for American childhood, but also because it provides an understanding of the formation of ideals and myths about American childhoods that were developed early in the nation's history. It is the perceived loss of these ideals that has led to this sense of declension which pervades contemporary rhetoric about American childhood (Buckingham 2000). In other words, it is the very nature of these narratives of decline and diminution that illuminates particular characteristics thought of as quintessential to the American childhood experience.

For Steven Mintz, this pervasive articulation of and belief in the decline and loss of childhood itself is an inherent feature of American attitudes toward childhood throughout history. He begins his 2004 book, *Huck's Raft*, by saying,

> For more than three centuries Americans have believed that the younger generation is less respectful and knowledgeable, and more alienated, sexually promiscuous, and violent than previously. Today adults fear children are growing up too fast and losing their sense of innocent wonder too early. Prematurely exposed to the pressures, stresses, and responsibilities of adult life, the young mimic adult sophistication, dress inappropriately, and experiment with alcohol, drugs, sex, and tobacco before they are emotionally and psychologically ready. (vii)

Indeed, Mintz believes the role of history is to debunk the myths that make such nostalgia and pessimism possible. Childhood has never been insulated from the world of adults, for most children childhood has not been an age of innocence, and for most of history the majority of American children were not well cared for, nor were their experiences idyllic (see Ashby 1997). Childhood generally was not and is not carefree—children have to cope with all types of pressures brought on by society at large. Mintz also argues that the United States is not a particularly child-friendly society despite idealized protestations otherwise: Americans were and are actually largely ambivalent about children.

Mintz's assertions point both to the relational and ideological constructions of childhood operating in the American past, and the ways that they are contested in contemporary and historical contexts. These historical studies further underscore these aspects of childhood in that they are just as much about parenting and family dynamics as they are about children. Particularly, histories of American childhood trace the changing dynamics of power between parents and children, especially the increasing parental investment in children over time. Including parents and families in studies of American childhood does not marginalize childhood as a topic, but rather provides a way to emphasize that children are active agents and participants in society and in historical and cultural change.

Beyond a pervasive tone of declension and the need to understand childhood in terms of particular cultural constructions, a sense arises from these works that there is a childhood that can be identified as particularly American. What is this American childhood that was once celebrated and is now lamented as lost? In reviewing these historical treatments of American childhood, I would argue that there are five distinct themes that emerge across the literature that can help define and problematize American childhood. These themes are not used to organize the subsequent chapters of this work but rather transcend and permeate the discussions of childhood that follow.

Theme 1: Risk and Opportunity

America is still often characterized as a land of opportunity where hard work and entrepreneurial spirit can lead to successes that would not and could not happen elsewhere. According to Paula Fass (2016), America was most certainly a land of opportunity in the nation's colonial period and early years as a republic, particularly for its children. She argues that American childhoods were characterized by flexibility and choice in many social arenas that were constricted in other parts of the world, supported by an abundance of resources that could be acquired by individuals growing up in the country, and enabled by relaxed legal strictures that limited the power of inheritance. In contemporary European societies, these same dimensions served to keep children following in the footsteps of their parents. Children were required to apprentice in the trades of their parents—a family dynamic underscored by surnames indicating occupations, such as Miller, Smith, or Baker. Land was scarce and only acquired through inheritance, which generally only applied to male children. Girls and women relied on marriage to determine their futures, and making a good marriage match for daughters was an important endeavor for many families. Children in America had the possibility of acquiring their own land and determining their own occupations and futures in ways that were unimaginable in Europe. Of course, striking out on one's own offered prospects and opportunities, but also came with considerable risk. Fass notes

Americans were prosperous and their opportunities seemed without limit. Their children could move in directions not even imagined by the previous generation. With seemingly endless landed resources, a dynamic economy, and laws that did not restrict them to following in their parents' path, succeeding generations could define their own futures. This appeared to liberate generations from each other to create a dazzling sense of change. . . . These images also conveyed risk, both for children and the parents. Parents had less influence and children were on their own. Parents would have less power to control: and children, fewer shoulders to lean on. (2016: 1)

The ability for American children to choose their own futures very much changed the meaning of childhood in the new nation, and altered relationships between generations. Obviously, this generalized view of opportunity and risk shifted circumstantially among the diverse families of America, but in general, members of each generation were offered at least the possibility of changing their circumstances and forging their own path. They also were offered the chance to make mistakes with significant consequences. Parental influence and power decreased in American families, and children lost some of the safety and security of tight intergenerational bonds accentuated by residential proximity. Outsiders such as Alexis de Tocqueville encountered American children and described them as uniquely independent and relatively empowered, noting that there was no need for a period of adolescence, because even young children exercised so much freedom from their parents.

Opportunity and risk are tied to ideas of freedom. They are also tied to broader ideas about the decline and loss of American childhood. As parents and adults began to reassert control over the lives of children during the late nineteenth and early twentieth centuries, the risks to their health, safety, and economic and social well-being were reduced, but, many would argue, so were the essential freedoms needed to become independent, opportunity-seeking Americans.

Theme 2: Diversity

It is impossible to conduct any social study of America, past or present, without tackling the idea of diversity. Diversity in American childhoods was the norm from the very beginning of the colonies (Marten 2007; Mintz 2004) when many different groups of Europeans arrived, bringing enslaved Africans from myriad cultural traditions and encountering diverse Native American cultures. Once established as a new nation, America became a place of opportunity and refuge and waves of immigrants have continued to enter into the country to this day. Who is a child? How should a child be raised? How are children included in shifting ideas of family and community identity? How are these ideas altered and modified as cultures come into contact and as that contact becomes sustained? The range of diversity in American childhoods is too vast for any one work to capture.

The chronological organization of historical works on childhood emphasizes the variability of American childhoods over time, as ideals about childhood and childhood experiences changed with the country. The second organizing principle of these works tends to be geography—comparing the urban with the rural, the East with the West, and the North with the South in one fashion or another. Pamela Riney-Kehrberg (2014) goes a step further and explicitly makes the case that geography is and was responsible for differences in childhood experiences more so in the large, vast nation of America than elsewhere in the world. Beyond these broad vectors of time and space for creating and capturing diversity, Mintz (2004) notes there are a variety of ways that the diversity of American childhood can be addressed, particularly age, gender, class, ethnicity, and religion. Because source materials are variable for different populations, it is impossible to address the diversity of childhood in all of its complexity, but it is essential to continually acknowledge that no singular experience of childhood has ever existed in the past, American or otherwise.

Diverse childhoods have always been the norm in America, but rarely have they been welcome by those in positions of power. Histories of American childhoods are filled with information about institutions and programs that, beyond whatever specific charge they were created to fill, were also attempts to minimize cultural diversity in America. Often children were particularly targeted by institutions, as it was believed that they could influence older generations of their families, or effectively be alienated from them and their traditions. Public schools not only became mandatory, but also were designed to assimilate immigrant children into the American "mainstream" (Berrol 1992). Orphanages, asylums, and poorhouses took in children deemed unfit, at risk, or tainted by the choices and actions of their parents, so they might be made productive members of society (Pazicky 1998). More perniciously, American Indian boarding schools physically relocated children away from their families in attempts to break cultural bonds and family ties in order to eradicate the intangible heritage of America's indigenous populations (Surface-Evans 2016). Ironically, these institutions, designed to eliminate cultural diversity, have become among the best sources for scholars seeking to understand the diversity of childhood experiences and ideals about childhood in the American past.

Theme 3: Consumerism

The relationship of children to material culture and consumer culture is an enduring theme in general historical treatments of American childhood (Calvert 1992) and is a subject that also has generated a large body of scholarship in its own right (e.g., Buckingham 2000; Cross 1997, 2004; Forman-Brunell and Whitney 2015; Jacobson 2008a; Ringel 2008). The material accessorizing of childhood from infancy through adolescence and beyond is also a critical part of contemporary popular American discourse about childhood. In 2008, Americans spent over five billion dollars on purchases for or directly influenced by children (Jacobson 2008a). How American children have become such a consumer power is of particular concern to historians as well as contemporary parents. This widespread concern is indeed very fortunate for archaeologists, as there is a rich context for understanding the material culture we encounter in the archaeological record.

America was not a nation for very long before the Industrial Revolution shifted populations to urban centers, transformed the production of material goods, and restructured society around markets for labor and mass-produced objects. By the late nineteenth century, mass-produced goods for children were becoming increasingly common, but these goods were still advertised to parents as gifts for Christmas and occasionally birthdays. The twentieth century saw a marked shift on the part of advertisers from targeting parents as the primary decision makers around children's toys and playthings, to relying on the "pestering power" of children to persuade adults to buy particular goods on their behalf (Jacobson 2008a). The purchasing of children's toys became a year-round event, and not one reserved for holidays. Department stores created large toy departments, and mail-order catalogues devoted an increasing number of pages to toys and objects for children. "Pestering power" as a tool for marketers was extended to other household objects beyond toys.

The fact that American children have long spent extended periods of time away from home in public schools has helped to fuel consumerism among children. Peer cultures that developed away from parental influence resulted in the development of longings for goods considered cool, desirable, and trendy (Cross 1997). While these longings may have been widespread, different circumstances of children and their families meant the ability to participate in consumer culture was not equal among children. Archaeologists have commonly interpreted toys and accessories for children as a deliberate choice and a prioritization of household funds on the part of parents, particularly to demonstrate an acceptance and awareness of childhood ideals operating in broader society. Because children consistently participated in social arenas outside the home, away from their parents, such material investments were important social signals to others.

Understanding these shifts in advertising strategies and changes in consumer practice is essential for archaeologists studying children in the American past. While toy types and styles may change little over several decades in time, the way these toys are advertised, the relative empowerment of the child consumer, and resulting family dynamics vary dramatically at different times in American history. Dialogues about the need to protect children from consumerism, from desiring material goods, and from the designs of crafty advertisers have accompanied these changes in childhood consumption, making toys and material culture central to understanding ideals about childhood and the relational constructions of adults and children throughout American history (Ringel 2008).

Theme 4: Space

Space is a natural theme for any archaeological endeavor, as it is an essential part of archaeological inquiry on multiple scales, including architecture, landscape, and social life (Pauls 2006). Space and place are also essential for understanding American childhood. The United States is a geographically expansive country that affords a multitude of diverse lifestyles to its citizens. Much of the nation's history has been characterized by expansion either in growth of available land or changing technologies enabling the exploitation of new resources. American children growing up in an expanding and expansive nation have developed particular sensibilities about space and place underscored by contemporary and historical understandings of possibility and opportunity fueled by geography. Ideas of possibility and opportunity in relationship to geography have changed over time, whether the initial expansion of colonists and pioneers to the West, or the contraction of agricultural populations into urban, industrial centers. Children and adolescents experienced these changes as broad national trends and also highly localized experiences of personal landscapes.

Historically, childhood experiences of space and place were geographically diverse but were differentiated along social lines as well. According to Riney-Kehrberg (2014: 3), "Children's experiences of the places in their lives were mediated by a number of factors—geography, class, gender, race, and ethnicity to name a few. The influence of geography is perhaps the most obvious." In a geographic sense, it is clear a child growing up in rural Minnesota, in a gold rush town in Nevada, or a port city of the eastern seaboard experienced space and place in vastly different ways despite all having "American" childhoods. Experiences of place were also expanded or contracted depending on other social variables. Class, gender, and race were and are critical variables in the opportunities children have to use space. Prescriptions and proscriptions for using shared social spaces external to the home, the size and configuration of one's living space, and the landscapes provided for transportation, recreation, and education varied according to a child's social position and identity. These aspects of space had profound implications for children's health and well-being as well as social development.

Theme 5: Disruption Due to War and Warfare

Perhaps the most surprising theme to emerge from the review of the historical literature was the impact of war on American childhoods. It is worth noting that no generation of American children has grown up in the absence of war or its consequences. In earlier wars, teenagers were conscripted into military forces and younger children provided ancillary services to troops in camp and on the front lines. In all wars, children were parts of families and communities disrupted by the departure of (mostly) its male members. Homefront support efforts, the need to reorganize household and community labor, and the uncertainty of a war's outcome were parts of children's lives. For some families and communities, the need for more permanent reorganization of economic and social worlds persisted when those members who fought in the war never returned home.

Some of the earliest documentary sources of childhood in North America are stories of European children taken captive and raised by Native Americans and First Nations groups in the context of war with colonial arrivals (Mintz 2004). The American Revolution resulted in major social disruption, conscription, and a reorganization of society that had a significant impact on children and the nature of childhood (Marten 2009). Children served on both sides of the U.S. Civil War, and lived in homes disrupted by the absence of male family members. Orphanages and reform institutions were inspired by the demands for child labor and fractured family structures that were in large part consequences of the Civil War (Fass 2016). These trends in disruption and societal restructuring and the impact of being a "home front kid" continued during the world wars of the twentieth century (Tuttle 1993). Change in American childhoods can certainly be seen, in part, as connected to subtler and more gradual cultural changes, but the abrupt, disruptive, and persistent presence of war and its social and economic consequences are an essential part of understanding American childhood at any given moment, and over time.

This constant presence of war also has had a profound impact on the material culture developed for children, particularly objects designed for young boys. Toy soldiers, guns, and army-themed playthings have been common since the eighteenth century and particularly popular throughout the nineteenth and twentieth centuries (de Melo 2011). Toys encouraging young boys to pursue math, science, and technology, such as erector sets and home science kits, have been entangled with the need for future generations to keep the nation ready for changing technologies of war, more so than for times of peace (Pursell 2015).

The Archaeology of Childhood as a Field of Study

The archaeology of childhood has its own particular development as an area of study and distinct body of scholarly literature to support its foundations. Beginning around 1990 and gaining traction in the early 2000s, scholarship emerged that critiqued the absence of children in archaeological interpretations and the biases that prevented archaeologists from seeing children both as valuable members of past societies and as viable subjects of archaeological inquiry (Baxter 2005; Crawford 1991; Kamp 2001; Lillehammer 1989; Roveland 2001; Sofaer 1994, 2000). The majority of authors engaged in this critique were coming from prehistoric and classical archaeology, but historical archaeology was certainly in the mix. The timing of this emergent interest in children was not exclusive to archaeology (see above) as scholars from a variety of disciplines in the humanities and social sciences were building on work focusing on gender and identity popularized in the 1970s and 1980s, and applying similar ideas and critiques to children and childhood (Baxter 2008). The emergence of childhood studies from gender studies was a logical extension of intellectual movements concerned with the consequences of ignoring populations previously considered "invisible" by researchers (e.g., Moore and Scott 1997). Simultaneously, researchers themselves were, and arguably are, living in a time when concerns for and about children are paramount, and an abundance of discourse surrounding children permeates popular culture and media. With children carrying such a place of prominence in society, it is no wonder that academics followed, tacitly or deliberately, in these interests.

Certainly, archaeologists mentioned children before the archaeology of childhood became an area of inquiry, but such mentions were largely in service of understanding the worlds of adults. Recognizing children as individuals with unique cultural knowledge and experiences, and acknowledging the agency that children exercise in the production, modification, and replication of both tangible and intangible culture, is central to the ways archaeologists studying childhood think about children in the past. The formative literature that led to this perspective for so many archaeologists can be summarized into four main points (Baxter 2015b).

First, children are absolutely everywhere. There is no documented society where children are not present in significant numbers, which means almost all archaeology involves children whether or not archaeologists choose to acknowledge their presence. Given this fact, not including or considering the possible presence of children when evaluating the archaeological record creates a biased and most likely inaccurate interpretation of life in the past. Historical archaeology in the United States is no exception, as at no time in American history have people under the age of 15 been less than half the population (Baxter 2000) and at times that demographic has been nearly two-thirds of the nation's populace (Marten 2007).

Second, archaeologists are significantly biased in their understandings of childhood because of their own upbringings in modern Western societies that tend to characterize children as people who are primarily learning to be adults. Recently, Baxter (2016) has argued that childhood is different from other categories of identity studied by archaeologists (see Clark and Wilkie 2007) because all nonchildren were once children themselves. The relational nature of childhood and the trajectory of human ontogeny combine in a way that means that all adults (or nonchildren) experienced childhood firsthand at some point in their lives. This experience gives people some sense of empathy and a feeling of understanding about how childhood is and should be. In most Western cultures, people only are considered significant contributors to social, economic, and political worlds once they reach adulthood, and an empathetic projection of such ideas about childhood into the past has marginalized the archaeological study of children.

The fact that childhood is culturally constructed not only means that expectations and understandings of contemporary childhood cannot be extended into the past, but also that there is the potential for significant variation in the definitions of who is a child and beliefs of what childhood should be like. Archaeologists have turned to ethnographic evidence to demonstrate that cultural constructions of childhood vary significantly across cultures. Some cultures elaborate the category of childhood to include multiple subcategories and embellish childhood as a distinct cultural phase, while others minimize differences between adults and children (Kamp 2001). Ethnographic sources also illustrate that children are important cultural actors and often make substantial economic and social contributions to their families and communities. Children also structure adult lives, resources, and priorities in variable but significant ways.

Finally, since the publication of Grete Lillehammer's 1989 article, considered by many to be the very first article on the archaeology of childhood, it has been demonstrated that every category of archaeological evidence analyzed to understand life in the past can and does reveal information about the lives of both adults and children. Children do not need to be "found" or "discovered," but rather archaeologists need to change their perspective to one that acknowledges the presence and value of the contributions of a variety of cultural actors, not just adults or those assumed to be important.

Substantive literature on the archaeology of childhood has grown significantly over the past two decades, and has expanded well beyond critique (Baxter 2017). When the first monograph on the archaeology of childhood was published there were fewer than 30 sources on children in archaeology, and approximately a third of those sources made the case for children being unknowable or archaeologically invisible (Baxter 2005). As this same work is entering into a second edition (Baxter forthcoming[a]) there are over 300 works on the archaeology of childhood in print including monographs, edited volumes, dissertations, master's theses, and an array of articles in archaeology and bioarchaeology. This tenfold increase in literature includes works that explore cultural constructions of childhood and age-graded categories in archaeology and bioarchaeology; address relational approaches to understanding social dynamics between adults and children in households and communities; engage the relationships among children, material culture, and landscape; interpret the intersection of childhood with other categories of identity such as race, gender, and class; investigate diet, health, and mortality in childhood populations; and present the power of children as idealized symbols in art and iconography. All of these works are examples of the types of rich interpretation that can come from recognizing the powerful perspective of childhood to understand life in the past and from complicating the archaeological interpretive sphere to include cultural actors of multiple ages and genders.

It has been argued that archaeology of childhood has a somewhat different trajectory within the discipline of historical archaeology, as Suzanne M. Spencer-Wood (2014) recently noted that most research on children typically has been integrated into broader research topics, such as parenting, social status, and education or in the investigation of broader socializing institutions such as schools and orphanages. Children certainly do make appearances in earlier literature in historical archaeology, but this does not mean that children or childhood have been included as an integral part of research until relatively recently (Wilkie 2000). For example, practitioners of historical archaeology have long defined the discipline and often championed it as a form of research that restores lost voices to history. In the well-known and groundbreaking work *Those of Little Note* (Scott 1994), children are not found in the index, and they are not an active subject in any of the chapters, even those that discuss institutions for children such as kindergartens. Similarly, the 1994 book *A Chesapeake Family and Their Slaves: A Study in Historical Archaeology* (Yentsch 1994), which has children depicted on the cover, has virtually nothing to say about the family's children in the pages of the volume. Even more recent works by historical archaeologists addressing constructed identities in the past do not give much time or space to children (e.g., Voss 2006). This is not an exercise in fault finding, but rather a way of pointing out that archaeological approaches that are truly inclusive of children are also a very recent development in historical archaeology as well.

Laurie Wilkie (2000) levied such a critique on the field when she noted that previous nods to the study of childhood in historical archaeology were not because of any "superior or enlightened interpretive or theoretical frameworks, but rather an artefact of the material culture that historical archaeologists study" (2000: 100). Wilkie was referring to the fact that beginning in the mid-nineteenth century, objects readily identified as having been manufactured, marketed, and sold with children in mind enter into archaeological assemblages, making children easier to recognize in the past and at the very least demanding that an acknowledgment of their presence be included in archaeological interpretations. Historical sites also include institutions such as schools and orphanages that are known to have been developed specifically for children, which also requires an acknowledgment that children were present.

At the time of her critique, Wilkie (2000) noted that there was much to be done with the material culture of childhood that historical archaeologists so often recover, and offered several ideas about how to interpret material culture for children in ways that have been influential in subsequent studies. She argued that toys serve as a valuable medium of symbolic communication between adults and children, and among children themselves. The material provisioning of children with particular types of objects and the investment in institutions for children also served to send messages between families and the broader community. Dialogues of control and resistance between adults and children and between families and communities are an essential part of how the relational and ideological boundaries of childhood are maintained and altered. As dialogues are two-sided, such an approach empowers children as independent social actors and not simply the receivers of adult ideas, objects, and agendas. It is these types of studies that make up the core of the material presented in this book—those that engage the idea of children as actors, interpret archaeological sites with children present in the past, and consider the relationships between children and adults as dynamic and multifaceted.

The Organization and Contents of This Book

This book is a departure from the extant literature on American childhood in that it is not organized first and foremost by chronology. Instead, this work is structured by the available archaeological literature on children in historical archaeology, and is organized by the types of archaeological sites where evidence for children has been interpreted and published. This strategy emerged from a review of the literature itself, which has its own inherent limitations and biases.

This work replicates a very traditional and unfortunate divide in archaeology of the historic period in America as it largely, but not entirely, omits archaeological and historical studies of Native American children (Lightfoot 1995). This omission is due largely to constraints of space, as the diversity of Native American childhoods at the time of contact and throughout American history is too large a topic to integrate into this work. Focusing primarily on European immigrants and their descendants, as well as enslaved and free Africans and their descendants, creates ample challenges for representing the diversity of childhoods experienced in the American past.

One of the ironies of compiling a synthetic work on children in historical archaeology is the knowledge that there are quite literally thousands of archaeological sites where objects readily identified as relating to children have been found, but the overwhelming majority of those finds have never been published or are otherwise inaccessible. The chasm between the discovery of children's material culture and the reporting of such discoveries stems from, I believe, two major factors. First, the majority of historical archaeology in the United States is undertaken as part of cultural resource management (CRM) projects, and rarely are the results of those projects widely or publicly disseminated. Because CRM produces such a large body of literature, creating a systematic strategy to delve into reports to find small mentions and summaries of artifacts relating to children would be impractical. Instead, it is necessary to rely on reports that have been made accessible online or through other, personal channels. Similar issues have been encountered by other authors in this series, notably Rothschild and Wall (2014), who lamented the inability to access CRM-related data on urban archaeology in the United States, resulting in sporadic coverage of such work in their volume.

The second issue derives from a larger tradition in archaeological interpretation that favors the reporting of large assemblages of artifacts that can be analyzed using quantitative as well as qualitative means (Beaudry 2009; White and Beaudry 2009). This bias toward artifact types that are found in larger quantities often results in smaller assemblages of artifacts being ignored for reporting and publication. While children's artifacts are present at perhaps the majority of historical sites investigated in the United States, they are very rarely a significant percentage of the overall artifact assemblage and are therefore not elaborated on in reporting and publication. This bias in archaeological methodology means the majority of literature on sites where it is highly likely children were present, such as domestic households, rarely include children in their interpretations (e.g., Barile and Brandon 2004; Fogle, Nyman, and Beaudry 2015).

Despite these issues, there is ample work to draw upon, but it is important to characterize the limitations of the available sources used to develop this picture of childhood and adolescence in America through an archaeological lens. Published materials favor some sites and site types more than others, and at times publications are often the work of just a handful of dedicated scholars. Rarely, but when necessary, this book also taps into archaeological work conducted in Canada and the UK to round out ideas and understandings of childhood relevant to archaeology in the United States. This book is able to do a great deal with relatively few publications because of the quality of current literature available. Expanding literature to include more sites and site types as they relate to children will enhance archaeology's contribution to the study of American childhood in the future.

Using site types to organize this work provides a particularly archaeological approach to American childhoods, and it also helps to correct for the temporal imbalance in the archaeological study of children in the American past. Material culture for children does not become common until the nineteenth century (chapter 2), meaning while studies of children and childhood from earlier in the country's history exist, they do not occur in a frequency that allows entire chapters to be devoted to their summation. To help ground the work chronologically, chapter 2 presents a brief historical overview of childhood in the American past, with a particular emphasis on the material culture that accompanied historically documented views about children. This chapter explores more fully some of the dominant ideas held about childhood at different periods of American history. Such a background offers important contexts for archaeological work that provides insights to the daily lived experiences of children, and the commemoration of children in death that amplify and express some of these same ideals in the material world.

Chapter 3 explores children in their living spaces, as material culture for children is most often encountered archaeologically in such contexts. Domestic sites, broadly defined, vary significantly in economic and social structure throughout American history, and are further differentiated by region. These lines of difference are used to structure this chapter as a way of organizing broad types of children's experiences "at home." The material culture of childhood in domestic contexts offers insights into negotiations of childhood identities at the intimate scale of family life, as well as how families provisioned children with material goods for their interactions with the world outside the home. Domestic sites also offer an opportunity to explore how children contributed economically to the success and at times survival of their families, and point to their essential roles as household members. It is in this chapter that the disparity between excavated sites and published interpretations of children's material culture is most glaring. Despite thousands of domestic sites having been excavated across the United States, only a handful of archaeological cases are available to examine the lives of children in nineteenth- and twentieth-century America.

Children's lives are certainly not always tied to the household, and chapter 4 explores a variety of institutions that were created and operated with children in mind. Some institutions, such as public schools, became seen as a necessity for all American children as part of a healthy democratic society. Other institutions, such as orphanages or boarding schools, targeted specific populations of children considered particularly at risk or in need of institutional confinement and care. All such institutions were engaged in the care of children away from families, but were places where children were subjected to control and confinement to varying degrees by nonfamilial adults charged with their care. Simultaneously, institutions became places where children socialized and built bonds in the absence of parental intervention, and developed strategies for resistance and autonomy within the constraints of institutional life. Institutional sites are material incarnations of ideals about how children should be cared for, particularly in the eyes of reformers and activists reacting to the perceived risks to children's physical, social, and moral well-being. They also are important sites for interpreting children's agency, autonomy, and peer culture, and the discourse between adults and children in the American past.

Chapter 5 presents research about children who never had the opportunity to grow up with the country. The loss of children was much more common in the American past than it is today, but the death of a child has always been an emotional experience for the family and community left behind. Burial treatment and the erection of headstones and grave markers offer insights into how adult mourners chose to commemorate their children and how children came to symbolize important values in family and community life. While the bioarchaeology of childhood has taken off as a very prolific area of scholarship in prehistory, laws in the United States and elsewhere prohibit the exhumation of skeletal remains or the disturbance of known burials unless destruction is imminent. As a result, there are very few studies of children's skeletal remains and grave goods from the historic period in America and elsewhere. Studies of grave markers, consolation literature, mortuary art, and epitaphs are somewhat more common. This chapter also considers the awareness of mortality that children had in the American past, when the death of siblings and peers was not uncommon. How children were socialized to understand death, and the possibility of their own death, is an important final consideration of this chapter.

Chapter 6 is a departure from the nonchronological organization of this book, as it is devoted to contemporary archaeology and looks at childhood in the present and very recent past. This chapter is essential because it captures a significant movement in archaeological thought and practice, and also because popular and scholarly concerns about childhood, even in deep prehistory, are rooted in our interests in childhood in the present. Rather than relying on emotional, popular accounts that permeate the media, this chapter engages scholarship on how and why children have come to hold such a place of prominence in contemporary American society, and why American childhood is simultaneously viewed as being in a state of profound decline. Exploring how archaeologists and scholars of material culture view contemporary childhood provides useful insights into consumption, gender construction, and the migration of children's material culture from the physical to the digital realm. This contemporary perspective offers readers an opportunity to consider the historical trends that have brought American childhood to its place in contemporary culture, and also current scholarship.

~ 2 ~

Material and Social Histories of Childhood and Adolescence in the United States

American childhoods are diverse at any given moment, bound by particular themes that allow us to trace and explore change, and variable over time in both fundamental understandings of what childhood is and which Americans are considered to be children. The majority of documentary sources available for consideration tell less about how childhood was actually lived, and more about the ideals people held about childhood at any given moment. Legal codes, popular writing, and official records and documents provide an understanding of how childhood was structured and understood in relationship to adulthood. Such sources offer insights into what a period of childhood should entail, who was and was not a child, and the different recognized subcategories of child, including infants and adolescents. Where firsthand accounts of childhood do exist they generally are recorded as memoirs, oral histories, and recollections of childhood when individuals were adults looking back on childhood through the imperfect lenses of memory and nostalgia, thereby creating alternative, but perhaps equally idealized, views of childhood for historians to consider.

The historical record for American childhoods is dominated by the voices of those living in the northern, and particularly northeastern, United States. During the colonial period, Puritans were relatively prolific in their writings about childhood when compared to other communities, creating an enduring bias in how the history of American childhood has been written (Marten 2007; Mintz 2004). In later periods, publications about childhood were penned by what historian Daniel Rogers (1985: 7) refers to as "The Yankee Bourgeoisie." These individuals were wealthy Americans living in the Northeast who set the agenda for national initiatives, such as education, labor reform, and public welfare, and as a result had a hold over the learning institutions, canons of respectable values, and shifting ideas of work and reform that shaped public discourse. These individuals were the same people who, as parents of upper- and middle-class children, set the standard for child-rearing and defined the nature of childhood that was put forth in period literature such as mother's books, ladies' magazines, children's literature, and parenting guides to be disseminated across the expanding nation. As discourse about childhood became increasingly entangled with governmental and institutional authorities and scholars, dominant narratives of childhood continued to find most of their origins in the eastern and northeastern United States.

If the northeast largely dictated the national discourse through publication and writing, Chicago controlled the distribution of material culture through its large supply-house catalogue companies such as Sears and Roebuck and Montgomery Ward. While few artifacts for children were part of American colonial households, children became direct marketing targets of the advertising industry by the end of the nineteenth century and the number and variety of goods available for raising, educating, and entertaining children exploded into the marketplace. Whether few or many, artifacts are a far more ambiguous source for understanding childhood in the American past. Artifacts for children provided essential object lessons about social rules and norms at any given time, including age categories, gender roles, household roles, interpersonal relationships, and the values that structured them (Praetzellis and Praetzellis 1992). In many ways, artifacts for children reinforced the dominant ideals about childhood put forth in the documentary record. Once placed into the hands of children, however, these same artifacts became focal points for resistance, negotiation, rebellion, and a reconfiguration of some of those very same ideals (Casella 2011; Chudacoff 2007; Crawford 2009; Forman-Brunell 1993; Wilkie 2000). Similarly, families across the social spectrum could use artifacts for alternative purposes that undermined the systems of values their designers sought to uphold (e.g., Yamin 2002). This chapter sets the stage for thinking through some of these complexities in different archaeological contexts.

Changes in published American ideals about childhood and children's material culture are intertwined with two distinct timelines. The first of these timelines involves the major shifts in thinking about childhood that come from popular intellectual and social movements, often beyond the United States. Ideas from philosophy and science trickled down into popular thinking about children and had immediate day-to-day consequences for how children were perceived, accessorized, and raised (Calvert 1992; Fass 2016). These timelines of popular thought about childhood are not unrelated to the events of American history, but certainly do not chronologically trend alongside them. This chapter uses major periods in United States history as its fundamental organizing chronology and interweaves changing thoughts about childhood through this dominant timeline. Like most historical treatments, this chapter begins with the colonial period in the seventeenth century and continues through to the twentieth century. Chapter 6 of this book continues the timeline with its exclusive focus on twenty-first-century American childhood through the lens of contemporary archaeology.

Colonial Childhoods (1620–1750)

Young people were not scarce in the early American colonies, as birth rates were quite high, and by some estimates people under the age of 15 comprised nearly two-thirds of the population (Chudacoff 2007: 20). Infant and child mortality also were quite high given the risky nature of early settlement life when health was precarious and life expectancy short. Historically, some scholarship has suggested that this high rate of birth and death made parental and communal investment in individual children quite limited, and that individuals only became socially significant once certain thresholds of vitality were reached (Benes and Benes 2002). Current scholarship disagrees. Despite their relative abundance and their often very brief lives, children were incredibly important to populations trying to stake a claim in a "new world," and for those groups trying to maintain their homelands (Chudacoff 2007; Mintz 2004). Children were certainly given considerable care and attention, and colonial households and communities were organized in ways that considered their care and well-being. Children are often portrayed as being the future for any group of people, and in the early colonies this was particularly true.

Contemporary scholarship on children during America's colonial period embraces the cultural diversity that characterized early colonial interactions between Europeans, Africans, and native populations of the Americas (Chudacoff 2007; Marten 2007; Mintz 2004). While significant diversity existed among Native and African populations, including in terms of attitudes and practices around children, those documenting early encounters had limited interest in those populations' children and often culture in general. While scholarship is present and growing in this area, it is still quite scant (Marten 2007). Colonial American childhoods also varied significantly and ideas about child-rearing varied by region, religion, race, and ethnicity, as well as social and economic distinctions (Chudacoff 2007; Marten 2007). Despite significant variation in colonial populations, before 1770 religion was the dominant paradigm everywhere, and being obedient to parents and to God was paramount (Chudacoff 2007). This overarching religious worldview shaped ideas about children and child-rearing throughout the colonies.

Most scholarly literature on childhood reflects the imbalance of writing about children at the time, with the overwhelming majority of such prose originating with the Puritans in New England (Mintz 2004). Puritans and their descendants had powerfully strong convictions on how things should be done, and their preoccupation with children was the result of their religious beliefs and the social circumstances of being marginalized even among their fellow settler communities. This sense of moral superiority and social isolation shaped how the Puritans negotiated their encounters with entirely new peoples and places, and how they sought to perpetuate their society into future generations through their children. Mintz wrote:

> The Puritans were unique in their preoccupation with childrearing, and wrote a disproportionate share of tracts on the subject. As a struggling minority, their survival depended on ensuring that their children retained their values. They were convinced that molding children through proper childrearing and education was the most effective way to shape an orderly and godly society. Their legacy is a fixation on childhood corruption, child nurture, and schooling that remains undiminished in the United States today. (2004: 10)

The idea that Puritans, a powerful symbol of American origins, are the source of so many of the fundamental values associated with childhood in America today is noteworthy, and speaks to the origins of many deeply held beliefs about childhood in America. Simultaneously and, as he notes, ironically, Mintz (2004) argues that the opportunity offered by America (chapter 1) was particularly responsible for the erosion of the stringent patriarchal authority that held Puritan society together. American childhood was being shaped and created in the midst of its own budding demise.

Despite the Puritan fascination with children, for generations of early scholars colonial childhoods were characterized as being, for all intents and purposes, historically invisible (Beales 1975; Calvert 1992). This characterization originated, in part, from depictions of children in portraiture as "miniature adults" (figure 2.1). These images show children dressed in identical garb to their adult contemporaries and there is an absence of child-specific material culture accompanying them in the images. A similar lack of child-related objects in curated and family collections reinforced the idea that children were not only historically invisible, but also not differentiated as a category of personhood. The absence of child-specific clothing and playthings in combination with a relative dearth of writing for and about children when compared to later periods of American history codified this perspective for generations of scholars.

These ideas were challenged as later scholars took a less comparative view toward colonial childhood and sought to understand seventeenth- and early eighteenth-century society in a more relativistic manner. It was found that other types of primary sources make a clear distinction between childhood and adulthood. Seventeenth-century laws made divisions between adults and children into their teens. Records of religious conversion demonstrate that such events did not occur until an individual was at least 10 and more often around 14. And, accounts of apprenticeship systems indicate that young men did not obtain economic independence until the age of 17 or 18 (Beales 1975). These sources indicated that childhood and perhaps additional stages of identity, such as a type of adolescence associated with apprenticeship, must have been recognized in the seventeenth century. Those stages were not necessarily subjected to extensive material and social elaboration, however, resulting in the appearance of "miniaturization" of colonial, and particularly Puritan, children.

In her influential study of American childhood through material culture, Karin Calvert (1992) characterized colonial children not as miniature adults, but rather as inchoate ones (figure 2.1). Her analysis of portraiture suggested that children were not being portrayed as miniaturized versions of adults in their community, but rather were seen as incomplete

Figure 2.1. The work entitled *David, Joana, and Abigail Mason* is considered emblematic of the "miniaturization" of adulthood that typified seventeenth-century New England "childhoods." Painting attributed to the Freake-Gibbs painter. Wikimedia Commons.

human beings because of their inability to walk upright and their incapacity for coherent speech. Children who crawled on all fours and babbled in incomprehensible tones were to be reared out of these vulnerable, godless states and into the ranks of humanity as quickly as possible. Child-rearing practices included swaddling, which involved the wrapping of infants' limbs to make them rigid and to simulate an upright posture. Walking or standing stools were a common artifact type for children because they posed children in a standing posture and encouraged walking as soon as possible. Children's portraiture expresses a desire among Puritan parents for their children to move beyond this animalistic phase of development when their souls could not yet be redeemed. One way to assuage this parental concern was by dressing children not as adults per se, but rather as humans with souls that could be turned to God. Clothing simultaneously marked gender distinctions from infancy, which were upheld strongly throughout an individual's lifetime (figure 2.1).

Puritan life was structured around nuclear families with heavy-handed patriarchal control. Many historians have characterized these families as being scaled-down models of the church that governed the community, also through domineering, patriarchal leadership (Chudacoff 2007; Mintz 2004). Nuclear families were not the pervasive social structure elsewhere in the colonies, however, and religion was not quite so fundamentalist in nature. Children in other colonies were often indentured servants, and an abundance of laws and strictures interrelate age categories and this economic system of servitude. It was not uncommon for children to be indentured. A fee was paid to the parents, and the child was sent to the colonies to work off the debt without their families, who remained in England or elsewhere (Herndon 2009). The majority of the 307,000 white migrants arriving in the colonies from 1700 to 1775 weren't free, and, of course, nearly all of the half-million Africans weren't either (Chudacoff 2007). Economic systems of labor, apprenticeship, and slavery shaped how most young arrivals into the middle colonies were treated. In those colonies, there was a decided sex imbalance in favor of males, and the abundance of unchaperoned child servants and apprentices meant that child-rearing was often a collective effort. Children reared in families in the middle colonies and under milder forms of Christian doctrine generally experienced a childhood based on the premises of affection and early independence. Less work was expected of children at an early age than of Puritan children, and strict discipline was reserved for and directed at slaves, not a family's children (Mintz 2004).

Some leisure was afforded to children in the middle colonies, and there were some toys and games, such as penny whistles and cup-and-ball games, and early forms of what later became elaborate parlor amusements were also recorded. However, these were not child-specific activities, and both adults and children enjoyed such games as recreation. Items labeled as toys and activities categorized as games were not age-specific. Toys and activities conceptualized as play were forbidden for all members of Puritan society, and children were expected to engage in adult pursuits much earlier in life. Play was not terribly widespread in general, and it was felt it had to be tied to some kind of greater purpose, lest it be perceived as a type of "idleness" that carried negative religious connotations (Chudacoff 2007: 21–23).

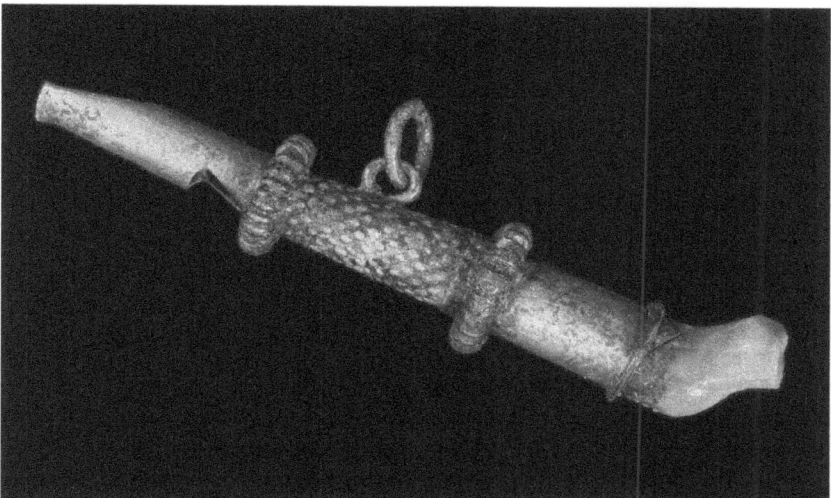

Figure 2.2. Baby whistle and teething stick excavated at Historic Jamestown. Image courtesy of Jamestown Rediscovery (Preservation Virginia).

Dressing children in the same clothing style as adults and restricting what activities were exclusively children's limits the material culture of childhood available for study in the colonial period. As archaeologists rely heavily on child-specific artifacts to make claims about the presence of children in the past, and most certainly to interpret the nature of childhood (Wilkie 2000), this is not inconsequential for the archaeology of childhood in America's colonial period. The only child-specific artifact identified in Calvert's (1992) study of children's material culture from this period was the coral and bells, an instrument that would have resembled a rattle or other handheld noisemaker for children (figure 2.2). These silver or bronze objects were provided to children in affluent households to engage them with the bright pink coral that was thought to protect them from disease and ill-health. The metal casing often took the form of a whistle with bells to hold a child's interest and encourage interaction between child and object so they could reap the medical benefits of the coral, particularly through teething and sucking.

Archaeological investigations into seventeenth-century sites have recovered examples of coral and bells, although they are quite rare. Archaeological work at early colonial sites in New England has yielded only one such item: a silver whistle from a set of coral and bells. The whistle bears the initials "E. W." and most likely belonged to Elizabeth Winslow, who was born in 1630 to a prominent and prosperous family of the early colonies (Beaudry, Goldstein, and Chartier 2003). A single whistle and coral piece has been found at excavations in Jamestown, Virginia (figure 2.2). Other child-rearing devices such as walking or standing stools and swaddling cloth are unlikely to survive in archaeological contexts, and instead are known through portraiture and curated museum collections.

The archaeology of childhood in this earliest period of American history presents a significant challenge for archaeologists. It is well understood that the very idea of childhood is a cultural construction expressed differently across time and space (Baxter 2008; chapter 1) including the possibility that childhood did not exist in some cultures (Rothschild 2002). Children were clearly important in the early colonial period, but the world around them was not designed to accommodate their small size or stature, their dress and clothing were not age-specific, and there were few objects that were designed for them alone. Relational approaches have been used in similar circumstances to evaluate how children would have interacted with landscapes and objects designed primarily for adults, and to which they would have been expected to adapt (Dozier 2016; Hutson 2006).

Baxter (2015a) has argued that one way to address working in periods where childhood is not a marked or elaborated category of identity is to engage singular, highly personal artifacts found in archaeological assemblages as advocated by others in historical archaeology (Beaudry 2009; Brandon 2013; Mímisson and Magnússon 2014; White and Beaudry 2009). Such approaches to the material record eschew the common archaeological practice of focusing on larger assemblages of similar objects that can be analyzed quantitatively, and instead engage closely with artifacts that hold particular poignancy because of their rarity and uniqueness. These types of artifacts are often highly personal and entwined with individual identities, and would have been connected to individual bodies and persons as adornment, as objects of personal practice, or as signifiers of intimate relationships. Such approaches emphasize the situated experiences of material life and the reciprocal shaping of objects and human experiences.

Even in periods where children's artifacts are much more abundant, child-specific artifacts are generally a small amount of any given assemblage. When such goods are all but absent, as in the colonial period, the idea of recovering childhood through the archaeological record is daunting. Even with a single artifact, however, such as a silver-and-coral teething stick, a variety of individual identities are represented, including a child who needs to be reared into human form in good health and in haste, and a particular class of individual whose family could afford a silver teething tool for a child (Baxter 2015a: 30). In some cases, children's initials were placed on the device itself, associating it with an individual of a particular gender as well. While children engaged all artifacts in the home, making all artifacts a part of childhood (Wood 2009), these personal, individual artifacts have particular power in periods with limited archaeological visibility for children.

Childhood in Revolutionary Times and the Early Republic (1750–1830)

Early colonial ideas about children certainly shifted as settlements became established, new waves of immigrants and settlers arrived, diversifying the population, and children grew up to find new, unique opportunities independent of their families. As the eighteenth century brought about political upheaval, revolution, and nation-building, intellectual thought turned to the Enlightenment, which emphasized scientific, rational thought. Works of two prominent philosophical thinkers, John Locke and Jean-Jacques Rousseau, entered into intellectual and popular discourse and transformed the way Americans understood childhood. Childhood became a distinct period of personhood with unique institutions, activities, and material culture to help parents raise their children to be respectable, responsible citizens of the new nation. The young country of America was future focused, and children were very much seen as the future of families and the country. These new ideas placed a greater emphasis on democratic ideals in the American family and highlighted the independence of children as a fundamental right. Changes in family life also enabled child-rearing and control over domestic spaces to become a source of empowerment for women within the household. Family life in the early republic came to embrace and mirror some of the core values underlying the American Revolution itself, albeit on a much smaller scale than the birth of a nation (Fass 2016: 17).

The scientific ideas that were popularized during the eighteenth century advocated for careful observations of the natural world and focused on the development of all things. Nature was predictable. There were patterns and cycles that could be observed and understood not just by scientists and thinkers but by everyday enlightened citizens as well. The more humans studied the natural world, the more it could be shaped and controlled. Humanity did not stand outside of nature in this paradigm, unlike in earlier forms of religious thought that elevated humans to something beyond the natural world. This rhetoric of science was applied to understanding humanity as well as the natural world, including critical social constructs surrounding race, culture contact, and child-rearing. It was believed that heredity could be shaped with the right intervention, and parents could channel and nurture the potential and possibility in their children through structured programs of child enhancement based on science.

John Locke's 1693 work *Some Thoughts Concerning Education*, which outlined his ideas about children, came into prominence during the eighteenth century, alongside his writings in political philosophy. His political writings helped to drive the American Revolution, and the popularization of his writings created a clear parallel between children and the American nation as both being young and in need of parenting and nurturance (Calvert 1992; Chudacoff 2007; Fass 2016). Locke believed children were a "tabula rasa," which didn't mean that they should be left to their own devices, but rather they could be actively shaped and molded by thoughtful adult intervention. Childhood was characterized as a natural state and children had natural tendencies that could be cultivated and tempered as needed (figure 2.3).

In this intellectual environment, Rousseau's 1762 work *Emile, or On Education* was more immediately received and incorporated into thinking about childhood. Children were not innately corrupted by original sin as earlier religious-based thinking espoused, but rather children were receptacles of human virtue found in a state of nature. Children needed care so they could develop reason in their own way, but play and exploration by children was seen as an essential part of their development. This thinking helped to codify childhood as an essential and significant part of human growth and development, and Americans developed an enhanced appreciation for the special innocence and vulnerability of children (Chudacoff 2007).

In practical and material terms, childhood became an important preparatory age that was to be enriched with experiences to encourage natural tendencies and promote growth and development (Calvert 1992).

Figure 2.3. Two children circa 1755–1760. This depiction captures a transitional moment in American childhood. The image engages emerging ideas about the natural state of children and childhood through their associations with the natural world, while also showing the younger child holding a teething stick popular in earlier decades and associated with ideas of child-rearing that were falling out of favor (see figure 2.2). Image attributed to James Badger, Boston Massachusetts. Wikimedia.

Earlier ideas and objects that restricted and restrained children, such as swaddling and standing stools, were abandoned, as was the idea that children were to be rushed out of an infantile or childlike state. Infancy and childhood became characterized as natural, the need for exploration essential for development, and play a way of learning and source of joy. Households became structured around two well-defined generations with distinct expectations and activities for each, and genders also were carefully separated as the different innate natures of men and women were considered equally observable and clear through these lines of scientific thinking. Clothing came to mark both age and gender categories within families, and children's clothing became less restrictive to enable movement, exploration, and greater activity (figure 2.4). Young boys particularly were distinguished in unique garb that was distinct both from adult

Figure 2.4. *The Artist and His Family* by James Peale, 1795. This image illustrates the distinctions between individuals of different ages and genders within the American family. It also shows a family in nature with the children engaging in relatively active pursuits in contrast to the parents' more reserved postures while demonstrating a focused interest on the children. Wikimedia.

males and their female siblings, marking the emergence of a particular cultural category of "boyhood" (Calvert 1992).

Play became an important aspect of childhood experiences, but it was believed that play should be structured to maximize its developmental potential (Chudacoff 2007). Portraiture from the time depicts children with their own material culture, including dolls and doll accessories with girls and hoops, wagons, balls, and toy soldiers with boys (Calvert 1992; Chudacoff 2007). Children also are often associated with animals in these images, including domesticated pets as well as tamed wild creatures, thereby emphasizing children's place in the natural world (figure 2.3). Some games and toys still were enjoyed by both adults and children, but there was a notable shift in the categorization of play objects. Certain objects became toys associated exclusively with children and shops began selling toys specifically with children as the intended audience. Other aspects of society shifted to embrace this new emphasis on childhood as well. Literature for parents offering child-rearing advice became more common. Options in public schooling increased and formal religious institutions were created just for children, such as Sunday school, where children attended alternative religious education while parents took part in church services (Chudacoff 2007: 45). Child care was characterized as tedious and hard work, especially for mothers. New medical products were introduced to soothe children and make them easier to manage to reduce parental burdens (Calvert 1992; Fass 2016: 36). All of these material, institutional, and philosophical changes worked to separate spheres of adults and children, creating unique cultural expectations, objects, spaces, and experiences for children and adults.

Comparisons to earlier American childhoods make these eighteenth-century ideas of childhood seem freeing and liberating for children. But early accounts of play suggest that children were seeking even greater independence from parents, and play in the hands of unsupervised children became a space of rebellion that included the defiance of adult ideals, the establishment of child-only secret places, and the pursuit of activities that courted danger such as chewing tobacco, consuming alcohol, and engaging in unsafe forms of play that resulted in injury (Chudacoff 2007: 63). Remembrances of childhood from this time emphasize the importance of being out-of-doors as a way to find unstructured and private places and times to play. Interior spaces were shared spaces, and recreation in such contexts often was intergenerational with reading, games, and puzzles being popular engagements. These sources suggest children were actively negotiating their childhoods through uses of space and material culture as greater cultural spaces for a distinct child-specific phase of life were established.

A leisurely childhood left to exploration and optimal development was not afforded to many of the nation's children. Systems of apprenticeship and indentured servitude persisted well into the eighteenth century and many children spent their childhoods working and learning their future trades or paying off their passages to the colonies. Children participated in all aspects of the Revolutionary War and are seen in engravings and images and recorded in accounts of being in battles, riots, protests, and revolts. It was also during the eighteenth century that American slavery underwent significant changes in scale and organization that kept large numbers of adults and children enslaved as laborers in all types of tasks and under dehumanizing conditions. The lives of enslaved children were incredibly complex. These children had to endure psychological abuses, sexual exploitation, and physical stresses from labor that was forced upon them at very young ages (figure 2.5).

On a most basic level, both documentary and skeletal evidence suggest that the health and nutrition of enslaved children was quite poor. Poor health began when children were neonates because of demands on maternal labor. Mothers had inadequate nutrition to nourish their own bodies, as they were subjected to hard labor late into their pregnancies. As a result, the loss of children at birth and miscarriages throughout pregnancy were quite common (Mintz 2004: 96). Inadequate nutrition also plagued enslaved children from infancy, as irregular access to laboring mothers and the resulting infrequent opportunity to breastfeed meant children were fed alternative foods containing lactose that were largely indigestible. Enslaved children also suffered disproportionately from tetanus and other diseases caused by unsanitary living conditions, and were generally developmentally delayed and physically stunted because of poor health and nutrition early in life. Mintz (2004: 96) notes that the treatment of enslaved infants and young children was at odds with the widespread recognition that the birth of children into slavery was a source of labor and wealth, as nothing was done to "cultivate" this source through attention to health and nutrition.

Once children could do the work of a full field hand their clothing and food rations improved, but labor for enslaved children began quite early in life. Work in service of their owners began as soon as possible. Children were expected to do small things such as rocking cribs, fetching things, or running errands. These tasks were not valued particularly for the labor itself, but rather emphasized and inculcated control and subordination at a very young age (Fass 2016; Mintz 2004). When children reached the age of 10–12 they could work alongside adults, but not for a full day, and it was at this age that many children began to learn trades paralleling the labor experiences of non-enslaved children who were beginning their lives as apprentices around the same age. While, arguably, gender mattered far less for enslaved children than white children living in families or working as indentured servants and apprentices, the likelihood of sexual

Figure 2.5. A group of men, women, and children being taken to a slave market, entitled *Band of Captives Driven into Slavery*. Children were not only born into slavery once in the American colonies, but also were taken captive as part of the Atlantic Slave Trade. Wikimedia via Wellcome Images.

exploitation as young girls reached puberty was far more common than for their male counterparts within systems of slavery.

In addition to physical deprivations, sexual exploitation, and a life of forced labor, the psychological strain on enslaved children was also quite significant. Children endured all of these difficult circumstances in a context of precarious family lives and population instability in their communities. Both parents and masters struggled to gain the loyalty and obedience of children, often placing them in positions of complex and consequential social decision-making when still very young. Perhaps most basically and most profoundly, enslaved children at some point during childhood had to recognize that others had absolute control over their bodies and future labor, and that adults in their community were unable to protect them from this fate (Fass 2016: 48–49).

Despite these incredibly difficult situations, communities of enslaved people made significant efforts to maintain an extended sense of family in naming practices, the teaching of traditions, and empowering and imbuing people in the broader community with family-like roles to support children (Chudacoff 2007: 44). Enslaved children also engaged in play and recreation as a way to cope with stress, and to develop a sense of self-worth, as well as community and peer relationships (Mintz 2004: 107). Play also taught children fundamental skills and offered an opportunity for some basic education, such as learning counting and alphabets, under circumstances that generally made more formal education impossible.

Historians also have noted the particular place that enslaved children played in the rhetoric of abolitionist movements. The insensitivity to family and children was a major appeal made by abolitionist speakers and writers when trying to persuade fellow Americans against the institution. Paula Fass (2016) notes that the heroine in *Uncle Tom's Cabin* (1853), Little Eva, is held up as an example of an innocent and angelic child who dies because her character is so at odds with the cruelty of the culture of the American South. In such instances, the symbolic and social meaning of children was upheld as more powerful than institutions based on racial discrimination and economic exploitation.

Childhood, the Industrial Revolution, and the Gilded Age (1830–1900)

The symbolic and social meaning of children became increasingly important as the industrial revolution brought about significant changes to how labor and family were organized in America. As families relocated to urban areas and people had to sell their labor in new factory and industrial work settings, the realities of children's lives changed dramatically (Matthews 2010), and so did their symbolic value as pure and innocent ties to heaven and to traditional home and family life (Baxter and Ellis 2018). Childhood became a time of innocence that stood in direct contrast to the modern world; children were morally pure and closer to heaven, and their very presence gave comfort to adults at a time of cultural upheaval and change (Cross 2004). Parenting was an effort to prolong goodness and innocence and to restrict access to the evils of the world beyond the home. Stages of childhood became more carefully delineated, and gender distinctions became emphasized under the rhetoric of maintaining sexual and therefore social purity (Calvert 1992; figure 2.6). The categorization of children based on age-grades also became more precise and segmented, which established more specific peer cultures for children, specialized material culture based on age as well as gender, and reorganized institutions such as public schools into age-based cohorts. The rise of childhood as an elaborated cultural category in America was helped along significantly by the ability to produce and market an extraordinary array of goods to raise and entertain children.

The exaltation and celebration of children that escalated in the latter half of the nineteenth century was a result of broad organizational transformations in family and community life, but it also reflected a dramatic drop in birth rates. This steady decline in birth rates is seen in census data where live births per 1000 women of birthing age (15 to 44—note the age range) dropped from 194 in 1850 to 87 in 1900 (Chudacoff 2007: 69–70). This demographic trend allowed for more time and energy to be spent on individual children and a stronger categorical distinction to be made between children and adults (Cable 1975; Calvert 1992; Chudacoff 2007; Somerville 2015: 277). This delineation was realized particularly in domestic settings, as smaller families meant people tended to live in single, nuclear family homes rather than multigenerational households. New living arrangements allowed parents to exercise a greater degree of

Figure 2.6. "Elsie Leslie as Little Lord Fauntleroy circa 1888." Little Lord Fauntleroy was a character in a novel of the same name by English-American author Frances Hodgson Burnett. The work was published as a serial in *St. Nicholas Magazine* from 1885 to 1886 and was adapted for the Broadway stage that same decade. The long hair and velvet suit was an iconic fashion for young boys, as it retained many of the feminine elements of the dresses they would have worn as younger children in the same style as their female siblings. This intermediate style of dress also retained many of the childlike elements of younger children's clothing while allowing young boys to begin to emerge into garb appropriate for the public sphere. Wikimedia.

control and order over daily routines and relationships within the home. This organization also meant that parents were able to improve the "quality" of each child's upbringing, and they were able to invest more time and energy in each individual child (Cable 1975).

Historian Priscilla Ferguson Clement (1997) identified dominant patterns of child-rearing that were prevalent in nineteenth-century family life that also capture contemporaneous themes and variations in how families defined and raised their children. As America expanded and diversified during this period, the physical and social geography of American home life became increasingly differentiated among regions, across urban/rural divides, and amid diverse ethnic, racial, and economic communities. While Clement (1997: 36) identified four such patterns of child-rearing, three are particularly germane here: (1) American, Protestant, middle-class families living in urban environments, and a variation thereof practiced by southern plantation families; (2) white, urban, working-class families who were mostly foreign-born; and (3) frontier and farm families living in the rural western and midwestern United States. The majority of available sources on the history of nineteenth-century childhood is centered on the first pattern of child-rearing, while sources detailing the lives of urban poor and rural children are much more limited. Urban, Protestant, middle-class and upper-class families of the eastern United States were the target audience for the copious child-rearing literature that emerged during the period. These families were also the dominant economic and social force in nineteenth-century America, and as such shaped popular ideals of child-rearing and inserted their ideals into political actions and community institutions for children. The second two forms of child-rearing noted above, while deviating from patterns set by middle- and upper-class families, shared many of the same ideas and aspirations for children.

Parenting became increasingly underpinned by science and scientific discourse about proper child-rearing methods (Fass 2016; Green 1984). Nineteenth-century publications on parenting regularly had columns on matters of health and hygiene, as well as home science experiments for children. The science of childhood, like any science, took place in the broader cultural milieu of which it was a part, including the moral and social constructions of childhood of the day (Green 1984: 122). Scientific ideas from earlier periods persisted, enforcing the sense that parents could raise their children for good or evil and also inform their moral and cognitive development through the implementation of proper child-rearing methods. Other ideas were new and transformative. The popularization of Darwinian evolution and the conception that evolution was a force of progress catered to parents' desires to purposefully and usefully intervene in the raising of their children's bodies and minds (Green 1984: 126–127). This evolutionary sensibility was extended to people's social lives through burgeoning ideas about the relationship between morality and social class as well as beliefs about the racial superiority of white Americans over others. Such views connected science to a moral imperative that could be displayed through properly raised children.

Child-rearing literature frequently presented advice that came from contemporaneous women's movements and movements for domestic reform as well (Wood 2009). Many of these movements sought to elevate the position of the mother in the home and underpin her authority in household management and in the care of children (Fass 2016). It became increasingly popular to advocate that a child's mother was the only natural and suitable choice of a primary caregiver (Beecher 1841; Child 1831). While many affluent families in the past had employed nannies and servants for child care, period literature stated that domestic servants were now considered potentially dangerous influences on children (e.g., Child 1831: 100–101). In response, the nature of domestic service changed. Instead of nannies, families employed cooks or laundresses, who freed mothers from other household duties, and enabled mothers to devote their time and energies to child-rearing (Cott 1978). While a mother's importance within the home environment was increasing, fathers worked outside of the home and maintained the public image of the family (Griswold 1993: 15). Fathers did, however, spend time with their children, and ideally served as caring and compassionate masculine role models in the home, particularly for their young sons.

Parents were instructed to invest time and care in their children with particular goals in mind, particularly to raise obedient, loving, moral, and Christian children (Clement 1997: 41). Middle- and upper-class children also were supposed to be taught the values of thrift, duty, and punctuality: all were considered important virtues to survive in the emerging industrial society of America, and to be active, responsible members of the country's fledgling democracy. These same values were taught in public schools. As Beecher (1841: 233) wrote, "There is no more important duty devolving upon a mother than the cultivation of habits of modesty and propriety in young children. Civilization depends on everyone and even babies must be taught to be decent members of society."

Parents considered their children to be innocent, angelic creatures not yet spoiled or sullied by contact with the adult world. The success of child-rearing methods was measured largely by the parents' abilities to prolong this innocent state of childhood, while cultivating skills appropriate for the adult roles that loomed ahead. Parents believed that the upbringing of children was best done by building on the innocence and good that was already present within them, and that children's inherent "Christian nature" could be cultivated through "kindness, love, and tender care by a mother who exemplified all the virtues that would adequately prepare the child for salvation and a life of moral responsibility" (Cott 1978: 22–24).

Children were socialized into gender roles through the teaching of the basic values and virtues that were to prevail in their adult lives. Parents emphasized values such as love, loyalty, and the importance of family as being important for a productive domestic life, a responsibility shared by both men and women. Virtues such as thrift, duty, and punctuality applied more directly to public life; however, it was important that both men and women should be aware of these behaviors and values (Clement 1997: 43). While parents imparted the same basic values to all their children, different skills and behaviors were cultivated in children of each gender (Chudacoff 2007; Fass 2016; Mintz 2004). Young girls were socialized to be ideal housewives and mothers, roles which required an emphasis on domesticity and maintaining harmony in family relations. It also was considered critical that young girls have the proper demeanor and moral virtue required to raise their own children properly, and to know when and how to exercise appropriate social skills and etiquette (McLeod 1984). As such, emotional traits such as anger and aggression were not tolerated in young girls. These emotions were accepted in young boys, however, because such traits were deemed necessary to be competitive and successful in the outside world (Sterns 1993: 37, 42–45). Also, young girls often were subjected to particular dietary regimens, which denied them meat, sweets, alcohol, coffee, and tea, in attempts to suppress their "carnal urges" and delay the awakening of their sexual desires.

In contrast to the behaviors and skills cultivated in young girls, the social skills of boys largely were developed outside of the home through peer interactions. Such interactions were encouraged by both mothers and fathers, and fathers took a special interest in cultivating masculine, social behaviors in their young sons (Griswold 1993). Boys were encouraged to partake in physical competitions and neighborhood play, which socialized them for the aggressive and competitive world that awaited them (Chudacoff 2007). Many of the feminine influences that characterized home life were in direct contrast to the all-male culture boys encountered in their peer groups. As Anthony Rotundo writes in his history of American manhood, boys had to move

> back and forth from a domestic world of mutual dependence to a public world of independence; from an atmosphere of cooperation and nurture to one of competition and conflict; from a sphere where intimacy was encouraged to one where human relationships were treated instrumentally; from an environment that supported affectionate impulses to one that sanctioned aggressive impulses. (1993: 52)

So, while young boys gained basic values for a productive family life at home, their worlds also were shaped by the opportunities and realities of the public sphere, a world to which their mothers and sisters were rarely exposed.

While upper- and middle-class families had the means to shield their children from many of the harsher realities of the world, urban working-class families were not afforded such luxuries. From a very young age children were in direct contact with adults in the family and the community, and were exposed to many unsavory aspects of urban life. Families living in such settings rarely were able to achieve the distinct, prolonged period of childhood innocence idealized in the nineteenth century. Like upper- and middle-class children, urban children were raised to be obedient, to respect their elders and their families, and to lead moral lives. However, among immigrant families, many of whom were Catholic, values and moral lessons were different than in Protestant homes.

In upper- and middle-class homes there was at least a theoretical distinction between work and home, and public and private spheres (but see Boydston 1990; Cowan 1983; Kerber et al. 1989). In working-class homes these boundaries were broken down, as mothers often brought in work, such as laundry or sewing, or lodged boarders to make ends meet (Clement 1997: 51). Children often helped their mothers in such tasks, even at a very young age. In addition to these income-related activities, mothers were required to perform routine household tasks, making it virtually impossible to devote the time and energy to child-rearing considered ideal at the time (Ewen 1985; Stansell 1986). Fathers often were absent from the home for long periods due to the rigors of industrial labor, and often were less of a presence in their children's lives (Griswold 1993:37). With parents otherwise occupied, child care often fell to other members of the community, older children, or extended family who lived in the same apartment or tenement.

Families tended to be much larger in working-class neighborhoods due to lack of available birth control and the value of children as a source of family income (Zelizer 1994). As a result, children received less individual attention and had very little privacy within the home (Fass 2016; Riney-Kehrberg 2014). Gender socialization was maintained through divisions of labor, and less through segregated spaces for play and social interaction. Urban streets often became a play space for children, primarily for boys but also young girls (Chudacoff 2007; Riney-Kehrberg 2014). Children also were expected to "work" while at play on the streets, scavenging for items that might be of value for family use or for sale (Ewen 1985: 142). The need for children's labor also often limited their access to education, even when it was free, public, and mandatory.

These families undoubtedly were aware of the discrepancies between their child-rearing strategies and those advocated by mainstream American culture. However, economic necessity, religious justifications, and the desire to maintain traditional child-rearing practices from home countries made it possible for some families to reconcile these differences (Fass 2016; Mintz 2004).

Childhood and child-rearing in the rural United States during the nineteenth century was in many ways an amalgamation of the upper- and middle-class and urban working-class patterns of child-rearing. Many parents in rural families embraced upper- and middle-class ideals about the uniqueness of childhood, the responsibility of mothers, the need to cultivate values of independence and self-reliance, and the importance of imparting distinct gender roles to their children. At the same time, rural families had to balance the necessity of properly raising children with the demands of a rigorous work regime. While parents worked in and around the home and were therefore a strong presence in their children's lives, the demands of farm labor occupied both adults and children on a continual basis (Clement 1997: 62; Riney-Kehrberg 2014; West 1989).

Because farming families were relatively isolated, child-rearing duties were shared among extended family and members of the outside community (Craig 1993). Children growing up on farms generally were allowed a greater degree of independence than other children of the time, and they were given their own chores and jobs to do that did not require direct adult supervision (Fass 2016; Riney-Kehrberg 2014; West 1989). While all children worked, their tasks were somewhat gender segregated. Both boys and girls were expected to help with work in the immediate yard areas, including the tasks of tending animals and harvesting garden crops for household consumption. However, heavier work in the fields was reserved for men and older boys. Household tasks such as cooking, canning, and sewing were reserved for young girls and their mothers. The tasks delineated for youngsters of each gender were designed to replicate the roles they would have later in life. Boys learned the cycles of planting and harvesting, and the economics of farming from their fathers. Young girls learned traditional household tasks, as well as the types of jobs that entered into the extended definition of housework on a farm, including the provisioning of the household with animal and garden products (McMurry 1997). Children of both genders went to school, although girls generally attended for longer periods of the year and to a greater age, as the nature of their tasks at home permitted greater time for education (Clement 1997: 72). Many of these farm-related tasks made it virtually impossible to maintain the ideal of a sexually innocent child, as children witnessed and were expected to understand the nature of animal procreation as part of their duties.

Despite these unique features of rural lifestyles, parents worked hard to maintain contemporaneous ideals of childhood. Most child-rearing literature was not directly available to parents in rural areas, and groups known as Mothers' Associations emerged so that mothers would be kept up to date on the latest child-rearing advice and techniques (Meckel 1982). These groups, often associated with Protestant churches, acquired copies of recent books and periodicals on child-rearing, and presented the latest in advice and devices for child-rearing. Some mothers attended meetings on a regular basis to discuss these ideas and ways that they could be modified and implemented effectively in rural areas. Mail-order catalogues, which became widely available in the latter half of the century, made it possible for parents living in remote areas to purchase many of the items advertised in current literature for children's use. Through exposure to this literature, parents sought to raise their children in ways similar to their upper- and middle-class urban counterparts.

Family life was only one area where concerns about childhood entered into American popular discourse in the later nineteenth century. The idea that there were minimum standards of care that all American children should receive, and the need to "save children" from lesser fates fueled political, religious, and secular reform movements. These reform movements focused on the children who were seen as not fully part of the nation's life, particularly those in immigrant families, those born to single mothers, and those being raised in poverty. Concerns of schooling, citizenship training, and anti–child labor laws as well as interests in healthy surroundings for play and recreation all became issues undertaken through government intervention and by private reformers (Marten 2014). These reform efforts were a direct response to industrialization, immigration, and the lingering disruption to families and communities in the aftermath of the U.S. Civil War, all of which threatened to undermine social coherence and national identity as well as the quality of life of all Americans (Fass 2016; Mintz 2004). This is not to suggest that reform efforts were enacted simply to maintain a sense of comfort among the nation's elite. There were real and pressing issues facing children. Street children and foundlings became common especially in urban areas, and many children suffered due to unsafe living conditions, demands on their labor, and inadequate nutrition and access to health care (Mintz 2004). Childhood was seen as a domain of influence where institutions and organizations could have a greater impact in people's lives, and children were central to ideas about reform.

One of the major reform efforts of the nineteenth century was to bring free, tax-supported education to all Americans. This effort was very successful, and school enrollments increased steadily throughout the century. However, the ability to partake in public education varied widely by social class, race, and geographic location. Appeals for common schooling were made on the basis of three main arguments (Kaestle 1983). The first appealed to people's Christian values. Reformers stated that all members of society should share moral values and virtuous lifestyles. They argued that the institution of public education would enable moral lessons to be taught not only at home and in church, but also in a school environment five days a week. The second appeal was made on a political front. Americans in the nineteenth century held a great deal of concern for the country's fledgling democracy. Reformers argued that public schooling, with a mission to educate all individuals, was essential for a successful democratic republic. The final argument used for promoting public education was the need for education in a capitalist society. Activists presented schooling as a useful vehicle to teach the values of industry, competition, and the sanctity of property. All of these lessons were thought to ensure the healthy survival of capitalism in the United States.

Because these schools emphasized Protestant values as an integral part of every lesson, many Catholics and Jews began their own alternative schools (Clement 1997: 83). Immigrants who were not able to attend these private and parochial schools found public school a harsh environment. Instructors are consistently described as antagonistic and disdainful in nineteenth-century accounts of immigrant schoolchildren (Berrol 1992: 47). English was the only language tolerated in school, making learning even more of a challenge for many. Schools also took a forward role in "Americanizing" immigrant children, so that they would go home and help in the process of assimilating their families. Selma Berrol summarizes this assimilating role of public schools as "apparently to everyone's satisfaction, immigrant children learned WASP etiquette, along with WASP speech, and dress from their teachers, who also brought culture into their lives" (1992: 50). Because "ethnic" food, dress, and language were not tolerated in the school environment, children were encouraged to go home and demand "American" cooking and clothing from their parents.

A second arena where children came into contact with the broader community was by entering the workforce. Children worked extensively in rural agricultural areas, and also in urban industrial communities. Children worked in mines and mills where harsh industrial conditions prevailed, and also in domestic service, agricultural activities, and street trades. In urban environments family poverty forced the majority of children into some type of employment at one time or another (Zelizer 1994). However, in many immigrant families putting children to work was not socially stigmatized, because child labor was common in Europe. Factory owners were desperate for a large workforce in many industrial towns, and they found children desirable because of their manual dexterity and submissiveness. To increase the number of children in their workforce many factory owners deliberately underpaid parents, and then offered them bonuses for recruiting additional family members (Schmidt 2010). Children also worked in nonindustrial settings. Young boys worked on the streets scavenging for ragpickers, running errands and delivering messages, and selling newspapers. Young girls were more apt to enter into domestic service, or work in laundries or other service industries.

Reformers worked to limit child labor throughout the nineteenth century. These activists were concerned for children's physical well-being and their moral condition (Fass 2016; Mintz 2004). However, many children still entered the workforce despite the many child labor laws and welfare institutions that were put into place. Legislation outlawed the employment of children in industrial settings, but many loopholes and unscrupulous factory owners kept children employed, although in dramatically reduced numbers (Schmidt 2010). These laws did not address the other types of child labor that were pervasive at the time, including agricultural work, domestic service, and street trades.

Community involvement in the life of impoverished and delinquent children also resulted in the development of institutions of childhood reform. Child-saving movements existed prior to the nineteenth century, particularly with the establishment of almshouses or poorhouses (Casella 2009; De Cunzo 2006). These institutions accommodated individuals of all ages who would have otherwise been homeless and destitute. As the nineteenth century began, and new ideals of the unique and innocent child emerged, concerns were raised among reformers about the potential for children's "corruption" that might result from such intimate exposure to adults (Clement 1997: 189–190).

Orphanages were developed to address this newfound concern. The purpose of these institutions was to house impoverished and delinquent children in an environment that would retain childhood innocence and promote moral virtue. These institutions were seen as surrogate families and as a means to remove children from the influence of inappropriate parents and communities. The majority of children in nineteenth-century orphanages had at least one living parent or extended family member, but orphanages tried to estrange children from these family members. Staff members either forbade or restricted family visits and censored all mail to and from the children. The main roles of the institution were to feed, clothe, educate, employ, and resettle children into new environments. This approach was designed not only to improve the lives of a current generation of children, but also to break the cycles of poverty and delinquency that plagued urban environments (Cohen 1985). Other ventures, such as orphan trains, relocated children away from their homes and families in eastern urban areas to rural areas where they were taken in by farm families seeking additional labor (Fass 2016).

Orphanages did not accept all children into their charity, but rather they focused on white urban youth. African Americans explicitly were denied access to the vast majority of these reform institutions. Both young boys and girls entered into orphanages and stayed until they were between 18 and 21 years of age. Many institutions were single-sex facilities, or they housed orphans of different genders separately so that the women who emerged from institutional care would still be perceived as marriageable. Women, thought to be the best possible caregivers for children, ran the majority of orphan asylums.

The childhood ideals put forth by families and communities also had material components. Parents used material culture, clothing, furniture, and playthings to mold their children in their image of an ideal child, and to protect them from contact with the adult world. In a society where a family's success in the material world directly correlated to their moral virtue and worth (McGuire 1991), a child who was inappropriately attired and presented, or who engaged in behaviors contrary to their innocent nature, was considered to be very telling about the true moral conduct of the parents (Calvert 1992; Clement 1997). Families made an overt, material expression of acceptance of contemporary ideals of childhood by outfitting their children appropriately. This expression would have been visible when the child left the home and entered into the public sphere at school, church, and play.

Material culture of childhood from this period is bound in understandings of innocence through the maintenance of sexual innocence and gender boundaries. The most obvious material expression of childhood was clothing. Clothing and hairstyles of the time were designed to present young children as androgynous beings (figure 2.6). The integration of traditional elements of boys' clothing, particularly long pantaloons, with dresses and frocks associated with young girls, came from fashions worn by children visiting from Europe. This new look did not catch on right away in America. While young boys had always worn dresses during their earlier years, the adoption of pants by young girls was seen as a case of females usurping masculine prerogatives. However, by midcentury an androgynous look was the dominant form of dress and was embraced and popularized in periodicals such as *Godey's Lady's Magazine*, and in children's literature such as Frances Hodgson Burnett's *Little Lord Fauntleroy*.

Parents created a unique material signature through this style of clothing that reinforced the concept of childhood as a separate stage of development (Calvert 1992: 99–103). At the same time the androgynous style denied or blurred the sexual distinctions between boys and girls. This was an important feature of such clothing as it was credited with disrupting the emergence of a child's sexual awareness, one of the primary mechanisms through which childhood innocence was lost. This view was expressed by Dr. Christian Struve, when he wrote that if young people were not dressed similarly, "the attention of children might be excited to the difference of the sexes, a circumstance which would deprive them, at an early age, of their innocence and happy ignorance." In actuality, however, children's costumes likely did little to prolong their innocence of sexual differences between men and women, because these differences were clearly visible in the adult world. What this new style of dress did achieve, however, was to bring the visual image of children into accord with social expectations of innocence, and served to reassure concerned parents (Calvert 1992:109).

Toys, unlike children's appearance, were gender-specific, and often replicated the tools and social skills required to perform the adult roles that loomed ahead (Calvert 1992; Chudacoff 2007; Heininger 1984: 8–9). Parents provided these gender-specific toys for two main reasons. The first reason was to reinforce messages about proper attitudes and behaviors in their children (Praetzellis and Praetzellis 1992; Rotman 2015). The second reason was that parents believed gender-specific toys would bring their children the most pleasure, as they considered gender-specific roles and behaviors to be an inherent part of human nature (Calvert 1992: 111). All forms of play became more structured, were designed to carry moral messages, and were developed to keep children isolated from the world of adults (Chudacoff 2007). Unsupervised, unstructured play was considered dangerous and limiting for appropriate intellectual, physical, and moral development.

Toys selected for girls provided domestic training and encouraged restful and solitary play. Dolls and doll accessories, such as toy cradles, tea sets, and furniture, were by far the most common types of toys marketed for girls (Forman-Brunell 1998; Mumma and Baxter 2018). Ideally, girls were to use dolls in two types of play. In the first type of play, a doll would serve as a baby, where a young girl could cultivate the skills of a future nurturing mother. In the second form of play, dolls were companions for tea parties and social events, which taught appropriate social behavior. These scenarios for girls were literally "womanhood in miniature" (Dawson 2003: 68). While it appears that girls in rural areas were allowed to play outdoors (Riney-Kehrberg 2014), most girls' play was centered on the home, and encouraged solitary, restful pursuits rather than physically active lifestyles whether they preferred this type of activity or not (Chudacoff 2007).

In contrast, parents encouraged young boys to engage in active and interactive pursuits, allowing them to develop their social skills, physical well-being, and mental alacrity (Chudacoff 2007). Toys such as marbles, balls, whips, guns, cannons, hobbyhorses, and wagons were all designed for social play, and to get young boys out of the home and into public spaces. Toys related to war and warfare were common. Parents offered their sons more toys, and more types of toys, to choose from than they did their daughters. This difference reflects the broader array of cultural roles that were available to boys as they grew into young men (Calvert 1992).

Educational toys and objects for children became common in the marketplace so that playtime would be useful morally and intellectually. These included board games as well as interactive toys (Barton and Somerville 2012; Somerville 2015). Children also used writing slates and pencils for educational purposes. Many infant-related accoutrements, such as baby feeders, rattles, and coral jewelry were used in the care of both boys and girls. Furniture and play spaces, such as nurseries and bedrooms for individual children, developed to contain and physically segregate children from adult activities in the home (Calvert 1992). These rooms were designed to be of central importance in children's lives, where they could be introduced to schedules and routines (Beecher 1841: 219).

The ability to mass-produce goods and the demand to develop new products and capture new markets resulted in an incredible proliferation of children's material culture both in quantity and quality. These toys and child-rearing devices reflected more than gender ideals and separate spheres for adults and children. They echoed subtler, yet highly significant, social sentiments of the moment. Mechanical and clockwork toys were quite popular as they used cutting-edge technology (clock gear systems) to automate movement in toys (Somerville 2015). Such toys were symbolic of industrialization itself, representing order, time, and mechanization, and were designed to be sold to middle-class consumers to emphasize those values that were prized in the new capitalist economy (Somerville 2015: 282–283). Mechanized toys were also relatively expensive and appealed to families wishing to display wealth through their children (figure 2.7). Other toys that were educational in nature helped to build basic skills such as learning letters and numbers, but also to help children learn

Figure 2.7. Mid-nineteenth-century mechanical toy carousel at the New York Historical Society. These toys represented industrial technologies and values on a small scale suitable for children and promoted core values of the American middle class. The Wikipedia Loves Art Project by Opal_Art_Seekers_4, taken by Flickr user griannan.

contemporary ideas about the broader world, such as history, geography, and moral lessons (figure 2.8). Other toys and accessories reinforced contemporary perceptions of social difference, such as racialized toys that portrayed African Americans, Chinese, and Irish in socially clichéd and stereotypical manners. Other toys inculcated children with a sense of patriotism and nationalism (Somerville 2015:288).

Historical sources also provide some insights into how play and material culture were used by children to challenge parents' expectations of them. Memoirs often recall the frustrations of young girls whose play was constrained and controlled, while their male siblings played more freely and actively (Chudacoff 2007). Many girls sought ways to engage in more

Figure 2.8. Mid nineteenth-century child's plate featuring the alphabet and depicting "Italians" as one of the "Nations of the World." Material culture for children emphasized education and learning, as material prosperity and moral virtue were entwined. A family could use such objects to display their social, economic, and moral standing through the appropriate display and use of such objects by children. Photo by Joseph Furbeck for the author.

active play, and bent or broke rules for their proper behavior to engage in more active, and more fun, recreation, including playing alongside their male siblings and relatives. Similarly, doll play became a space of rebellion where scenarios were created in which dolls were intentionally broken and damaged reflecting anger and frustration toward imposed rules and expectations placed upon young girls (Forman-Brunell 1998; Wilkie 2000). Even with their relative freedom, young boys moved past structured play into activities considered dangerous and inappropriate as ways of creating autonomous spaces for themselves (Chudacoff 2007). Many of these forms of resistance and rebellion are illustrated in the archaeological record as well.

Twentieth-Century Childhoods and the Emergence of Adolescence (1900–1950)

It is easy for someone with even a casual awareness of contemporary American childhood to see its roots in the later nineteenth century. The ideal of innocent children and the need to protect them from corrupting and painful dynamics of the "real world" are in constant tension with the need to shape and prepare children for their future roles as adults in the best way possible (Mintz 2004: 92). The careful balancing act of maintaining innocence while providing appropriate experiences and opportunities was the concern of nineteenth-century parents and communities, much as it is today. Using an arsenal of specially designed material culture and cultural spaces to shape and buffer these contrasting ideals is also a uniting thread of the past 150 years. The difference is, of course, in the details. Certainly, many changes in childhood took place in the early twentieth century, particularly as the Progressive Era was in full swing (Fass 2016). However, there are three important themes related to early twentieth-century childhoods that help to capture the transformation of broadly shared core ideas about childhood across a century of time: the role of science in child-rearing, increased government intervention, and the rise of the child consumer. Many of these transformations had their roots in the last decades of the nineteenth century and got fully under way during the twentieth. These elements also combined to expand and extend the acceptable period of social dependency and preparation for adulthood well into an individual's later teenage years: a period known as adolescence.

Beginning in the 1890s, science and scholarship about children replaced amateur reform and child saving movements, and reshaped popular discourse and understandings of childhood. In 1886 the American Pediatric Association was established, formalizing the idea that there were unique age-related standards for child health and development in physical, cognitive, and emotional dimensions (Chudacoff 2007: 70). Parents, teachers, psychologists, and social welfare specialists moved in to make sure children's play was functional, healthy, and safe—all in the service of helping children to make critical developmental milestones. These types of initiatives included interventions that historian Howard Chudacoff

(2007: 101) characterized as "the invasion of childhood." Organized sports, playgrounds, educational games, and toys all overseen by adults overtook significant amounts of children's leisure time, leaving less and less time for unstructured, child-generated play, imagination, and recreation.

Having scientists, educators, and doctors considered childhood "experts" enter into the discourse had another major consequence: it introduced the idea of an "Average American Child" (Fass 2016). The idea that there was a normal, average American child enabled the establishment of benchmarks and milestones for all types of development. The creation of an ideal, normal child meant that children could be measured against the average and be labeled as delinquent or superior against these norms. Parents now had a way of scientifically gauging their success as parents, depending on how their children measured up in terms of educational, emotional, social, and physical standards. The codification of such standards also systematically and scientifically undermined ethnic patterns of child-rearing popular in immigrant families, as those children rarely met standards for a normal American child because of cultural and linguistic barriers (Fass 2016). Ideas of average and normal also became tools to continually marginalize African American children as their families and communities reconfigured after emancipation and sought opportunities to raise their children into new and different futures (Mitchell 2010).

Steven Mintz (2004: 279) has argued that parental anxieties shifted at this time away from childhood mortality to producing socially ideal children. The most important question for parents was no longer whether or not their child would survive (because for the first time in history they most likely would), but rather what sort of person they would become. The goal of parenting was not just to produce a healthy, happy child but also a psychologically well-adjusted adult. The emergence of scientific standards for "normal" helped to cultivate this sense of anxiety. Children who were labeled as below average or not normal were seen as the product of bad parenting. Similarly, adults labeled as maladjusted or antisocial in some way were determined to be the products of deficient childhoods and negligent parents. By the mid-twentieth century, unifying material and cultural forces in the form of mass media gave Americans a sense of what normal looked like (figure 2.9). As parental anxieties swelled, fads in material culture and popular guides to empower parents, such as Dr. Spock's, became common in the marketplace. Trends and fads in parenting offered obvious behavioral and material ways to display an acceptance

Figure 2.9. *Leave It to Beaver*: The Cleaver family (Ward, Wally, June, and The Beaver) circa 1960. Idyllic notions of the American family are often reinforced. Image from ABC Television.

and awareness of what was normal at the moment, as seen on television and in other popular media outlets.

Parents were not left alone to worry about their children and the outcome of their parenting efforts, as during the first decades of the twentieth century the federal government became increasingly involved in insuring basic standards of care for all American children (Chudacoff 2007; Fass 2016; Mintz 2004). President Roosevelt convened the first White House conference on dependent children in 1909. Over 200 activists and experts attended to express concerns over the horrors reported in private and religiously sponsored institutions designed for child care, and the exploitation of children in the labor force. There was an appeal for a dedicated agency in the U.S. government to directly address the needs and concerns of children. The Children's Bureau, administered by the Department of Labor, was established in 1913 in response, and was an agency designed to work for the welfare of all of the nation's children. A second conference was hosted by President Wilson in 1919, a year he declared the "Children's Year" to turn the national spotlight on to issues relating to child welfare and labor and to energize governmental and private initiatives to support children. A third such conference, arranged by President Hoover, resulted in the declaration that a happy, healthy childhood was a fundamental right in U.S. culture. This attention to childhood resulted in programs, initiatives, and legal protections for children sponsored by the federal government, all designed to insure that all children in the United States received the basic rights of childhood.

The Progressive Era brought about major domestic reforms regarding children and childhood in the United States at a time when the country was emerging as a major world power. Historian Paula Fass (2016: 128) has argued that one of the major consequences of this domestic agenda and change in world stature was the establishment of high schools as a uniquely American institution that insured continued education not just for the nation's elite, but for everyone. High schools were an initiative tied to the American economy and developed in part as a strategy to help manage the enormous immigrant population entering the country. While all schools were different and certainly not equal, through particular common elements high schools offered a means to provide a unifying experience for every member of a generation. The importance of this fledgling institution to the nation can be seen in its persistence and stability throughout the Great Depression of the 1930s.

Much like parenting, high school education was all about the future. Comprehensive high schools were designed to produce literate and reliable citizens and also expose students to things beyond academics, including clubs, art, performance, sport, newspapers, magazines, and recreational activities. High schools were modeled on democracy, and empowered students with the possibilities of self-government and self-determination in the types of activities that took place outside a more standard academic curriculum. Enrollment in high school surged in the three decades after 1910, with enrollment rates increasing from 18 to 73 percent and the national graduation rate rising from 9 to 51 (Fass 2016: 135).

The pressure on parents to shepherd children into productive adulthoods and the unusual government investment in American children through expanded education programs combined to elongate the period of childhood dependency into a period of adolescence. The culturally defined category of identity known as adolescence seems relatively clear today. Individuals in adolescence often are referred to with terms like tween or teen, and are recognized as someone not quite childlike, but neither fully adult. While some version of adolescence has been identified cross-culturally in a great many cultures (Schlegel and Barry 1991), in America the construct of adolescence is seen as a historical development, often tied to G. S. Hall's 1916 "discovery" of the phenomenon. Hall believed that adolescence was age-specific and tied to the hormonal and physiological drives that began with the emotional turbulence that emerged with the onset of puberty and waned as an individual entered into their early twenties. His work was infused with the certainty of biological science, and postulated that adolescence was an inescapable feature of human development, despite no such identity being recognized in early periods of the nation's history. In Hall's characterization, adolescence was a time of "storm and stress" with drugs, delinquency, depression, and social and sexual deviance being typical.

Scholarship throughout the twentieth century continued to portray adolescence as a developmental imperative in the human life cycle. Famously, Erik Erikson (1968) advocated that adolescence was an essential time for an individual's identity formation. It was a period where individuals overcame uncertainty, and became more self-aware through a process of crisis (an "identity crisis") and self-reflection that led to self-definition. Because adolescence was seen as such a tumultuous time and teens were no longer fully adult, cultural attitudes about deviance and normalcy became codified in the legal realm as things like age of consent for sexual conduct and debates over minimum age for use of tobacco, alcohol, and driving became ways of delineating those who had not yet attained adult status from those who had (Luker 2006).

Biological and psychological explanations of a universal, inevitable adolescence reflect the growing influence of science in defining childhood and determining appropriate cultural responses to human development during the twentieth century. The social definition of adolescence that emerged in twentieth-century America came at a time when changing ideas and pressures surrounding childhood were pulling society in different directions. Extending parental responsibility to include the type of adults their offspring became prolonged the social and economic dependence of children on parents. Simultaneously, stretching education through the teenage years in high school offered increased social independence for children and adolescents as their time spent away from home in school and extracurricular activities amplified the influence of cultural forces beyond the family. Young people became cultural innovators and the generators of popular culture as "adolescence became a prolonged sojourn of development spent among other youth" (Fass 2016: 135). At a time when parents were feeling increasingly responsible for their children, they also felt they were losing control over their cultural worlds (Cross 2004).

The emergence of adolescence in the twentieth century demands attention because it is a historical shift in accepted categories of identity in American culture. Americans didn't always care that much about a person's precise age. What one could and could not do had more to do with one's circumstances, class, and ability rather than a strict chronology (Luker 2006: 39). The twentieth century ushered in a series of changes that oriented society toward knowing one's precise age, reaching milestones, and behaving accordingly as a bit of a cultural obsession.

It was during the twentieth century that children and adolescents became a significant consumer force, shaping the spending habits not only of their peers, but also of the adults around them. Targeting young people and their purchasing power did not originate in the twentieth century, however, despite an often held assumption that nineteenth-century childhood innocence included being separated from the consumer marketplace, especially for middle-class children (Mintz 2004: 76–77). Paul Ringel has recently shown that business interests were shaping child consumers as early as the 1820s through children's goods, including magazines (Ringel 2015), and that institutions to protect children from the dangers of consumption can be found as early as the 1870s (Ringel 2008). His work showed that antebellum adults often saw commodities to be appropriate tools through which children could be trained to succeed in an urban, market-driven world (Ringel 2015: 8–9). Inculcating children to be savvy, thoughtful consumers was a project undertaken through the use of magazines (Ringel 2015), books (Jacobson 2008b), and consumer trading cards (Schultz 2018) promoting products children might use, but also products for the home in general. Still during this time, most children's material culture was purchased by parents for children and only for special occasions (figure 2.10). The acquisition of toys and playthings was not a quotidian transaction as often it is today, and it was not directly child-driven.

The direct targeting of children and adolescents as consumers, and its many consequences, is often tied to the maturation and entrenchment of consumer capitalism at the turn of the twentieth century (Cook

2004; Jacobson 2008a). One way producers and advertisers sought new markets was to target entirely new demographics for their products, and children and young adults were as yet a largely untapped consumer force. By 1905, advertisers were writing openly about the "pestering power" of children in their campaigns to cultivate desire among children for toys and playthings and products for their homes and families as well (Jacobson 2008a). Department stores created special sections for toys that were available year-round, offered babysitting services in such departments while mothers shopped, and hosted special events for children to cultivate their sense of desire for particular products and objects (Pursell 2015). In the 1930s, stores deliberately lowered counter heights and the positioning of mirrors to accommodate children, and staff were trained to treat children as consumers, offering age-appropriate incentives that emphasized children's autonomy in the marketplace (Jacobson 2008a). The material landscape of shopping became altered to accommodate children as independent consumers. Print advertising in children's magazines, advertisements on the radio and television, and marketing for toys that could only be acquired through the purchase of an unrelated household product (such as breakfast cereal, laundry soap, or other everyday item) all became ways of cultivating child consumers and pressuring parents to comply with their perceived needs and desires (Cross 1997; Jacobson 2008a; figure 2.10).

Parents were and are always a "silent partner" in most any transaction involving children because of economic power and the ability to grant or deny consent over a particular purchase, but the empowerment of children as a driving economic force changes dramatically over the course of the twentieth century (chapter 6). I would argue that an awareness of the changing status of children as consumers is imperative for archaeologists analyzing children's material culture. Many types of toys, such as dolls, for example, do not change radically in form or character during this same period when consumer power is being reconfigured between adults and children. Very similar objects found in deposits just a few decades apart may have been acquired in radically different ways by the children who used them. Understanding transformations in the later nineteenth and early twentieth century around the dynamics and contexts of consumption is essential for the interpretation of children's material culture encountered archaeologically.

Twentieth-century material culture for children was shaped by decades

Figure 2.10. Christmas advertising in the *Chicago Tribune*, December 13, 1896. This advertisement for Lloyd's leads with goods for children and uses the lure of visiting Santa in the store and the chance to be "surrounded by toys" as an enticement. This proliferation of toys and playthings, as well as a special area for children within department stores, was a new phenomenon in the late nineteenth century. The advertisement ties the consumption of toys to special occasions, particularly Christmas, which was the accepted way for children to acquire toys throughout most of the nineteenth century. *Chicago Daily Tribune* (1872–1922), December 13, 1896. Display 10.

Figure 2.11. Advertisement for Erector Set toy, *Popular Science Magazine*, November 1952. Advertisements such as this show the growing trend to emphasize the preparatory nature of boys' play in the burgeoning technologies of the twentieth century. These ideas of technological preparedness on the part of young children were tied to greater narratives about keeping America at an advantage in technology in times of war and peace. Photo by Flickr user Joe Haupt (CCby).

of warfare and the rapidly changing world of technological innovation that was ushered in largely by the First and Second World Wars. Simultaneously, toys were a vehicle to create a sense of continuity to a traditional American past creating a tension in the values being communicated to children. The need for the United States to maintain technological superiority over other nations and to have a home front that could mobilize in a war effort shaped not only formal education but also the types of goods made available to children for play. Young boys particularly were encouraged to use toys that were scientific in nature such as engineering and building tools, chemistry kits, and home science experiment sets (Onion 2016; Pursell 2015; figure 2.11). By the mid-twentieth century, some of these toys contained actual radioactive material to help make children feel comfortable in the atomic age, and to encourage scientific experimentation, espionage against imagined enemies, and the prospecting for uranium as part of their play repertoire. War toys were actually somewhat controversial, as anti-war toy movements helped to shape the design of and discourse around the continuous influx of soldiers and later soldier "action figures," toy-sized war vehicles, and toy guns, swords, and other weaponry into the marketplace (Cross 1997; Rhodes 2017). Toys for girls emphasized the importance of the new popular science of home economy, with miniaturized suites of domestic furnishings such as play kitchens and toy vacuums and ironing boards becoming popular. Dolls remained ever popular tools to inculcate young girls into the realm of domesticity, and, when technology allowed dolls to become more lifelike, took on biological and social characteristics of real babies. Kitchen toys also developed to include technology for basic cooking on a miniaturized scale to help insure young girls were ready to assume the role of home front housewife as needed (Onion 2015; Pursell 2015).

Another feature of twentieth-century child and teen consumption was that of media, particularly media produced exclusively for their use and enjoyment. Organizations that emphasized peer interaction, such as scouting and 4H, produced periodicals that were targeted to the organization members—not their adult leaders and facilitators. Other similar periodicals such as *Co-Ed*, *Seventeen*, and *Highlights for Children* were launched and became popular in the mid-twentieth century. Television shows such as *The Mickey Mouse Club* brought a collective sense of American tween/teen culture into homes across the country (figure 2.12). The programming of such shows and the contents of such periodicals directly addressed the concerns of children and teens, and, while produced by adults, they all offered the chance to hear voices of peers asking questions, offering advice, and creating a shared sense of age-specific experiences that excluded those younger and older than the targeted audience (Baxter 2016). These types of media experiences cultivated a sense of identity with objects and groups that were outside the home, creating a formalized sense of peer-culture that was not tied to family or to school.

Material & Social Histories of Childhood & Adolescence in the U.S. · 65

Figure 2.12. Photo of the Mouseketeers from the television program *The Mickey Mouse Club* circa 1956. Shows such as *The Mickey Mouse Club* helped to underpin the power of peer culture for twentieth-century adolescents and children by featuring content that specifically addressed their concerns and were sponsored by advertisers offering products directly to them. Wikimedia.

These insights into childhood from historical sources offer a sense of how American childhood has transformed throughout the nation's history. This historical approach will be continued in chapter 6 as this narrative is developed through the lens of contemporary archaeology and contemporary material culture studies. This background is also foundational for understanding how the lived experiences of children, as seen through the archaeological record, are connected to popular discourses about childhood throughout the nation's history. Ways in which American childhood is constructed, idealized, transformed, and "lost" can be seen in even a cursory historical overview such as this one, and the significant role of material culture in all of these constructed ideals is indicative of the potency and potential of archaeology to illuminate childhood and adolescence in the American experience.

~ 3 ~

Children in Their Living Spaces

Nineteenth- and Twentieth-Century Domestic Sites

Almost certainly, any archaeologist who has worked on a nineteenth- or twentieth-century domestic site has encountered artifacts readily identifiable as toys or child-specific objects (figure 3.1). These assemblages almost always include marbles, toy tea set fragments, and doll parts, and perhaps some metal parts from mechanical toys or cast-iron toy soldiers. Occasionally, pieces of dishware for children (figure 2.8) and some fragments of writing slates and slate pencils (figure 4.2) will round out the assemblage. At twentieth-century sites, plastic and its predecessors allow for many children's playthings to remain for archaeological discovery. There generally are very few artifacts that fit into this category of child-specific objects, even from the largest and most extensive excavation projects.

On the one hand, these objects are a kind of crutch, offering archaeologists an easy way to acknowledge the presence of children without having to really look for them (Wilkie 2000) but most often, like other artifacts found in limited numbers, child-specific artifacts are dutifully reported but not interpreted, as such energies tend to be spent on artifact types found in abundance, such as ceramics, glass, and zooarchaeological remains (Beaudry 2009; White and Beaudry 2009). It is not uncommon for archaeologists to acknowledge the presence of children at domestic

Figure 3.1. A "typical" assemblage of children's artifacts found at a nineteenth-century domestic site: doll parts, doll accessories, marbles, and parts from metal clockwork-operated toys. Most archaeologists working on nineteenth-century domestic sites encounter similar assemblages of artifacts that are few in number but represent the objects purchased for and used by the children in the household. From "The Archaeology of a San Francisco Neighborhood," Sonoma College.

sites, and authors tend to present children, when mentioned, as integral to household activities and structures, but they are rarely specifically addressed as independent actors within the domestic sphere (Barile and Brandon 2004; Fogle, Nyman, and Beaudry 2015; Groover 2008; Rotman and Clay 2008; Tomaso et al. 2006). The state of affairs can be summed up thus: archaeological evidence for children is found at nearly every excavated site in America, but the number of published sources that can be used to interpret children in domestic contexts are few. As the sources highlighted in this chapter suggest, however, taking the time to work with these small assemblages of artifacts to explore the lives of children in household contexts provides rich and rewarding narratives about the American past.

Historical archaeology's disciplinary penchant for studying those underrepresented in the historical record is evidenced by the types of domestic sites most commonly studied, and the ways households are interpreted as economic as well as social units. Upper- and middle-class households are rarely the focus of archaeological investigations, and most scholarship is directed toward working families, whether at farms, plantations, industrial sites, or urban neighborhoods. This bias is in part due to the relative abundance of homes of working families on the landscape, but the ways in which they are interpreted as households reflect a consistent underlying disciplinary concern for class and class struggles in the American past, regardless of the specific issues being addressed in any particular study. Many authors have directly integrated children, how families made choices in providing for their children, and the value systems that informed those choices into their understandings of households, particularly in the context of middle-class hegemony and the realities of working class life.

Before the industrial revolution, households and often entire communities were organized around labor and production, and families shared the same vocation. Labor was the responsibility of all members of a family, and the differentiation of work and home was minimal as multiple generations worked together in support of their household. American opportunism worked to break this system down while it persisted in Europe (Fass 2016; chapter 1), but the real shift came when industrial production all but dissolved the home workplace. A major consequence of this shift in production and the circumstances of labor was that all working people became responsible for raising children independently (Matthews 2010; Wall 1994). Children became a major focus of the lives of families as, "given the multitude of difficulties attendant to procreation, from childbearing and birth itself to costs of food, clothing, shelter, and health, to the responsibility of transmitting values—children are typically and rightfully the central focus of parental life" (Matthews 2010: 13). The significance of raising children cannot be overemphasized when thinking about domestic sites. Children define a family household and demand physical, financial, and emotional resources that structure and reproduce social and economic orders.

Childhood itself was transformed by capitalism as children became symbolic and public representations of respectable domesticity and parenting that were tied to practices in and of the home (Fitts 1999). Raising children "appropriately" in the dominant discourse became synonymous with middle-class values, and those values could be directly displayed in the material world (chapter 2). Domestic rituals, such as mealtimes, were an important aspect of socializing and training children to emulate these values and ideas and were regarded as "three opportunities a day for teaching punctuality, order, neatness, temperance, self-denial, kindness, generosity, and hospitality" (Fitts 1999: 49). Mealtimes became important family reunions as families now spent days apart. Middle-class children were at school, mothers tended the home, and fathers went to work. Family bonding and cohesion occurred over meals, not over work, and the role of women in overseeing the preparation and serving of meals elevated their position in the household.

Training for children would be ineffective if not carried out with appropriate matching tableware and an array of vessel choices for specific courses and dishes. The cultural knowledge of not just what to eat but how to eat it was a chance to display understandings of class and to perform class within and beyond the home. Having specialized dining sets for children was a part of an ideal middle-class household dining ensemble (Fitts 1999), and their presence in archaeological assemblages has been interpreted in relationship to class and class aspirations of particular households (e.g., Rotman and Clay 2008; Walker 2008). The daily rituals and mundane furnishings of everyday life became essential expressions of class identity, and children provided very clear evidence for the appropriate lessons and values being taught in the home. These standards of middle-class genteel respectability provide a useful way of considering how children in other types of households were a part of social and material discourse around the nature of childhood, particularly as it related to family identity and dynamics of class and ethnicity (see also chapter 2).

Assessing the quality of families was not left to passive performance, and literature was developed and organizations formed not only to support institutions to help those deemed to be in need (chapter 4) but also to intervene directly in working-class families and households for their betterment (Spencer-Wood 1991, 1996). Many of these domestic reform movements were the purview of middle-class women who found empowerment in their newly redefined roles in the household, and sought to promote agendas where the domestic sphere was seen as equal to the public sphere of men, giving women a domain of equivalent power. The agenda of the middle-class reformers was steeped in religion and Americanizing immigrant families. Working-class families had to choose to participate in reform, and power did not lie solely with reformers. Values were always in dialogue, and working-class women had agency in these exchanges. Some of these exchanges were certainly about childhood. Reformers advocated for particular activities for children, such as gardening, participating in tea rituals alongside adults, structured play, and home schooling (Spencer-Wood 1996). Ideas of reformers included rethinking the spatial dynamics inside and outside the home that allowed for women's work and children's play to co-occur (Spencer-Wood 1996). Other reform movements sought to transform women's family and mothering roles into socialized child care and education in public cooperative housekeeping institutions, including day nurseries, kindergartens, and kitchen gardens (Spencer-Wood 1991). These reform movements were not confined to urban areas, as women's guilds brought the latest reform literature to rural areas as well (Clement 1997; chapter 2).

Rural Childhoods and Farm Life

America began as a largely rural nation taking advantage of the enormity of the available landscape and variety of regional climates to produce a diverse array of products for both local subsistence and international trade. Perhaps the primary value of America as a colony in the seventeenth and eighteenth centuries was as an agricultural outpost in the European economy. Children living on farms experienced fundamentally different worlds than their urban counterparts (figure 3.2). Immersed deeply in the day-to-day rhythms of farm life and the natural environment, rural children were exposed to nature in all its tempers, engaged in activities that blurred boundaries of work and play in the out-of-doors, and worked alongside adults in seasonal tasks (Riney-Kehrberg 2014). Rural childhoods emphasized freedom and play in nature, and historians suggest the material culture of play was often far less formalized, with children creating their own playthings more often than using mass-produced goods. Ideas of optimal gender separation presented in reform and parenting literature and practiced in more populated areas were not always possible in rural areas, as there were fewer options for "suitable" peers for play (Chudacoff 2007: 51). Education, considered an essential part of American childhood, particularly in rural communities (chapter 4), was suspended during times of peak demand for labor in the agricultural season.

72 · Archaeology of American Childhood & Adolescence

Figure 3.2. The sod house of Martinus B. Olson circa 1886. This image depicts children in front of their sod home as America spread westward in the nineteenth century. Courtesy of North Dakota State University Archives and the Digital Horizons: Life on the Northern Plains project.

Rural children had a much greater likelihood of surviving to adulthood than children living in cities, because despite potential risks and dangers of farm work and vulnerabilities of living so close to nature, the open spaces and relatively hygienic conditions reduced exposure to pathogens that could sweep efficiently through densely packed urban populations (Riney-Kehrberg 2014: 11–21).

Children had mixed views of farm life, and over time many opted to move away from their rural roots and make their own futures in cities, as illustrated in the rapid urbanization of America in the last decades of the nineteenth century. At the same time, adults, particularly those living in cities, believed that rural life was perhaps the only place to raise happy, healthy, and moral children. This idealized view of rural life was at the roots of many reform movements, perhaps most famously C. Loring Brace's "orphan trains" that relocated orphaned, neglected, or poor children from eastern cities to live in rural communities from the mid-1850s through the 1920s (Fass 2016; Riney-Kehrberg 2014: 25). Within local communities, formalized organizations such as 4H and the Future Farmers of America emerged to encourage more children to remain on farms and maintain and develop technologies and lifeways for living effectively and efficiently away from city life.

The archaeology of farmsteads is incredibly common in America, particularly as part of cultural resource management (CRM) projects taking place before farmlands are transformed into suburban housing (Groover 2008). In her book on agriculture in Delaware that draws on both academic and CRM archaeology, Lu Ann De Cunzo pointed out many of the challenges particular to archaeological research on farmstead sites. She wrote,

> Historical archaeologists cannot excavate a two-hundred-acre farm, even when the entire property does lie within the construction boundaries of a CRM project. But neither can we understand the cultures of agriculture if we only excavate in and around the houses, barns, and outbuildings and in the trash heaps of historic farms, as has been our wont. (2004: 4)

Agriculture is a social enterprise that transforms entire landscapes, and the economy of farmsteads is deeply tied to the social and political processes that make such work possible.

Archaeology at the Felton Farmstead in Wayne County, Michigan, identified children's play activities on the farm in places that underscore the importance of focusing on areas both around the central buildings and also further afield (Baxter 2000). While children's artifacts were found in discrete areas in the farmyard, reflecting gender-segregated play, other assemblages of children's artifacts were found well beyond the built area of the farmstead. The play that took place around the different buildings was in clear sight of work areas and the farmhouse windows, suggesting that the surveillance of children by adults was possible as they were accomplishing their own work at the farm. Artifacts found further afield suggest that children were finding places for play where they could avoid the gaze of adults. The assemblage from this site was very small, reinforcing the idea that most play was undertaken as a component of work, using found objects, and engaging the natural world. The patterning of the limited mass-produced goods indicates social ideals of gender were being upheld even in a rural population, but also illustrates the wide-ranging opportunities for play that rural life afforded to children.

Comparative archaeological work at farm sites tends to defy historical ideas about the paucity of commercial toys at such sites, and in fact archaeological assemblages indicate that mass-produced goods for children were quite common on American farmsteads. Catalogues enabled sales of toys and goods for children directly to parents and families, and the merchandising of toys to rural shop owners for holidays meant that children's goods were widely available for rural consumers (Mumma and Baxter 2018). A comparison of urban and rural sites in New York State showed incredible parity between urban and rural assemblages of children's toys, including a concomitant shift toward more toys and a greater diversity of toy types after the Civil War (Bunow 2009). This work suggests that other factors, such as class and class emulation, had a greater effect on how families were furnishing their children with toys and playthings rather than a sharp rural/urban divide.

In a comparative study of agricultural homesteads in Delaware, toys including dolls, marbles, toy firetrucks, toy pistols, and musical instruments were found in excavated deposits at farm sites of elite, middle-class, and tenant-farming families (De Cunzo 2004). This pattern reinforces the ubiquity of mass-produced material goods for children at farmstead sites, and their widespread availability to farm families across the economic spectrum. These toys may have been broken in play, but may have also been discarded when children died or married and moved into their own homes. When explored across the racial divide, comparisons of white and African American farmsteads led to some interesting conclusions. Socialization of white and African American children, particularly males, seemed to focus on different types of activities, suggesting sons were being socialized into two different masculinities. The presence of white dolls in white households was interpreted as objects of play, and opportunities for adult socialization and childhood imagination. The presence of the same kinds of dolls in African American households was more puzzling given that darker toned dolls were available on the market at the time. If young girls in African American families wanted such dolls, they could have been purchased or could have been easily made and sewn within the household. De Cunzo (2004) argued that these white dolls imported from Europe may have been used for dressmaking models by a seamstress instead of for play by her daughters.

A final study of children in rural contexts focused on a twentieth-century site in the town of Shabonna Grove, Illinois (Dozier 2016). This research provided an interesting model for studying children in the absence of mass-produced, child-specific material culture, which has been an enduring problem for archaeologists wishing to study children in the American past. Shabonna Grove was founded in the nineteenth century as a farming community, but was a town where the railroad came too late, and that fate left the community in a state of economic collapse as a marginalized town outside of Chicago.

This particular study focused on a pit feature found on the edge of a parcel of family land during an archaeological project. The pit contained toys from the 1960s that were intentionally buried there. The pit may have been constructed by adults for some purpose or by children to create a secluded place for play, not unlike the remote play spaces identified at the Michigan farmstead (Baxter 2000). The pit was highly secluded on the landscape, covered by bushes and vegetation, and was not a place on the landscape that was easy for adults to access. Within the pit, alongside the mass-produced children's artifacts, was a small cache or collection of seemingly random household objects and object fragments dating from the early years of the 1900s through the 1960s. The remote area of the pit makes it unlikely as a place for a trash-dumping episode from a household, but it does make sense that this was the collection belonging to a child or group of children who were augmenting the toys that had been bought for them with found objects. Dozier (2016) suggested such a collecting strategy may have offered children a chance to exert control over some aspect of the world at a time when economic collapse and social change was leaving them with very little sense of control. As we will see in other instances in this chapter, play, when examined archaeologically, can often be interpreted as children exerting control or engaging in acts of resistance in reaction to the world around them.

Children on Plantations

Children raised on plantations also experienced rural childhoods with a closeness to nature, but the social organization of plantation economies defined not only by class but also by race and the enslavement of African American peoples created unique dynamics around childhood and child-rearing (chapter 2). Archaeologists have considered these dynamics surrounding children from two perspectives: mothering and child-rearing, and the alternative meanings of mass-produced goods that emerged as they were used in African American households, both by enslaved peoples and emancipated sharecroppers living in the segregated American South.

Mothering and child care were arenas where racial and social divisions that defined plantation life became blurred in very complicated ways. Enslaved women were often put into service as wet-nurses and caretakers of children, giving them extended periods of intimate time with children of planter families. Stewart-Abernathy (2004: 72) noted that white children raised by enslaved women shared greater physical and emotional energy with these women than their own mothers, but their biological mothers exerted control and dictated the terms of these relationships. African American dolls were often given as wedding gifts to women who were to become the wives of planters to reinforce bonds of emotion and ownership and to symbolize the dynamics of power in a plantation household (Edwards-Ingraham 2001). Enslaved women had experience with children but no authority, and the reverse was true of their mothers (Stewart-Abernathy 2004: 72).

Enslaved women also became mothers of their own children. Motherhood was a radical action for enslaved women (Edwards-Ingraham 2001). Child care was at odds with the demands of labor, and child care had to be integrated into the demands for labor being placed on women by their owners. These demands often meant childhood was a precarious time in terms of health and well-being for enslaved children (chapter 2). Becoming a mother also subjected enslaved women to the role of wet-nursing children, which wasn't a choice, but often did change the types of labor expected from them. The decision to become a mother and motherhood itself was bolstered by a particular ideology developed among slaves, who were often captured from matrilineal African societies (Wilkie 2003). The powerful social roles of women in families were connected to motherhood in ways that gave women esteem and power in the household. Wilkie (2003) reports on excavations of the well and yard at the Perryman house site in Mobile, Alabama, where equipment from a community-mothering midwifery business was found. She argued that remains of four white dolls/figurines, white ceramics, and a toy tea set found at the site represent both the family's desire for upward mobility and the sanctity of motherhood, rather than the emulation of whites.

The role of enslaved women as mothers of their own children and caregivers to the children of white planter families often brought children together who lived on the same plantation under very different circumstances (Mintz 2004). Enslaved children were often expected to serve as playmates for white children whose rural homes did not afford them many nearby playmates who shared their social standing. These social encounters likely meant that enslaved children also had experiences using the types of mass-produced toys and playthings that were common at the time, but the dynamics of play also would have underscored the disparities and divides among the children temporarily brought together as companions and playmates (Chudacoff 2007). As noted in chapter 2, enslaved children were regularly expected to complete small tasks and acts of labor as ways of cultivating a sense of obedience and loyalty and socializing them into a life of slavery. Children of planter families would have been raised in households aware of ideals and trends in middle- and upper-class child-rearing and would have emulated appropriate material and social performance to reinforce class and race-based distinctions (chapter 2).

Mass-produced toys have been found at sites where enslaved people lived, both on and off of plantations (Leone 2005; Wilkie 2000), as well as sites where African Americans were living as free citizens (e.g., De Cunzo 2004; Wilkie 2000, 2003). As seen above, interpreting these objects requires a contextual understanding of the social dynamics of plantation life, and an appreciation that the meanings and messages of material objects, including toys, were both widely understood and open to interpretation and manipulation by both enslaved peoples and their owners. Enslaved and emancipated African Americans saw child-rearing as an opportunity to develop social worlds on their own terms, and engaged the material and social practices of the dominant society in ways that reflected their particular circumstances and values (Bernstein 2011). Brandon (2004: 206–207) argued that households, particularly emergent middle-class households in the postbellum South, were the places where children could learn rules about racist society and develop a critical stance toward it.

Wilkie's (1994, 2000) work at Louisiana's Riverlake and Oakley Plantations remains as one of the most important studies focusing on children living on plantations during slavery, but mostly after emancipation as sharecroppers. Her work at both plantations illustrated that while toys were marketed toward white families, they also were found in archaeological contexts indicating they were used by African American children.

This archaeological evidence suggests that, despite being employed as laborers at a very young age, there was free time during which play was allowed and facilitated by toys. Oral histories used in her work affirmed these archaeological findings, particularly emphasizing memories of children making their own toys and playing imaginary games. Her analyses indicate that the meaning of these toys shifted significantly when brought into the context of African American households and children's lives.

At Oakley Plantation, archaeological excavations were focused on the home of the Freeman family, who worked as house servants for the Matthews sisters. The proximity of the Freeman family home to the home of their employers and the distance from the field quarters, which were over a mile away, socially isolated the Freeman children. Wilkie (2000) postulated that the toys found at the Freeman home were likely gifts given to them by the Matthews sisters. Toy tea sets, which in white households were designed to emphasize feminine gentility and household ritual, could have been bestowed on the Freeman children to encourage individual play and teach service and servitude. The toys recovered from the Freeman household included tea sets and doll parts, which were found in poor condition underneath the raised cabin floor. The provenience and condition of these objects suggest that the children did not treasure these gifts from their employers, but rather discarded them as trash, perhaps as an act of resistance and rebellion against acculturation and the roles being dictated to them (Wilkie 2000).

At Riverlake Plantation, the assemblage of children's toys was far less gendered, with marbles being the dominant toy type. According to Wilkie (1994, 2000), the marbles were probably purchased from the plantation store, which was stocked by the plantation owners, thereby limiting the types of goods available for purchase and use. The owners might have chosen marbles as an object to sell to children as a way to foster communal play that would help train future sharecroppers for their roles in communal work gangs (Wilkie 2000).

Urban Children and Childhoods

America as a nation began to industrialize in the early nineteenth century, resulting in a significant population shift into urban areas. By 1920, the U.S. Census Bureau had declared the United States an urban nation, meaning over half the population lived in cities and towns. This trend has continued unabated to the present day as Census Bureau statistics report that 81 percent of Americans now live in urban and suburban areas.

Riney-Kehrberg (2014: 41) noted that at the close of the nineteenth century, despite a movement to urbanization, it was not always easy to define the difference between urban and rural areas, particularly in smaller cities and towns. In both types of places, many families lived without electricity, plumbing, or central heat, and livestock were prevalent. Populations in urban neighborhoods often retained the types of interpersonal connectivity and mutual reliance considered essential and common in rural areas. For children, while age and gender certainly played significant roles in how activities were experienced and enjoyed, children were relatively unrestricted in terms of movement in both urban and rural communities, and peer relationships and the exploration and development of relationships to areas outside one's home were common.

Certainly, it is possible to identify areas of significant difference between these types of spaces as well. The majority of urban-dwelling children were a part of working-class families, and tended to live in small, cramped, overcrowded apartments and tenements, making the interior spaces of homes largely unsuitable and undesirable locations for much of their activity. Places external to the home were crowded and congested, dirty with sewage, litter, and industrial waste, and as a result filled with hazards for the children who both worked in such spaces and used them for play and leisure. These conditions gave rise to many of the later nineteenth-century reform movements that developed playgrounds, play lots, and organized clubs and activities for children (figure 3.3) whose improvised play in shared urban spaces was considered dangerous, inappropriate, and even immoral (Riney-Kehrberg 2014; Valentine 2014). Such activities were often considered inconvenient and an impediment to the activities of adults as well.

When children were not on the streets, many were working, as they became a prime source of unskilled labor, particularly after the U.S. Civil War (Shackel 2009: 90). The use of children as laborers was often blamed on the moral failings of their families' immigrant cultures who did not understand civilized American culture (Shackel 2009: 92). In fact, child labor supplemented many families' incomes, even though children made a fraction of the wages an adult male would earn. While reformers felt children should be nurtured and protected from the workplace, and others called for education for all, this was not the reality for many children.

Figure 3.3. Stevens School playground, Allentown, Pennsylvania, 1903. This image is a good example of how urban children became separated from the rest of the city during their leisure time. The creation of these playgrounds was at the heart of many reform efforts seeking to improve the health and safety of children living in America's cities. Wikimedia.

Working-class households, particularly urban households, were at the nexus of these contested ideas.

Stephen A. Mrozowski's (2006) discussion of working-class communities in the first planned industrial community in the United States, Lowell, Massachusetts, began with an oral history of Blanche Pelletier Graham, who lived in a Boott Boardinghouse as a young girl in the early twentieth century (2006: 64–66). She recalled playing house in the mill yard as well as her many jobs helping the woman who ran the boardinghouse, such as taking lunch pails to the mill workers and helping the housekeepers set and clear the table. Her recollection was one of a happy and favorable childhood in terms of food and care and atmosphere.

The Lowell Mills were developed around a scheme to use the unskilled labor of young women in their fabric mills so as to circumvent contemporary concerns around child labor which were already present in the early nineteenth century in America, and to avoid stripping male labor from nearby family farms. Boardinghouses early on were designed for this demographic of single women, but later shifted to include families and children. The archaeology of the boardinghouses illustrated the deterioration of conditions in worker housing and an increase in unsanitary conditions over time. These conditions had deleterious effects on not only the health but also the well-being of children in residence there. For example, Mrozowski (2006) posited that children of working families likely faced a great deal of discrimination while attending public schools simply because of their class. Issues around poor academic performance were often considered a prime example of class or ethnic differences between children of workers and middle-class families. He also suggested, however, that in addition to discrimination, basic environmental issues leading to malnourishment and lead poisoning could have caused learning disabilities and put children at an educational disadvantage. Being physically unwell and socially maligned could have affected self-esteem and self-worth among working-class children and families, diminishing the sense that capitalism offered opportunities for intergenerational betterment for workers as their children struggled physically and mentally (Mrozowski 2006: 150). Such insights linking the social and the environmental are crucial for thinking about children and families living in these working-class communities.

Undoubtedly, the most widely discussed group of children in historical archaeology are those that resided in the Five Points Tenement in New York City during the nineteenth century. This large project, undertaken by John Milner and Associates, unearthed an area that was once the location of densely packed tenements inhabited by various European immigrant communities along several city blocks. Children in this neighborhood generally were not working in factories, but rather were apprenticed to various tradesmen and worked in the streets selling and scavenging all kinds of goods (Yamin 2002). Shackel (2008: 48) notes that these salvaged goods may have created the "bank accounts" of recyclable clothing, buttons, bottle glass, and bones found in archaeological deposits associated with tenements. These deposits are relatively unexplored as products of children's labor.

Children spent very little time indoors at home as their homes were crowded with tenants and adult labor, in which they also sometimes participated (figure 3.4). Play was also based in the streets (figure 3.5) and communities that were divided by age, gender, and ethnicity often structured the worlds of children but those structures did not separate them from the world of adults. Paul Mullins (2008) has noted that children used community landmarks, such as corner stores, as gathering places

Figure 3.4. Children working at night inside an urban tenement in New York City. Photo by Lewis Wickes Hine. Courtesy of Preus Museum; Library of Congress; National Child Labor Committee Collection.

in Midwestern urban communities, and these kinds of public landmarks were important in creating meaningful landscapes for children in urban environments (chapter 4).

Given all the opportunities for a wide variety of interaction and engagement with the world around them, toys were perhaps not as important in these bustling urban communities as they might have been elsewhere (Yamin 2002). The Five Points project yielded only a small assemblage of children's material culture: 124 toys from six features, with marbles being 75–85 percent of the toys recovered from each feature. While most of the marbles found were among the least expensive varieties available, some of these marbles were of a more expensive variety imported from Germany in the mid-nineteenth century. Frozen Charlottes (an inexpensive doll type without movable parts), toy tea set fragments, wooden tops, and gaming pieces rounded out the toys in the tenement assemblages. Slate pencils also were found, and, while commonly interpreted for children's education, they could have also been used in commercial establishments found on the ground floor of many buildings (chapter 4).

Figure 3.5. "Playground in Tenement Alley, Boston MA 1909" by Lewis Wickes Hine. This type of unstructured, urban play was the target of reformers who sought to contain children's places safely away from the activities of adults. Courtesy of the George Eastman House International Museum of Photography and Film (CCBy).

Artifacts for children also included children's drinking cups personalized with names and/or adorned with moralizing messages for their consumption during mealtimes. These cups have been associated with German immigrant families rather than Irish immigrant families due to patterns in overall consumption, and were interpreted as an attempt to give a child something that was specifically theirs in a world of few personal possessions (Yamin 1992: 121). Labeled, individualized possessions offered children an opportunity to learn about private property (Praetzellis and Praetzellis 1992), a particularly poignant lesson for children living in densely packed apartments and tenements that afforded little personal space or privacy.

The children's artifacts at Five Points have been debated by scholars. The first wave of scholarship associated with the site interpreted the presence of toys in tenement deposits as suggesting variation in childhood experiences, particularly that some children didn't have to work or scavenge and instead could engage in play and leisure more typical of their middle-class counterparts (Griggs 1999). This interpretation has been scrutinized and largely rejected by subsequent scholars. Matthews (2010) has argued the presence of toys at working-class sites such as Five Points does not indicate an absence of children's work, but rather illustrates how under capitalism play became temporally constrained. Toys and engagement with them were limited in the lives of children who had other obligations, and "play time" became a structured segment in a day filled with multiple demands. Toys were a training tool for those who would later be in the labor market, by creating a material marker of time that was free and your own that stood in contrast with work when your time was being sold to an employer. This latter view was embraced by Charles Orser (2007: 121–122) in his study of the racialization of Irish American families. He argued that for the children of the Five Points toys such as ceramic tea sets, dolls, mini cannon, and marbles were symbolic of freedoms being constrained and of economic disparity between themselves and mainstream, middle-class America.

Rebecca Yamin's (2002) work on parents and children at New York's Five Points neighborhood compared these tenements to sites excavated in the Irish Dublin neighborhood of Paterson, New Jersey. Children in this neighborhood also had to work, due to the precarious economic circumstances of households, but, as in Five Points, parents also invested in toys so that children had time to play and things to play with. In Paterson, 111 toys were recovered from six features and despite knowing some history there is no way to know if these artifacts are associated with building owners or tenants, which would help determine some of the differentiations within working-class communities. As at Five Points, marbles were the most common, but there were no expensive examples of these toys and they were mostly made of unfinished clay and limestone—the cheapest kind available on the market. Toy tea sets and dolls were also found with inexpensive, immobile Frozen Charlottes being the most common type of girls' toys. Yamin (2002) argued that these artifacts were an investment in children as children and not just a means to socialize them. These toys allowed children the freedom to play in a world defined by work. She also interpreted the abundance of writing slates and slate pencils as evidence for home education as immigrant families attempted to eschew the powerful influences of public schools.

Yamin's (2002) analysis directly confronted class and its many dynamics in working-class neighborhoods. She argued that middle-class reformers made it very clear that working-class parents exerted too much control over their offspring and were perpetuating degenerate conditions into the next generation. Working-class families had different means and different values in how and why they provided for children as they did, and the values they expressed and articulated were not the values attributed to them by reformers. Working-class parents struggled to give material goods to children and also to control their time. Children in these neighborhoods worked and long hours, often beginning as young as age eight. Parents knew children needed rest and good meals, but also wanted them to be educated so they could understand the circumstances under which they were expected to live. Opportunities for children provided by the middle class such as Sunday school and public education were unwelcome interventions into the lives of children as they sought to turn value systems toward the middle class rather than the values informed by their actual living circumstances. Yamin (2002) asserted that the middle-class rules and expectations of play that have been the subject of scholarship (e.g., Calvert 1992) simply do not apply for archaeologists analyzing the material culture of working-class households. The provisioning of children with toys may not have reflected middle-class desires for gender inculcation, but rather simply to provide an opportunity for play.

It is far more common for archaeologists to interpret the presence of toys and playthings at urban sites as an investment in children, especially as a vehicle to demonstrate class aspiration and express an embracing of middle-class American ideals about childhood. For example, when looking at two nineteenth-century sites in working-class Minneapolis, Minnesota, McCarthy (2002: 145) considered the "investment in childhood relative to the construction of social identity and class structures more broadly" as one of four key themes in interpreting the use of material culture identified in these deposits. The first site, known as the Bridgehead Site, was comprised of structures identified as mixed commercial, what might be called "light industrial," and residential. Excavations of these structures included associated privies in an area used by first- and second-generation workmen and their families. Children were identified based on the presence of a very small assemblage of toys, writing slates, and pencils with a total of 41 artifacts or .15 percent of the overall assemblage being termed child-specific. He argued that children may have been working and playing in the context of apprenticeship or during the course of a work day at businesses such as barber shops or shoe stores. These same children may or may not have lived in the residences associated with these businesses. The presence of toys suggested certain indulgences toward children in the community.

The second site, the Courthouse Site, had particular children documented in census records, with 6 children under the age of 10 residing there in 1880 and 3 children under the age of 10 in residence in 1900. Sixty toys and children's objects were found at this site including toy dishes, doll parts, marbles, and writing accoutrements. While also a small part of the overall assemblage (.43 percent), the presence of more and higher quality artifacts at the Courthouse Site when compared to the Bridgehead Site was interpreted as indicating larger investments in children and greater aspirations toward the middle class. The differences in children's artifacts also seems to correlate to the relative separation of work and home documented for the two sites. Where work and home were conflated at the Bridgehead Site, childhood was less elaborately defined through material culture. At the Courthouse Site, children were moving in and out of the home and there was a daily transition between public and private spheres. In this case, children were given more elaborate middle-class culture that kept them more in line with the norms of middle class.

Other studies of urban populations have sought to investigate the ways that families of different ethnicities distinguished themselves among the closely packed households of urban landscapes. Stephen A. Brighton (2008) examined households from the same two neighborhoods as Yamin (2002), with a specific interest in exploring Irish ethnic identity, and this had some implications for understanding childhood. He found that in Paterson, where the church became well established, children in the community became elevated in status, enabling them to attend school well past the age when the children at Five Points had been sent out to work. The Irish were clearly seen as subordinate to the dominant culture (Orser 2007), but the church was a seen as an important elevating and moralizing force both within and beyond the community in a way that allowed proud community identity to be built around ethnic heritage. This offered greater opportunity for the community's children.

Anne Elizabeth Yentsch (2009) studied the households of Jewish families in San Francisco, California, and found that, as a community, families used kin networks and emphasized practices that enabled upward mobility over generations—a value that inherently implies an investment in children. Jewish households demonstrated upward mobility through a significant increase in property holdings over time, but there was little archaeological evidence of wealth in these households with children's toys being the only nonutilitarian artifacts recovered. The choice to defer gratification for adults and instead invest in property and provide for children's experiences was a way that wealth was being stored and invested. In New York City, Jewish families created in-house industries to provide services to the broader community when most immigrant communities were selling their labor. These house industries mimicked preindustrial patterns of families working and living together, creating different household dynamics for adults and children when compared to other ethnic groups living in the same urban areas (Rothschild and Wall 2014: 91–94).

African American communities in New York City also show considerable diversity, despite a scholarly tendency to represent a homogenous "African American community" that was juxtaposed with white American and immigrant families on the social landscape (Wall et al. 2008). Little Africa and Seneca Village were two enclaves that were differentiated by class, and each had a population that was approximately one-third children. At least one school operated in Seneca Village, and records show that about three-quarters of the children in the neighborhood were attending, as opposed to Little Africa where only half the children were attending school. Barriers to school attendance included fear for children's safety after the 1834 riots (see chapter 5), the need for children to work, and the inability of families to provide children with the appropriate clothing to attend school. The authors argued that variations in school attendance and values around children reflect the variation of economic circumstances in families as well as priorities of households within the African American community. Difference in school attendance was seen as a way to access class dynamics within the community and to help structure questions for future archaeological research.

A final insight from urban sites comes from Wilkie's (2000: 103–4) reporting of excavations in Santa Monica, California. Her work at the former home of Ernest and Katie Cords included the recovery of a notable overrepresentation of broken doll parts in a pit feature on their property. The many broken dolls were attributed to the actions of their eldest daughter Irene Cords, who was born in 1916 or 1917 and who was five to seven years old when the trash pit was in use. The archaeological remains in question were highly fragmented doll heads that had been brutally and intentionally smashed in clear acts of violence. Wilkie argued that the destruction of dolls could have been a very clear statement of resistance and frustration on the part of Irene toward her parents. Perhaps the arrival of a new younger sibling, or some other frustration, drove the young child to use her toys as a means of expression in a way that directly destroyed gifts associated with her parents as givers.

This vignette is a significant way to end this segment as the narrative of urban, working-class childhoods from history and archaeology reveals a very challenging lifestyle for adults and children. Environmental conditions affected health and hygiene and may have had implications for children learning and performing well at school and work. The demands of labor on children were constant and the economic stresses of their households were likely not kept in secret. Reformers even with good intentions enacted interventions for children that ultimately labeled them as deficient and in need of care, and offered programs that attempted to alienate them from their families. The lives of children were stressful, and Irene's story tells us that the archaeology of children may offer ways to understand how the many challenges of working-class life were felt by the youngest members of families and households.

Children at Sites of Industry and in Industrial Communities

Working-class families did not reside only in densely packed urban communities, but also lived in towns that sprung up near sites of resource extraction and processing endeavors, such as mines and mills. These sites are often interpreted using the same rhetoric of class that is commonly employed to understand sites in urban neighborhoods. In such contexts, children are often presented as symbols of family aspiration as well as valued members of households. For example, Jamie Brandon's (2004) excavations at Van Winkle's Mill in Arkansas uncovered a large quantity of toys from the workers' living quarters, including fragments of porcelain dolls, alphabet plates, and a cast-iron pistol as well as two clay marbles, and small black rings. He suggested that such objects are signs of upward mobility and an increase in the importance of education for children in working-class families, but that at the same time the abundance of toys could possibly be an indicator of parents' desire to provide their children with a childhood they never had.

While the emphasis on toys prioritizes children's recreational activities and the aspirations of parents and families, archaeological work at the site of Ludlow, Colorado, has situated children in the midst of a complex world of class negotiations, labor action, and family strife. The Colorado Coalfield Strike of 1913–1914 climaxed in the Ludlow Massacre on April 20, 1914, where men, women, and children were killed (Saitta 2007). The United Mine Workers Association (UMWA) delivered a set of demands to the coal companies seeking improved working conditions and compensation, and 90 percent of the workers at the coal mines refused to work. As a result, the workers and their families were all evicted from company housing. Tent colonies rented by UMWA in advance of the strike allowed workers and their families to live near the mines and block routes of potential strikebreakers into the area. The largest of these was Ludlow.

Women and children were an integral part of this community of solidarity. The UMWA provided its workers with food, medical attention, and strike relief based on the composition of the household. When the activities of the workers met with violent suppression, the Ludlow Massacre became nationally famous, particularly because of the death of so many women and children, including the shooting of an 11-year-old boy and the suffocation of a group of women and children when the tent under which they were hiding in a dug pit was burned. The potency of women and children being identified as innocents and the resulting outrage found in the reporting of the incident across the country speaks to widespread cultural attitudes about children at the time. The victimization of even the poorest, immigrant, working-class children that in other types of sources might be disparaged or labeled as deficient was seen as an unconscionable act of violence.

When archaeologists excavated the Ludlow tent colony, among the remains found were a lid from a child's tea set and part of a porcelain doll (Moore 2007). These artifacts had migrated with a child and her family from their home in company housing to the refuge of the union-sponsored tent colony. These artifacts are notable not because of how they were interpreted, as aspirations for the next generation or as teaching tools in the socializing of young children (Moore 2007), but because they illustrate the importance of being connected to broader cultural norms and trends even in a relatively isolated community. Such objects also speak to their importance in the lives of children, as toys could easily be labeled as "nonessential" in a time of upheaval and eviction. The continued presence of an object in the life of a child may have been a source of comfort and continuity that was acknowledged and indulged by the family at a tumultuous time.

Children's toys were 2.4 percent of the artifacts recovered at Ludlow, which is a very small assemblage acting as the representative of 40–50 percent of the population (Devine 2014). Children's lives are not exclusively about playing with mass-produced toys, in any context, and certainly not in the context of the Colorado coal fields. Children worked and attended school in the company towns, and, once relocated, children contributed to households at Ludlow and were actively participating in the strike alongside their parents.

Children's interest in the strike and relationship to the companies were not entirely formed through the lens of parental employment. The Colorado Fuel and Iron Company (CF&I) started a new branch called the "Sociological Department" in 1901 in reaction to a miner's strike and as way to deal with the ethnic diversity of the company's employees (Devine 2014). While they made claims against paternalism, the aims of the department were assimilating immigrants, which was hardly unique to this company during the Progressive Era (Camp 2013). The company organized clubs including American sports and offered cooking classes featuring American cuisine. CF&I's assimilation efforts were directly targeted at the children of its immigrant workforce and were designed to create goodwill with its employees through the purchasing of American toys for children at Christmastime and the creation of kindergartens for children to teach them American values (Devine 2014). These values were at odds with the heritage traditions and identities being taught at home, and meant children were experiencing the strain of operating in a world where they were being presented with two different sets of values and being asked to cultivate two very different sets of loyalties. The children of Ludlow may have found comfort and continuity in some of the objects provided as a benevolent gesture on the part of a coal company, but ultimately found themselves aligned with their parents in a violent clash with company forces.

Children at Home at Military Sites

A handful of archaeological studies in the United States and elsewhere have focused on the discovery of small assemblages of children's artifacts, particularly toys and items of clothing, at military sites (Venovcevs 2016). Often, in such contexts, items identified as toys are interpreted as recreational materials for soldiers, while in other cases they are presented without interpretation or as a "surprising" indicator that children were living in and among military encampments, forts, and installations. The presence of children's materials in such archaeological deposits should not come as a surprise, however, as documentary evidence suggests that upward of 20 percent of a military camp's population could consist of women and children who were the families of married military personnel and civilian contractors (Venovcevs 2016: 716). Children and adolescents also were active participants in wartime activities in American history. For example, Steven Mintz (2004: 120) reported that upward of 5 percent of the armies on both sides of the U.S. Civil War were comprised of individuals under the age of 18. Military sites in either of these contexts were as much a home to these children and adolescents as any of the other domestic contexts routinely examined by archaeologists.

One of the earliest articles in historical archaeology specifically focusing on children detailed the artifacts attributable to children excavated at military camps on both sides of the Revolutionary War (Cohn 1983). According to the author, these toys were originally misinterpreted as having been used by soldiers as amusements or pastimes when not engaged in military activity, or, in other cases, the excavated toys were overlooked altogether in the analysis and interpretation of the sites. A reinterpretation of these finds presented toys divided along gender lines. Toys interpreted as being used by boys included marbles, whizzers, whistles, and an incorrectly numbered die fashioned from a bullet. Artifacts interpreted as being for girls' play included earthenware sheep, doll parts, and play tea sets comparable to those found at more typical domestic sites of the period. Some of the recovered dolls' heads were hand carved from a wooden furniture post. The presence of commercially available and homemade toys in the same assemblages is a notable feature of the children's artifacts from these sites.

Archaeological evidence for children is also mentioned in studies of gender, women, and domestic life at eighteenth-century British military sites in New York State (Starbuck 1994), early nineteenth-century American garrisons (Clements 1993), and U.S. Civil War camps (McBride 1994: 130). As is common in such earlier publications (chapter 1) the presence of children was noted in passing but was not integrated into broader research questions or concerns.

Recent work by Anatolijs Venovcevs (2016), on the Canadian site of Fort York Ordinance Supply Yard, offers important new directions for interpreting children's lives in the context of military sites. His work draws heavily on contemporary archaeological theory of children's roles in shaping social and physical landscapes to assert the need to include them as important members of military communities and as contributors to the archaeological record of military sites. He cites patterns of evidence from domestic assemblages that show marked differences in the composition of household goods when families are and are not present, suggesting that children affected the day-to-day life of military communities in intentional and unintentional ways. Children at Fort York created their own landscapes of play and activity in and among the military and domestic operations of the fort as evidenced by the distribution of their toys and playthings and their appearance in historic photographs. Undoubtedly, children were interacting with adults and shaping the spaces they shared with them as they moved around the grounds of the fort.

These types of interactions are reinforced by recollections of adults who grew up at U.S. military installations in the nineteenth century (Devine 2012). These individuals recall performing household chores and engaging play and leisure that would have been considered typical for children of the period. Activities for children at these sites extended beyond their own domestic sphere. Boys and young men were able to watch and apprentice with military craftsmen, and at times accompany their fathers on military expeditions and training exercises. Girls and young women assisted in chores and worked in some of the military buildings as well. The soldiers on the base actively interacted with the children, and children considered them to be a part of an extended family.

Jamie Devine (2012) presented these recollections in her work on the spatial distribution of children's artifacts at Fort Garland, Colorado. Fort Garland was the base for troops that took part in several major military campaigns protecting the American gold and silver fields from the Confederates, and later housed regiments engaged in the Indian Wars until the fort was abandoned in 1883. As a relatively isolated encampment with comparatively few engagements, the presence of children at the fort was considered a welcome comfort and entertainment (Devine 2012). During the course of a full pedestrian survey at the site by Adams State University in 2011–2012, hundreds of toy fragments were found across the site surface, particularly in the large trash dumps containing military and household debris. The distribution of children's material culture was interpreted as reflecting potential idealized play zones (Baxter 2005) across the fort landscape as a whole, and suggested potential variations in gendered play as well as restrictions of play among children whose parents were from different classes of military personnel stationed at Fort Garland.

Some Thoughts

Reviewing the available literature of children at American domestic sites reveals both a richness and a certain paucity at this moment in scholarship. Given that material culture for children is available from nearly every excavated site in America, the limited bibliography and the domination of a few key cases in our archaeological understanding of children is disappointing. This limited body of published literature does, however, offer considerable insight into the diversity of childhood experiences in America, but also the unifying views of children that were being disseminated across the country through child-rearing literature, reform movements, and material culture.

One of the great challenges of working with mass-produced material culture is the tendency to fall into certain tropes of interpretive thinking, and there is a certain redundant quality to the interpretation of children in these studies. All of these studies in one way or another rely on toys as the means of interpreting children's lives. The tyranny of toys in these interpretations tacitly reduces children to their play, and represents very large populations of people through only a very small proportion of the artifacts they encountered and engaged with in their daily lives. While often the innovative and imaginative nature of children's activities that would have brought objects other than mass-produced toys into meaningful contexts in their worlds are mentioned, this is rarely explored with any rigor or depth. Historical records offer insights into the diversity of children's lives beyond the scope of play, and there is great potential in relational approaches to landscape and more nuanced consideration of entire household assemblages to further integrate children into the lives of their families and households. These studies demonstrate that studying households is much more than understanding the gentility of domestic ritual, and illustrate that studying the domestic sphere is a rich springboard into the complex lives of individuals negotiating complicated issues from survival to identity in the dynamic social, economic, and political landscape of America.

The focus on toys as a way of understanding children and childhood has also led to a distinct pattern in how these objects are interpreted as being symbolic of adult intentions. Parents or in some cases paternalistic companies and benevolent organizations were the providers of most mass-produced goods for children, and certainly there were multiple agendas and values in operation when such gifts were being bestowed. The work in this chapter identifies several. First is that toys served to symbolize the class status or class aspirations of a family or household. Second is that toys served as a way to signal a family's interest in participating in American culture and their understanding of what was appropriate and expected in child-rearing. And last is that in some sense toys functioned as an investment in children that reflected emotional and nurturing sentiments of parents, tied to offering opportunities for betterment through a more enriched childhood. The recurrence of these ideas across a variety of contexts reflects the homogeneity of the material culture being used to present children's lives, but it also demonstrates the emergence of a comfortable interpretive trope in the discipline which can be resolved with deeper attention to specific contexts and by further thinking of these objects from a child-centered perspective.

Children were incredibly important in American families, not merely as symbols in an adult discourse, but also as individuals having lived experiences. Children who were not from upper- and middle-class homes were being directly and deliberately targeted by the assimilation efforts of reformers, companies, and public education. These agents used objects, experiences, and knowledge as ways to transform children and isolate them from their families, their heritage, and the values being taught in their homes. Simultaneously, children were living and working in households where values, heritage, and identity were essential ways of coping with the pressures of being in often precarious, dangerous, and uncomfortable social and economic positions. Mass-produced objects for children may have spoken to ideals of childhood innocence and middle-class gentility, but, in most households studied by archaeologists, they are artifacts that were embroiled in a struggle for the minds and hearts of children and for the futures of families and the nation. Children were hardly innocent, but rather were in a position to accept or resist ideas being presented to them, to choose the messages to which they would listen, and to form their own identity in the next generation of Americans.

4

Institutions for Children and Children at Institutions

An exploration of childhood in the American past requires an engagement with historical and archaeological understandings of institutional life. Many institutions of the modernizing world, such as poorhouses, prisons, asylums, hospitals, and schools were integral to many children's experiences and certainly were central in many adult discourses about how childhood should be (De Cunzo 2006). Often such institutions were not designed for children, such as in the cases of prisons or almshouses, but children were among the residents at such places because of the circumstances of their parents or adult caretakers. Other types of institutions, such as schools and orphanages, were developed as deliberate attempts to shape the future of young people who for one reason or another were seen as needing institutional care. Some of these institutions, such as public schools, were and are considered a necessity for all American children and the collective care and maintenance of these institutions is tied to public discourse about the future of a healthy democratic society. Other institutions were designed with specific populations of children in mind, particularly those considered poor, abandoned, disabled, or criminal, and whose need for material and moral uplift became the concern of reformers and society at large.

The origins of American institutions lie in the early monastic communities of medieval Europe where confinement and regimented living were seen as important tools for cultivating moral and spiritual uplift for the residents (Casella 2007, 2009). The concept of confinement was taken from these religious institutions, imported to the colonies, and applied to caring for those considered poor, disabled, and/or criminal by the dominant society. During the colonial period, concepts of institutional confinement were paired with a mindset that there were "deserving" and "undeserving" populations eligible for confinement based on the moral standards and conditions of the person being confined. Variations in institutional types and conditions reflected this notion of deservedness. By the early nineteenth century, enthusiasm for institutions grew and a proliferation of institution types and their overall numbers swelled on the landscape—a period Casella (2009) referred to as the "Golden Age" of incarceration in the Western world. The twentieth century saw a souring of public opinion toward many types of institutions, and alternatives to social segregation and residential confinement were sought by new waves of reformers. Public schooling, however, became increasingly embraced on national as well as local levels, leading to ever increasing standardization and regulation by state and federal governments that determined the nature of local student experiences.

Clearly, institutions are highly variable in nature, but they do share some common features that allow them to be considered collectively. Lu Ann De Cunzo (2006: 167) has referred to institutions as "places of reformation, surveillance, confinement, protection, control, ritual, punishment, resistance, inscription, segregation, labor, purification, and discipline." Institutions strive to create self-directed, moral, normal individuals through an experience transpiring in the confines of an authoritarian, routinized schedule and place (De Cunzo 2006) and often involving a deprivation of liberty (Casella 2007).

Archaeological explorations of institutions have focused on these sites as places of social power. On the one side, institutional life can mean a loss of autonomy, material positions, individual expressions, community and family life, and potentially basic personal security (Casella 2007: 2). On the other side, individuals confined in institutions develop and carry out coping strategies to exist in such an environment, which need to be consolidated so they create alternative systems of meaning that counteract the hegemony of the institution itself (Casella 2007, 2009). These two sides of institutional life combine to create a dynamic of social power that can be seen as domination and resistance, as embodied engagement in place, or as forms of subversion (Casella 2007). The archaeology of institutions has been both functional and experiential in perspective, and both approaches have combined to look at dynamics of institutional control and personal and collective resistance in ways that are not inherently visible in other types of sources (Casella 2007, 2009, De Cunzo 2006). The range of institutions explored in this chapter arc along a wide spectrum of control and resistance, but all reveal cultural ideals around children and childhood at different points in America's history as well as offer insights into the lived experiences of children in places designed to control, improve, and inculcate them.

Children at Adult Institutions

Institutions for adults have taken many forms over the course of America's history, and often material and moral poverty were conflated in ways that made the work of institutions not only the care of an individual's basic needs such as food, clothing, and shelter, but also the moral instruction and uplift of impoverished individuals (Casella 2007). The decisions, circumstances, and judgments of adults determined to need such care were often transferred to the children in their families, marking certain children as deficient simply by association (Luker 2006). Archaeologists investigating institutions designed for the care and reform of adults have regularly encountered evidence for children, both through the identification of children's skeletal remains during intentional disinterment and burial relocation programs, and through the identification of children's artifacts in excavated assemblages. Much like domestic sites (chapter 3) the presence of children's artifacts at adult institutions are considered noteworthy, but often remain unanalyzed. As such, this treatment includes a few representative references of a much larger body of literature where children are mentioned but not studied as part of communities that once resided at institutions for adults.

It would be fair to say that many authors report finding evidence for children at adult institutions surprising, but it is decidedly common. One early report of children comes from the Uxbridge Almshouse, a public almshouse that operated from 1831 to 1872 in Worcester County, Massachusetts (Elia and Wesolowsky 1991). The site was a poor farm that offered subsidized housing and agricultural labor opportunities for men, women, and their children. When the burial ground was excavated as part of a development project, seven children were identified in a population of 32 individuals, characterized as disproportionately elderly. One of the reported burials was of a double inhumation of a young woman and a neonate. Reports of children in such burial populations appear with some regularity, but only recently have they become the subject of a rigorous, focused scholarship.

Jennifer L. Muller's (2017) recent work on the skeletal remains of over 60 children in the cemetery associated with the Buffalo Plains Erie County Poorhouse, which operated from 1851 to 1926, is one such example. Her work draws on Michel Foucault's concept of biopower to address how children defined as impaired and disabled were characterized and treated as residents of the poorhouse at a time when children's inclusion in mixed adult-child populations at institutions was being actively questioned. She identified an 1875 law that required the removal of all children between the ages of 3 and 16 from poorhouses in the state of New York, as it was believed such institutions corrupted children's bodies and souls, provided inadequate education, and established circumstances leading to hereditary pauperism. The children that were allowed to remain, however, were those categorized as unfit for society or familial care because they were labeled as "unteachable idiots, defectives, or otherwise deformed and/or diseased" (Muller 2017: 122). Her research carefully analyzed the health and pathology of the skeletal remains of infants and young children in the context of these societal views of childhood and disability, and considered how those in power make decisions about the right to life and survival of others.

Like children's bodies, artifacts identified as child-specific are relatively common at adult institutions. Children's artifacts, both toys and clothing, have been found in archaeological assemblages at penitentiaries, particularly women's prisons (Casella 2007: 93) as well as almshouses (Baugher 2001; Casella 2007). The eighteenth-century New York City Almshouse had a population that was nearly 30 percent children during its time of operation (Baugher 2001). Historical sources detail the training and schooling provided to children along strict gender lines by philanthropic organizations, and archaeological excavations recovered toys, suggesting play and recreation also were encouraged. This particular almshouse was furnished with fashionable, although mismatched, tablewares for the time, which suggests the sponsors were actively attempting to cultivate an enriching and elevating environment for residents (Casella 2007: 107). As with many institutions, the presence of objects specifically purchased for and given to the children at the almshouse by philanthropic donors is indicative of a particular investment in children that goes beyond attending to their basic needs. Undoubtedly, such objects were used by children as recreational objects, but also served as important vehicles for cultural indoctrination and social training as envisioned by adult donors and staff (chapter 2; Mumma and Baxter 2018).

Japanese Internment Camps

Another type of institution where adults and children lived together were the Japanese internment camps of the mid-twentieth century, but in this case both adults and children were the intended residents of these communities from their inception. After the attack on Pearl Harbor in 1941, the loyalty of Japanese Americans living in the western United States became a subject of scrutiny and suspicion. President Roosevelt signed an executive order permitting the U.S. Army to designate exclusion zones across the West Coast and, in 1942, 120,000 Japanese and Japanese Americans were removed from their homes and placed in assembly centers. Ultimately, they were moved to "relocation centers," more commonly known as internment camps (Camp 2016; Casella 2007: 49). Ten relocation centers were built in seven states, and all shared basic facilities, including gridded dirt roads, mess halls, laundry facilities, barracks, and gender-segregated latrines (Casella 2007: 50), but there were local differences based on physical environments, populations, and administration (Kamp-Whittaker 2010). The camps were designed to be self-contained facilities with all the amenities of a town, but surrounded by barbed-wire fencing and surveilled by guards in towers. Access to camps was limited to a single road, and each camp was buffered from surrounding populations by farms or swampland.

During their use, these basic facilities were improved by the residents as a means of making them more aesthetically pleasing and comfortable, but also as deliberate demonstrations of resistance. The very act of beautifying and personalizing an institutional facility can be seen as an act of defiance, but there were also deliberate acts such as creating graffiti that expressed Japanese ethnic identity and American patriotism. The people being relocated were told to bring bedding, toiletries, clothing, dishware, and personal items, but they were limited to what they could personally carry in two bags. Given these institutional constraints and the choices made by individuals within them, the material remains of these internment camps are very enlightening about this national incarceration effort, and such camps have attracted the scholarly interest of many archaeologists. Significant archaeological work has been conducted at several of these camps, including those in Idaho, Arizona, and Colorado (Camp 2016), and comparable archaeological work has been done on Canadian internment camps in British Columbia (Muckle 2017). According to Stacey Lynn Camp (2016: 169) these sites pose unique methodological and interpretive challenges because of the site size, brief occupation, mixed deposits, and histories of abandonment. Simultaneously, these sites allow for active collaboration and co-interpretation with former residents who often work side by side with archaeologists and/or provide oral histories in conjunction with archaeological research.

Children's lives at the Amache Internment Camp in Colorado were the subject of a master's thesis by April Kamp-Whittaker (2010) that combined archaeology, oral history, and archival research to examine children's lived experiences as detainees as well as adult efforts to socialize children within an institutional context. She argued that, while the camps themselves were isolated, the population density within them would have created an environment similar to an urban neighborhood. It was within this context that she explored how children were interacting with the physical, social, and political landscapes of a densely populated, ethnically segregated detention facility. Children's worlds included playing with American war toys, participating in patriotic organizations, and gardening (victory gardens), which all connected to contemporary political dialogues. While much of their material experience would have been focused on their "Americanization," there was also ample opportunity for learning Japanese intangible culture.

Her work showed that age and gender affected how children were able to move around the camp. Some of this movement was determined by the landscape design, such as the location of playgrounds for structured play activity and the placement of schools in the community. Preschools were numerous in the Amache camp, a feature which meant the youngest children had very short travel distances between home and school, while older children had to traverse much more of the camp to attend their classes and to use the playground facilities. Archaeological evidence indicated that children preferred to spend their recreational time away from the playgrounds, however, based on the relative number of toys recovered in play lots and elsewhere. The greatest number of children's toys were found in low-traffic areas, gardens, and other nonresidential areas of the camp. Toys designed for use by girls were consistently found much closer to the barracks than those attributable to boys, suggesting gender-segregated play that tied girls closer to home. These findings were corroborated by oral histories, in which former residents noted that boys had much greater freedom to roam, explore, and play with their friends than girls did. Former residents also reported that social networks and identities were created within the residential blocks, and children actively defended and policed territories considered to be the exclusive domain of their social/residential group. In some instances, children had greater mobility than adults, as they were often permitted to leave the fenced area of the camp since they were not perceived as a threat. Kamp-Whittaker concluded that the patterns of movement and dynamics of play in these institutions mirror those of contemporary urban youth, a finding that may be unexpected given the emphasis on the isolation and remoteness of these camps (Kamp-Whittaker 2010: 76).

The toys recovered at Amache can be traced back to catalogues of the 1940s and reinforce the gender and racial climate in America at the time. They also are comparable to the assemblages of toys excavated at other internment camps. The toys all were inexpensive and would have been purchased in sets, most likely via catalogue, reflecting the limited income of families and the restrictions on the quantities of personal goods that could be brought to camp. The very presence of toys suggests an investment in children even under difficult circumstances, and Kamp-Whittaker (2010) argued that these items would have very much been a luxury and status item in the community. Toy types included miniaturized domestic objects, marbles, war and military-themed toys, vehicles, and educational items as well. Many of these toys, particularly military toys, were advertised or contained imagery that depicted "Japs" as the enemy of American people. Consuming and using such toys were tied to contemporary political dialogues that would have engaged children with their outsider position in the larger cultural climate while experiencing Americanizing messages in the camp.

The internment camps also contained other institutions designed specifically for children. Schooling was mandatory and promoted the Americanization of children and their families in curriculum, structure, language, and cocurricular activities. It was also believed that schools would normalize life for children in the camps, serving as a source of stability in a difficult environment (Kamp-Whittaker 2010: 94). Artifacts from the school at Amache were mostly architectural, much like schools elsewhere (see below). Stationery supplies were also common, including pencil fragments, paper clips, and thumbtacks, which were not found in residential debris. While there were some personal artifacts related to hygiene and adornment, no toys or playthings were found at the school. This is not typical of other school sites (see below), suggesting a particular regimentation of children's time within the institution that kept school and play more strictly segregated.

The elementary school sponsored the creation of a large victory garden on its grounds, where children participated in modifying the landscape of the camp, learning traditional gardening practices, and developing agricultural skills under the tutelage of adult supervisors. Children also participated in extracurricular enrichment opportunities including organizations that taught them about their Japanese heritage, and others, like scouting, that were focused much more on American values. Participating in these latter organizations in the context of the internment camps was actually empowering for many of the children, as in mixed schools leadership positions were always held by white children and in the camp Japanese American children could move in from the margins and take on leadership roles.

Other institutional features of the camp were modified by residents to reflect the values of Japanese American parents. The social rules of dining halls were altered to keep families intact and parental control paramount. Family dining was expected as the norm, and if children wanted to eat with friends both sets of parents had to grant permission. This kind of layering of intangible values onto the physical landscape—in this case, communal mess hall dining—offered a way for institutional spaces to be transformed as places of learning about heritage and culture in the context of heavily structured institutional living.

Indian Boarding Schools

Japanese internment camps were not the first foray into creating institutions for specialized populations by the American government, particularly institutions for children. Indian boarding schools became a popular institution type in the later nineteenth century, at a time when other institutions operating in the United States were beginning to be viewed with skepticism (Casella 2007: 35). As part of what Sarah L. Surface-Evans (2016: 574) has termed an "internal colonialism policy," American Indian children were removed from their families and brought to reside in one of over 100 boarding schools modeled on military-style living. Such education became mandatory in 1893 and was a project in forced assimilation, designed to immerse children in values and practical knowledge of mainstream American society with the desired byproduct being a new generation of patriotic and productive citizens who would no longer require aid from the United States government.

At school, children wore uniforms, lived in barracks, and were subjected to physical conditioning drills as well as corporal punishment. English was the only language allowed at these institutions and children were provided academic and vocational training, particularly skills for agricultural labor and domestic service. This effort, backed by philanthropic organizations and individuals, was designed to alienate these children from their native languages, customs, and religions, and prepare them for menial jobs in mainstream society (Surface-Evans 2016). Despite these stated goals, there is little evidence that children at many of these schools received any education at all (Bassett 1994) and the emphasis was more often on labor (Lindauer 2009; Surface-Evans 2016). Surface-Evans (2016) argued, however, that schools were still considered educational because the labor at Indian schools was rarely profitable and instead the value was seen in the creation of reformed, disciplined, compliant bodies that benefited the overall social order of the country. "Education" was not measured in learning outcomes or skills attained, but rather the cultural and social compliance of the school's residents.

These schools did cause a sense of alienation between children and local tribal identities, and it was often difficult for students to return and cope and fit back into their communities. A related and certainly unintended impact was the bonding of children from different tribes through shared institutional experiences that helped to establish a transcendent notion of "American Indian" identity that illuminated underlying shared struggles and created a basis for a pan-tribal sense of political and social solidarity (Casella 2007; Lindauer 1996). Two published archaeological studies document the lives of Native American children at Indian boarding schools: the Phoenix Indian School (Lindauer 1996, 2009) and the Mount Pleasant Indian Boarding School (Surface-Evans 2016). These studies document not only the goals and designs of the institutions, but also the lived experiences of children and the strategies they developed for resistance against these programs of assimilation.

The Phoenix School in Arizona operated from 1891 to 1990 in an area of the country where Indian boarding schools were quite common. The school was originally labeled as an industrial school to teach "productive trades" and academics to its residents; however, details of the school's operation suggest that children were used simply as a source of labor both at and beyond the school (Lindauer 2009). The full-time job of the institution in reality was the indoctrination of students into mainstream American culture and the forced linguistic assimilation of a largely non-English-speaking population of students.

Archaeological evidence illustrated ways in which the school worked to break down collective identities that were a common feature of tribal cultures and replace them with more individual and self-reliant senses of self among students. Clothing remains at the site were the remnants of military-like uniforms that could be decorated with highly visible emblems of individual achievement. Gendered toys were provided to students that encouraged individual and small group play, and created a separation of boys and girls, making gender the primary dividing line in the school's population rather than other affiliations and identities. Dining halls required the use of dishes and utensils on a regimented meal schedule as a means to teach social order, courtesy, and health awareness. These same features also served to introduce children to ideas of wealth. The food on your plate was not to be shared or redistributed even if someone needed or wanted it more than you—it was owned. Providing toys to children that became personal property and that were tied to achievement introduced systems of material inequality among the students (Lindauer 2009: 95–97). Objects of personal hygiene were found engraved with individual names or other markings of personalization, emphasizing ownership. All of these were ways of enforcing the idea of self above others, and were contrary to the types of traditional value systems that were present in children's native communities.

Interestingly, however, some of these same objects are illustrative of acts of resistance on the part of the school's residents. The personalization of many objects was achieved not using students' English names assigned at school but instead alternative symbols or markings. Not using the required English to claim an object was a powerful act of resistance

(Lindauer 2009). Archaeological investigations also found hidden objects that were traditional to children's homes and cultures, such as fetishes, charms, and clan totems. The possession of these objects would have been strictly forbidden and caching them for personal use was a dangerous and defiant act. Some of these objects were brought from home, and others were made by children at the school, including flintknapped bifaces that were found in the dump. These acts of creating, caching, and symbolically retaining elements of traditional culture at the school were day-to-day activities that defied the institutional work of converting children's identities and values. More extreme and exceptional acts, such as attempting escape, also were documented, suggesting resistance took place through multiple avenues and on different scales.

A complimentary study of the Mount Pleasant Indian Boarding School in Michigan shows similarities in children's experiences at Indian boarding schools, but also applied different approaches to studying children's lives in these institutions, particularly an emphasis on landscape. The study combined documentary evidence with oral histories and archaeological excavation to study the dynamics of internal colonialism and resistance to institutional hegemony (Surface-Evans 2016). Mount Pleasant was the only off-reservation school that operated in the state of Michigan, and thousands of children from at least six different tribes attended school there. The architecture and landscape of the school was clearly designed to have a transformative effect on students and was integral to the highly regimented lifestyle they were expected to live. Regimented living and imposing architecture were designed to disorient students coming from tribal communities, and to promote a sense of order that appealed to donors and outside observers. Photographs of students, carefully posed and dressed with toys and accessories for "appropriate" western play, used the landscape strategically as an orderly backdrop that showcased a lifestyle that likely never or rarely transpired for students (Surface-Evans 2016: 577).

The reality of children's lives could not have been more different than the images produced by the school for dissemination. Children were drilled regularly in military-like exercise, and physical and sexual abuse was not uncommon. Children were often sick and injuries occurred with frequency. Vocational training prepared students for only the most menial of jobs. Boys performed farm labor, but also were given the freedom to roam the forested portion of the school grounds to hunt and fish. Girls were inculcated into contemporary middle-class standards of domesticity and motherhood and were constrained to the built areas of campus. Girls were instructed in sewing, cooking, and nursing as training for a life in domestic service, as evidenced by sewing- and laundry-related implements in the residential and instructional areas of the school. Further archaeological evidence from the girls' areas of the school included bisque doll fragments and pieces of decorative teawares and table sets that were inconsistent with those provided for the students by the school, but were appropriate in the training of girls to serve in middle-class homes. The production of traditional beadwork was allowed and encouraged, much as the children at the Phoenix School (Lindauer 2009) were allowed to create traditional ceramics because such objects had economic value to the school and were seen as a way to limit more destructive and subversive behaviors by students (Surface-Evans 2016: 584).

Such subversive behaviors certainly did exist at the Mount Pleasant School. Former students recall actively resisting the assimilation programs of the school by speaking their native languages, refusing to eat, and misusing and destroying school property. Students developed a system of contraband tokens that served as a currency, and strategies for acquiring, circulating, and retaining this currency took many forms. For example, students held powwows and pipe ceremonies in nonsurveilled spaces such as basements and wooded lots, and a button or marble as a form of token currency was the cost of participation. Archaeological excavations found these types of objects all over the school grounds, pointing to the widespread nature of this otherwise forbidden exchange network. Some students attempted to run away from the school, while others, particularly girls, used arson as a way of expressing their dissatisfaction with institutional life. Repeated attempts at arson were documented at the school, including that of the laundry (run by the girls as part of their training) and the girl's dormitory in 1899.

Schools and Educational Institutions

American interests in schools are and were not confined to the assimilation of Native American or Japanese American children. Public schooling arguably is the most widespread institution for children in the country, and has been for some time (chapter 2). Historians trace the origins of American public schools to the philosophies and practices of the Puritans

(Mintz 2004), and much of the impetus behind public schools can be traced to an extension of Christian ideas about morality and betterment of the self, including the notion that providing schooling for others in the form of publicly funded schools was a vehicle for social uplift and charitable action. Even more of the rhetoric around public schooling had its origins in the earliest days of the Republic, where education was tied to ideals of democracy and the need to create an informed citizenry (Finkelstein and Vandell 1984). This strong, enduring philosophical viewpoint took time to emerge, however; as Finkelstein and Vandell (1984: 66) noted, "A belief in the power of schools not only to oversee moral development but also to nurture good citizens, prepare young people for labor and extend therapeutic advice emerged only gradually."

During this time, the development of schools was an uneven and exclusionary practice in the country, and children's access to education and literacy varied between urban and rural communities, and by gender, racial, and ethnic divides. Robust and focused efforts to expand public education in America began in the nineteenth century with the influx of immigrant families and children, the upheaval of the industrial revolution, and the general atmosphere around social reform that resulted (Fass 2016). Building learning communities in specialized educational settings became seen as imperative so the moral and cognitive capacities of children could be tended to and cared for, with different standards of tending and care depending on the specific population and their perceived needs (Berrol 1992). Simultaneously, schools could offer a kind of standardized morality through books, school design, and other required features that provided a degree of consistency and social control. Public schools were a vehicle for assimilation for immigrant families (Berrol 1992), reflected concerns of racial segregation (Helton 2010), and reinforced gender roles (Beisaw and Baxter 2017; Helton 2010).

Archaeological research on schools does not reflect their importance in American history, or the central role education has played in the lives of most Americans. There has been some limited archaeological research at seventeenth- and eighteenth-century community schools (Baugher 2009) and no reported work has been done from the consolidation era that typifies most of the twentieth century after the advent of motorized transportation. Archaeological research on nineteenth-century schools is more common, particularly one-room schools that were a ubiquitous feature of the American landscape. One-room schools are regularly encountered in cultural resource management projects, but rarely make their way into the published literature (Beisaw 2009). This phenomenon is in part because, while common on the landscape, one-room schools are notoriously difficult to study archaeologically, with low artifact counts that offer little basis for interpretation, particularly when compared to rich domestic assemblages (Beisaw 2009; Beisaw and Baxter 2017; Beisaw and Gibb 2004; Catts and Cunningham 1986; Gibb and Beisaw 2000; Peña 1992). Landscape studies are also difficult at one-room schoolhouses because what were once larger parcels of land that contained features such as privies and outbuildings are often significantly altered in subsequent development, leaving the original schoolyard landscape unavailable for archaeological study (Helton 2010: 120). Despite the archaeological challenges of school sites, archaeologists have studied site formation processes, analyzed artifacts primarily identified with educational institutions, and explored the role schools played in American rural communities, using the archaeological record.

Perhaps the most influential scholar in the study of one-room schools has been April Beisaw (2009), who consolidated information from seven CRM reports and articles and identified common themes in archaeological findings to develop a site-specific formation model for one-room schools. The available sources for this project were limited in number and a small sample of such excavations, but were notable for their geographic diversity from across the United States. She found that all reports of one-room schools shared the following four characteristics: (1) architectural debris dominates archaeological assemblages; (2) areas within and around the schoolhouse foundations produce the most artifacts; (3) archival work is essential for understanding the building events represented in the archaeological evidence; and (4) clear research questions were seldom informing the excavation of school sites, which led to reporting but little analysis.

The results of this literature review were tested using two one-room schoolhouses in Michigan. Beisaw (2009) found that a particular pattern of construction, renovation, rebuilding, and demolition, as opposed to discard, dominated the deposition of materials at one-room schoolhouses. There were few artifacts that related to the daily use of school sites as educational facilities, which may relate to the nature of the institutions themselves. Some educational implements and toys were reported at these sites, but they are a very small percentage of excavated assemblages and

Figure 4.1. Archaeological work at the Old Edgebrook Schoolhouse, now located on a Cook County Forest Preserve Golf Course in Northwest Chicago, was typical of many one-room school excavations. The structure was significantly renovated and repurposed as a residence in the 1930s after school consolidation, and most of the schoolyard is now part of the golf course, including a modern snack shop and restroom facility, making the search for former outbuildings largely impossible. Archaeological findings related predominantly to the architectural history of the site with a limited number of educational artifacts, toys, and food-related artifacts recovered. Photo by the author.

are much less numerous than conventional wisdom would suggest. Concurrent uses of school buildings for noneducational purposes, such as community gatherings, and post-abandonment decay and repurposing, contributed only moderately to the archaeological signature of such sites (figure 4.1).

This pattern has been upheld by subsequent work at one-room schools (Beisaw and Baxter 2017; Rotman 2009, 2015). It is possible that public schools may have emphasized value systems that kept sites "clean," with children being encouraged to model particular values around cleanliness and order and having access to certain types of objects limited during the school day. Deliberately encouraging students to keep the schoolhouse and yard neat and tidy and conserving school supplies as coveted resources may have been practices that served to limit the artifact counts encountered by archaeologists. Other practices seem to limit the types of toys and playthings children brought to school. While toys are found at school sites, they are limited almost exclusively to jacks and marbles—small portable toys that could have been easily carried from home to school, and which encouraged small group play. Dolls and doll accessories are very rare findings at school sites, suggesting certain types of children's toys were not making the commute to and from school with their owners, perhaps because of their breakable nature and/or because of the types of play they encouraged or discouraged. Emily Helton (2010: 122) also has argued that it is likely that toys are underrepresented in assemblages at one-room schools because in rural areas much of the toy culture was homemade and improvised, and therefore not archaeologically visible. The identifiable mass-produced toys at rural schools are undoubtedly a subset of children's objects that were used during their scheduled outdoor and indoor recreation.

An analysis of artifacts from the Wea View Schoolhouse in Indiana reflected how the limited nonarchitectural assemblages at one-room schools can be used in site interpretation, and offers insight into the types of goods found in these notoriously small assemblages (Rotman 2009, 2015). Educational items at the schoolhouse included writing slate fragments, a variety of pencil types, ink bottles, chalk, and a fragment of a textbook page. Jacks also were found and were the only toys recovered in the excavations. Other items recovered came from community activities that took place at the schoolhouse, including a pressed-glass punch cup, cutlery, and smoking-pipe fragments. Other items, such as pins, needles, and buttons, could have been educational to teach children (girls) sewing skills, or may have been for social sewing events for women in the community. Three privies were found on the property, divided by gender: one for women and two for men, with gendered artifact assemblages associated with each. Deborah Rotman (2015) noted that dual use of the schoolhouse as an educational facility and as a place of community gathering reflected an underlying unified value system of gender segregation and gender roles that consistently permeated community life, educational practices, and site use.

This finding of gender segregation mirrors historical work done in conjunction with archaeological research at a one-room school in New Philadelphia and Hadley Township in rural Illinois (Helton 2010). Census data from 1850 to 1880 showed an initial prioritization of male students in the educational system that moved toward gender equity regardless of household income over time. Concomitantly, schools were redesigned to keep boys and girls separate in many key features of their school day, including

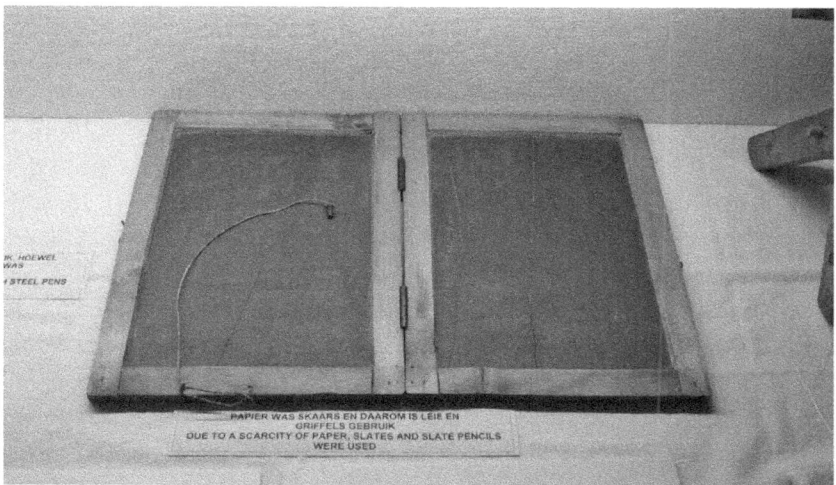

Figure 4.2. Writing slates and pencils are the most common type of educational artifact found at nineteenth-century school sites, although their immediate association with children in domestic contexts needs to be undertaken with care. Photo by Lynn Greyling at Publicdomainpictures.

gender-segregated privies and vestibules for removing coats and outdoor shoes.

Other archaeologists have analyzed artifact types associated with educational institutions, particularly writing slates and slate pencils. These artifacts are ubiquitous in archaeological deposits at educational sites (e.g., Napton and Greathouse 1997), as well as domestic sites (Howson and Bianchi 2014; Swords 2008; Yamin 2002), where they are often interpreted as being used for homework and homeschooling, and are considered identifiers of children's presence in a household (Baxter 2005). Writing slates and slate pencils were the preferred option for use in public schools until pulp paper was cheap and widely available in the 1890s, although their use endured much longer in some rural areas. Gibb and Beisaw (2004) conducted an analysis of slate pencils from one-room schools excavated in Michigan, and found children could use pencils as an effective writing implement until they were one inch in length, and then they were discarded. Oral histories document that children used knives to carve pencils into sharp points and to make a ring around the non-writing end for a string tie to affix the pencil to the writing slate (figure 4.2). Some students also used knives to line their writing slates if they could not obtain a version sold with lines.

Writing slates and writing pencils certainly had other uses including military, industrial, and recreational purposes, making their association with children likely but not inevitable (Swords 2008). This wider use of these implements is evidenced by their inclusion in a general "stationery supplies" category in the 1897 Sears and Roebuck catalogue, although the contemporary 1895 Montgomery Ward catalogue advertised writing slates and pencils as a school supply. Individual writing slates were offered alongside full-sized blackboards and chalkboards for communal use. One of the features often touted in these ads was the "noiseless" quality of certain brands, as the sound of a slate pencil on writing slate was quite unpleasant (Swords 2008: 45) and a classroom full of studious children would have been a cacophony. Slates also varied in size, some were lined or etched for graphing, and some opened and closed in book form (figure 4.2). As Swords has noted (2008), attention to the archaeological context of these artifacts is essential, as the universal association of children with slates and pencils should not be automatic. Other scholars have argued that other types of artifacts, such as desk hardware, may be better indicators of a site's educational function, as desks are less portable than pencils and were a consistent feature of schools and schoolrooms (Structemeyer 2008).

While some archaeologists have looked at the artifacts of schools in detail, others have explored how schools functioned in the context of communities. Recently, Beisaw and Baxter (2017) investigated the relationship between schoolhouses and communities by looking at one-room schools as sites of local autonomy, value expression, and resistance. In the nineteenth century, schools were funded and constructed by local communities and their location, appearance, and design were all potent material representations of the values placed on children, education, and community investment. Decisions to improve schools, to embrace changes offered by state and federal standards, and to retain aspects of local tradition and culture were all heavily debated at the local level in town meetings and by school boards. Archaeology offers the chance to evaluate the decisions that individual communities were making about children and education, particularly in light of documented standards being imposed by governmental authorities as the century progressed. Looking at these specific aspects of schools in the past can be extremely important for communities in the present, as one-room schools are often critical in contemporary dialogues about heritage, memory, and identity

(Beisaw 2009; Beisaw and Baxter 2017). The significance of these places can be seen in the presence of one-room school museums that are abundant across the country. While schools are frequently presented using generic tropes about education, oral histories from former students and donated memorabilia are often featured in exhibits. Archaeology offers a very powerful way to create community-specific interpretations of a truly American institution, and can bridge oral history, documentary records, and family history to place childhoods into specific local contexts that connect education to community and family life.

Campus Archaeology and the Long Adolescence

The archaeology of American education has focused mostly on one-room schools and sites of primary education. Some students attended these schools into their teenage years while others left at much younger ages having attained basic skills in literacy and mathematics. The extension of America's public school program in the twentieth century to publicly funded, mandatory high schools was, according to historian Paula Fass (2016; chapter 2), a uniquely American investment in the education of all of its citizens. This investment also is inextricably linked to the cultural recognition and elaboration of the period we know as adolescence, or a prolonged intermediate developmental stage where an individual is neither a child nor an adult (chapter 2). High schools have not been explored in the published archaeological literature, but institutions of higher education have (Skowronek and Lewis 2010; Wilkie 2010). Archaeological projects are common on college campuses, as they have become very easy sites for student training that can be richly contextualized with other types of documentation and readily coordinated and disseminated with the public in mind. While some of these sites explore the campus lands from periods long before the establishment of the college or university, others have focused on tracing the evolution and history of the academic institution.

When thinking of the archaeology of childhood and adolescence these sites are very germane. Individuals of college age who do not attend a university often live independently of their parents and take on the full responsibility for their own household. They are generally socially and culturally regarded as "full" adults. Students at institutions of higher learning exist in a particular kind of liminality that extends dependency on parents and other institutional structures, in essence prolonging their adolescence. At the same time, attending college most often includes leaving home, and such separation offers opportunities for exploring independence and comparing ideas and values with peers with a greater degree of immersion and intensity. Access to higher education and the ability to prolong entry into the workforce has always perpetuated and accentuated divisions of gender, race, and class in America. The tensions around this adolescent/adult divide can be seen in how boundaries are debated in social, political, and legal arenas. Issues including age of consent for sexual conduct, participation in military service, and debates over the minimum age for use of tobacco, alcohol, and motorized vehicles are used to delineate those boundaries, and they shift over time (Luker 2006).

Laurie Wilkie's (2010) work on the Zeta Psi fraternity particularly addresses the tensions around a prolonged adolescence that existed in the context of fraternity life from the late nineteenth to the mid-twentieth century at the University of California. Her narrative uses the vehicle of Peter Pan and the Lost Boys, a classic children's tale about boys who will never grow up, to contextualize the lives of young men who resided in the fraternity house on campus. Her work illustrated how fraternities were significant communities that helped to define changing ideas about masculinity and femininity over time while emancipating men from the domestic sphere. This all-male community was reliant on women as servants who cleaned, cooked, and cared for them as they spent their time going to school and doing the work of "growing up." Fraternities such as Zeta Psi also have traditionally focused on secret rituals and practices that connect members across generations in ways that allow adult men to remain connected to this particular part of their adolescence throughout their lives.

Much of the archaeology of academia has focused on the institutions themselves and the evolution of higher education on particular campuses and in general (Skowronek and Lewis 2010). Of course, none of these types of questions can be well understood without a focus on student life, but other projects have focused more specifically on the lived experiences of students in these institutional contexts. Perhaps one of the most extensive and best-known campus archaeology projects is one that took place at Saint's Rest on the Michigan State University campus (Lewis 2010; MSU Campus Archaeology Blog; O'Gorman 2010).

Saint's Rest was the first residential facility and dining hall on campus and operated from 1856 to 1871. During the earliest years of the college, the surrounding area was swampland and students were relatively isolated. Part of their educational costs were covered by helping to build the campus in the afternoons. The presence of educational artifacts such as ink bottles and pen nibs indicates they were also spending part of their day engaged in coursework and studying. Saints' Rest burned to the ground in 1876 and the site was not reused by the university, creating a temporally discrete deposit of mid-nineteenth-century campus residential life. Archaeological excavations at the site have been intermittent since 2005, and have revealed much about the life of the first students attending the new college.

These earliest students were all male, as the school did not become coeducational until 1870, but much like the fraternity house at the University of California the staff of the boarding house was comprised of women. Accounts at the university record the "dining room girls" purchasing personal and clothing items through university accounts that were then charged against their pay (Saint's Rest, MSU Campus Archaeology Blog). Many of these items were clothing related—garters, corsets, ribbons, parasols, and hoop skirts, while others were more practical items such as medicine. Documentary sources recorded the male students and "dining room girls" socializing in the dining room during nonmealtimes, suggesting there was fraternizing between students and staff on the isolated campus. It also seems the girls took an interest in their appearance for those visits, as the items they were purchasing were not for clothing and accessories that would have been worn in their assigned tasks of cooking, cleaning, and serving the residents.

The men who resided at Saint's Rest had their meals served on simple ironstone vessels, but with a variety of embossed designs and flourishes, suggesting a nod was made to elevating dorm living and dining experiences. The variety of vessel types also suggests that tables were set with an array of dinnerwares that would have reflected a certain degree of class-based knowledge about how to dine in a socially appropriate manner. While not the materials of a wealthy household, the dorm furnishings appear to have been comfortable and a bit nicer than the most basic of table settings. Other more forbidden comforts such as alcohol and tobacco were also evidenced in the archaeological record in the form of liquor bottles and smoking pipes. In many ways, the material signature of Saint's Rest is indistinguishable from a middle-class household, which says something about the expectations and aspirations of the students and their families sending them to college. The particular nuances of the assemblage, such as the forbidden nature of some of the objects and the gender dynamics of residents and staff, can only be understood in the broader documentary context for the site (Lewis 2010).

Much like the fraternity brothers at Zeta Psi, the students who resided at Saint's Rest were exposed to a very gender-segregated lifestyle. Men pursued their education and engaged in the manual tasks of building the university, while women were responsible for the domestic sphere of the dormitory. The isolation of the new campus was buffered by attempts to replicate patterns of diet and dining that would have been familiar to many of the students, and by bending accepted rules and norms around drinking, smoking, and socializing. When considered in the context of the emerging recognition of adolescence occurring in the later nineteenth century and the role education played in creating these liminal spaces between childhood and adulthood, archaeological work at places like the Saint's Rest dorm and the Zeta Psi fraternity house reveals how institutional structures helped individuals both stay young and grow up while away at school.

Orphanages and Children's Homes

A final institution type relating to children where archaeologists have conducted research is orphanages and children's homes (chapter 2). While orphanages were a common type of institution in many countries in the nineteenth and twentieth centuries, it has been argued that historical circumstances served to create unique relationships between America and its orphans (Pazicky 1998). Diana Loercher Pazicky (1998) has studied the trope of the orphan in American literature, and argued that the imagery of orphans in American literature is inextricably tied to familial imagery. Rather than seeing the family as a microcosm of the nation, she suggested that the family is held up as the paradigmatic institution that defined cultural values for the nation as a whole. This familial, and particularly patriarchal, system of values served as a metaphor between the government and its citizens, where particular populations including Native Americans, African Americans, and immigrants were cast as cultural orphans at different times in American history. The American literary orphan is most often depicted as a threat to the dominant culture, with the positive outcome being the return of the orphan to the "family fold."

Figure 4.3. An example of a nineteenth-century institution for children. Sister Irene and children at the New York Foundling Hospital circa 1888. Photograph by Joseph Riis. Library of Congress.

This recognizable metaphor was important as the country struggled to bring orphan populations "under control." Simultaneously, the proliferation of institutions for individual orphans by philanthropic organizations of social reform offered everyday Americans the opportunity to constructively engage with the nation's "orphan problem" (figure 4.3). Orphans were not necessarily without parents, but were without a home and support network deemed adequate by social reformers. Once removed from inadequate living situations, children could be molded into citizens who embodied traditional American values of hard work, industry, and discipline. The individual orphan and orphan cultures were symbolic parallels in America.

Orphanages, like one-room schools, were a very common institution in the nineteenth and early twentieth centuries. As childhood became a more clearly delineated phase of life and the value of maintaining a child's innocence and purity became a cultural ideal, institutions that provided care and training for children but kept them socially separate from potentially destructive adult influences became common (Calvert 1992; Chudacoff 2007; Fass 2016; Muller 2017; chapter 2). Most of these institutions were racially segregated and operated exclusively for the children of European immigrants and working-class white families. These institutions varied in scale and were operated by a variety of charitable organizations and later government agencies, each with their own funding, philosophies, and resources that were translated into material and social worlds for children. Larger-scale organizations, including most government-run institutions, were housed in structures and on grounds deliberately constructed for their institutional purpose, while others run by religious or charitable foundations often took over extant structures and modified them for use. Some of these institutions, therefore, lend themselves more to architectural and landscape approaches than others, based on the relationship between the institution and its physical location (Przystupa 2018).

One example of the former type of institution was the Magdalen Asylum in Philadelphia, which operated mostly during the nineteenth century as a privately sponsored institution, and was designed to be a home for moral reform through productive labor. There were workrooms, infirmaries, kitchens, and different lodging rooms that structured the institutional space (De Cunzo 1995). During the early nineteenth century, the asylum was designed as an institutional home of temporary accommodation for young, unmarried women, but the organization's mission gradually transformed and the institution became predominantly a home for the improvement of wayward girls. The goal of this institution was to be preventative rather than punitive, meaning it proactively provided girls with vocational training and garden work as forms of regulated leisure and productive industry (DeCunzo 2001). Through these efforts in productive labor, moral transformation would take place. This process was designed to take young girls in who needed temporary respite and convert them into productive, moral young women who could go into the world as upstanding adults.

The Rhode Island State Home and School also occupied a building and landscape designed and constructed specifically for the institution. This school was one of many government institutions resulting from determined political actions by women of the Progressive Era focused on reform (Spencer-Wood 1991). The home operated as the first public orphanage in the state, and more than 10,000 children lived there during its operation from 1885 to 1979. The archaeologist at Rhode Island College, where the remains of the home are located, noted "the Progressive Era women who lobbied for the creation of this place viewed it as a temporary home, or an alternative to the almshouses, poor farms, and asylums of the late 1800s" (E. Pierre Morenon, quoted in Urbanus 2014).

These types of institutions that were housed in purposefully built architectural facilities are the focus of current dissertation research by Paulina Przystupa at the University of New Mexico, who is comparing institutional plans and layouts of orphanages and Indian boarding schools, using a space syntax approach. Her work is designed to compare how the assimilation and socialization of children differed between orphanages and Indian boarding schools, based on social constructions of race and ethnicity in nineteenth-century America (Przystupa 2018). While still in early stages, this work will begin to systematically approach the built environment at institutions specifically designed for children.

An example of the latter type of institution was the orphanage at Schuyler Mansion that was operated by the Daughters of Charity from 1886 to 1914 in the former mansion of the Revolutionary War general Philip Schuyler, located in Albany, New York. The eighteenth-century mansion was modified to house orphans and many of the services deemed essential for their care, and outbuildings were also repurposed, modified, and added to accommodate the children in residence. Most of the children at the school were Italian immigrants. Those termed "infants" ranged in age from newborns to age six and were full-time residents at the orphanage. Children older than six were sent to school to learn skills so they could support themselves upon reaching the age of 18 (Feister 2009). Several years of work by state archaeologists as part of site development plans recovered information about the lives of the orphans and operations of the orphanage by the Vincentian sisters. The house is now a New York State historic site and museum.

Archaeological investigations at all of these residential institutions shared a common finding of abundant material culture for children's recreation and care, suggesting the children residing at these institutions were not living in austerity. All of these institutions included education and training programs that fit with the means, circumstances and values of the organizations operating them, but children also had access to toys and playthings that would have been common for children living with families as well. At the Rhode Island State Home, toys were the most common artifacts discovered, including marbles, jacks, toy trucks, soldiers, and roller skates (Urbanus 2014). Archaeological and photographic evidence illustrate that children at the orphanage at Schuyler Mansion were provided with toys and had time for independent play and leisure (Baxter 2000; Feister 2009). One letter to Santa from a child at the orphanage made a request for a very specific type of doll, suggesting that the children believed it was at least possible to wish for a specific toy and not just a generic toy given to all the children at the institution. The diversity of the types of toys recovered at the site suggests this possibility was realized for many of the children (Feister 2009). Account records at the Schuyler Mansion orphanage also show that, after operational and food costs were covered, toys and treats such as candy and ice cream were sometimes provided to children with budgeted funds.

The abundance of toys at orphanage sites suggests that children at institutions were engaged in play and recreation, and had childhood experiences involving material culture that would have been typical at the time. These toys were not provided just for recreational purposes, but also for the types of behaviors and values they imparted to children on behalf of their adult caretakers and benefactors. While this is arguably true of toys found in domestic contexts as well (chapter 3), institutional concerns of moral, spiritual, and social well-being would have made this aspect of toys even more pronounced and deliberate in institutional settings. A spatial analysis of the toys at Schuyler Mansion reflects gender segregation in play, which would have been considered socially ideal and appropriate (Baxter 2000). Almost all of the toys typically associated with girls (93 percent), such as dolls and doll accessories, were found in the mansion's gardens. Toys advertised and more likely used by boys also were found in the gardens, but 40 percent were found in deposits scattered across the grounds. This pattern suggests that the young girls at the orphanage were typically engaged in more sedentary play in direct view of the staff operating indoors or directly around the main building, while the boys had wider ranges of play on the grounds, which did not necessarily involve adult supervision. These distributions of artifacts at the orphanage look much more like those found at domestic sites (Baxter 2000) than at other institutions, such as Indian boarding schools (Surface-Evans 2016), where children were photographed with toys, but they do not appear in contexts of use in the archaeological record. The widespread presence of appropriate and fashionable (although not necessarily expensive) toys and their distributions in socially acceptable locations for play found at domestic sites (chapter 3) indicates that children at orphanages were engaging in some activities parallel to their age mates living at home.

Some Thoughts

The archaeology of institutions offers powerful insight into the American past generally, but also can be revelatory about childhood and adolescence. The intentional and deliberate design of institutions, the types of material goods used to furnish them, and the structured activities and programs that shape daily life within them are often connected to clearly stated goals, values, and beliefs about what and who is normal and desired in society. Certainly, no institution operates in complete self-awareness, but institutional design and philanthropic organizing are intentional practices that add transparency to the value systems that inform them. This aspect of institutions is seen in the well-documented Americanization agenda of Japanese internment camps, the internal colonialism and assimilation policies that governed Indian boarding schools, and the mission statements of philanthropic organizations dedicated to "saving" those in need of intervention. When institutions are developed for children, these deliberate intentions reflect cultural ideals about childhood and children as well. Identifying certain children as being in need of care, reform, and/or education and having definitions and standards for successful outcomes of institutional exposure can help illuminate deeply held cultural ideals regarding children and adults in society.

Extant research on institutional life also demonstrates how the study of institutions can reveal more tacit, symbolic values surrounding children held by the dominant society at any time. The symbolic parallel of reforming individual orphans and turning them into proper American citizens as a metaphor for orphan populations in need of the same return to the "family" fold, or the need to shelter children in their own institutions to maintain their innocence from the adult world as a reflection of their unique, pure status in nineteenth-century society, are two such examples. The deeper, unspoken dimensions of race, gender, and class and the desire for a population of compliant and patriotic individuals aren't to be found in any mission statements or reformers' propaganda, but they are analytically accessible through design and operation of these intentional and calculated institutions for American children.

Simultaneously, archaeology can tell us about the activities of children at institutions that fall outside the recorded schedules and programs designed for them. How children used institutional spaces in the course of their daily lives is a significant narrative that imbues children with agency in their own lives even in the context of institutional structures. In what ways did children express resistance to institutional design? How did they develop or maintain identities on an individual and community level? The work at Indian boarding schools is a potent example of how children taken from their communities were able to develop their own strategies of resistance, systems of meaning, and networks of support independent of adult intervention and guidance. This type of work is a powerful testimony to the potential of archaeology to reveal the worlds of children and how those worlds influence and shape culture as a whole. These kinds of narratives do not keep children at the margins, but rather illustrate their power as social actors.

Finally, it is clear that institutions have a profound impact on those who experience them, and this may be particularly true for children who move on into lives beyond institutional care as adults. Perhaps the most widespread example is the phenomenon of the "high school reunion" where people travel great distances at marked intervals to reconnect with classmates and celebrate their shared experiences of public education together. With less benign institutions (although many would argue high school in America is far from benign), sentimental reunions are not the preferred activity for those looking back. Many children who went to Indian boarding schools became activists fighting for rights for all Native Americans, and seeking justice for the abuse those institutions inflicted. Former residents of Japanese internment camps, perhaps most famously the actor George Takei, have become outspoken advocates for equality and the protection of all American citizens from oppression regardless of their identities. One aspect of many of the archaeological projects studying institutions is the eager participation and engagement of former residents. Many adults come back to participate in excavations and/or share their stories in the context of these archaeological projects. The archaeology of institutions provides a meaningful way to connect communities to their past and to interpret the archaeological record in ways that acknowledge the fundamental importance of childhood experiences in the lives of American adults.

~ 5 ~

Children's Bodies and Commemorations of Children

For some American children, childhood is forever. Cemeteries dating back to the earliest days of the country and the colonial era hold commemorative monuments to individuals identified as children and infants who did not live long enough to become adults. Diseases, pathogens, epidemics, poor sanitation, and limited medical knowledge were factors affecting all Americans in the past, but these factors disproportionately affected children, especially infants. The definitions of "child" and "infant" in death records vary significantly over time, and vital records were not kept consistently for most of American history. However, one can say with certainty that with the advent of public health initiatives and development of vaccines and medical interventions, the rate of childhood and infant mortality has declined significantly in America. A few reliable statistics can help give a sense of this change. According to data compiled by the NIH (Field and Behrman 2003), the infant mortality rate (individuals ≤1 year in age) in 1850 was 261 for every 1000 individuals, and in 1900 it was 165 for every 1000 individuals. In 1999, that rate was 7 for every 1000 individuals. In 1900, 30 percent of all recorded deaths in America were individuals aged 18 and under, while in 1999 individuals under the age of 18 were 1.4 percent of the total recorded deaths in the country.

Children's Bodies & Commemorations of Children · 125

Figure 5.1. A series of nineteenth-century headstones for individual children lost to a single family located behind the main headstone marking the family plot. The children's stones are mounted on a single slab and all share the same motif of a sleeping child, a common metaphor for death during the later nineteenth-century "beautification" movement. The unity of their headstones and their proximity to their parents in death emphasizes the importance of home and family. These types of monuments are material reminders of the high infant and child mortality rates that have been common throughout most of American history. Photo from Graceland Cemetery, Chicago, by the author.

Historians looking back from a period where the death of a child is a very rare event to a time when it was quite common have grappled with the question of how family members connected to young children given the precarious nature of children's health and the likelihood of their survival (figure 5.1). Much of the early scholarship on this topic suggested that high mortality rates meant that a meaningful emotional attachment to children by parents and families was deferred to a time well after birth when it was more likely that a child would survive (Beals 1975; Benes and Benes 2002). These types of studies emphasized the economic value of children in families, noting that children provided necessary sources of income, labor, and security (Zelizer 1994). Having many children, knowing only a few would survive to adulthood, was not an uncommon pattern in the American past, and it was extrapolated that love and affection for any particular child was diminished or absent under such circumstances. Family practices reflected on mortuary monuments, such as the use of the same given name for sequential children in the same family, often were cited as evidence for a lack of investment in any particular child, and rather that families were simply hoping for a child to survive to adulthood. Such interpretations essentially suggested that ideas of personhood and individual identity did not become realized until later in a child's life.

More recent scholarship has rejected this earlier depiction of parents and families being disconnected and unfeeling toward infants and young children as a way of buffering themselves against the likelihood of loss. Fass (2016: 42) has investigated personal writings and found that the losses of children and siblings were significant disruptions to households and genuine sources of grief. Americans in the past lived with the knowledge that infant and child death was common, but the loss of any particular child was a very real loss in time, energy, and resources (Matthews 2010) as well as hopes and aspirations for the future (Baxter 2013, Tarlow 1999). Puritan families tried to rush their inchoate children into a state of full humanness to help insure the well-being of their bodies and souls, not only if they lived but also if they died (Calvert 1992). In the nineteenth century, when childhood mortality was still quite high, the death of a child was elevated to the apex of an elaborate mourning culture where a child's death was simultaneously denied through metaphors of sleep and rest, and also celebrated and commemorated in photographs, monuments, consolation literature, and extended periods of culturally prescribed mourning (figure 5.2).

Archaeologists who study burial treatments, skeletal remains, and commemorations of children through monuments and ritual practices recognize that the death of a child is generally considered to be disruptive and against the natural order, even in times and places when its occurrence was quite common (Baxter 2013; Mays et al. 2017; Thompson et al. 2014). This particular quality of children's deaths—being untimely,

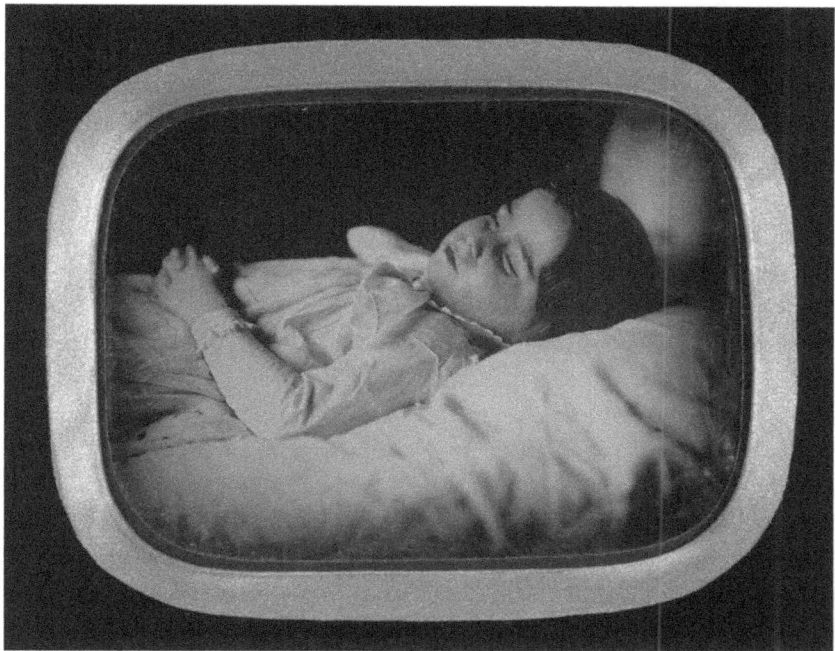

Figure 5.2. Taking photos of deceased children was a common nineteenth-century practice as a way to commemorate their brief lives, keep them included in the family, and depict them in ways that denied death in favor of the popular euphemism of being asleep or at rest. Carl Durheim, Postmortem of a Child, circa 1852. Wikimedia.

too soon, or in a sense unnatural—is reflected in the types of mortuary treatments and commemorations practiced by the communities that remained to mourn them. While certainly some children are unwanted and abortion and infanticide are and were widespread cultural practices, most children are born into communities hoping for their survival and invest time, energy, and resources into this outcome.

Mortuary studies of children (and all populations) in the American past fall into two broad categories: studies of excavated burials including mortuary assemblages and skeletal remains, and studies of headstones, grave markers, and the material culture of bereavement and consolation found above ground in cemeteries (Baugher and Veit 2014). These two types of sites reflect strong cultural divides operating in America that allow some memorials and burial grounds to be seen as sacred and untouchable, while others are seen as suitable for disruption and disturbance as community needs change. Setting aside land as sacred or as consecrated ground that cannot be disturbed is a form of collective sacrifice either for a family setting aside a parcel of their private land or as a community that weighs the need for such spaces in light of other types of amenities and development. Honoring that sensibility across generations takes a maintenance of the values that set aside those spaces as special and deserving of care in the first place. Erecting durable monuments that are recognizable as markers for the location of human remains requires an expenditure of time, energy, and income, and maintaining that marker extends an obligation of care across generations.

Children whose families were able to bury them in a space formally and legally set aside for the interment of the dead, and who could provide a long-lasting headstone to mark the location of their grave, tended to be white, whether native-born or immigrant, and from middle- or upper-middle-class American families. Their graves remain undisturbed over time in family plots or public or private cemeteries and are known to us today through their monuments and location on the landscape. While the relocation of marked cemeteries does occur, it is rare that they are the more affluent burial grounds of wealthier citizens. Children whose families were not able to bury them in places collectively recognized as sacred, or who could not afford monuments, or who came from cultural traditions where such burial practices were not the norm, often were buried in places that were disturbed and developed as towns and cities grew. Such graves are often still subject to disturbance and considered suitable for relocation if a significant development project requires their removal to proceed. Poor children, African American children, Native American children, and others are often studied using above-ground monuments, but also are more typically studied through excavated remains and bioarchaeological studies.

It should be noted that such studies are not common, as laws do protect the disturbance of known burial grounds, whether marked or unmarked. Studies of children's memorials are not abundant either, despite a long history of research on headstones and grave markers in the United States. Despite being limited in number, the available research in this area illuminates the diversity of childhood experiences like no other source. Dynamics of race, ethnicity, and class as well as how ideals of children become embodied and materialized are central to the archaeology of those who are forever children.

Children's Bodies and Burials

Archaeological studies of mortuary populations from the historic period of America's past are quite limited. Federal, state, and local laws prohibit the excavation of known burial grounds in the country, and when the removal of burials is required due to impending development, rarely are skeletal remains studied and curated in detail; rather, they are immediately reinterred elsewhere. Analyses that are completed tend to prioritize the identification of the individuals who are being disinterred so that descendants and family members can be notified and have input on the reburial process. Research on these early cemeteries is often impeded due to missing, fragmentary, or otherwise limited documentary records, and subsequent development of these sites can make matching the limited documentary records to the archaeological remains encountered during recovery efforts nearly impossible. The majority of these types of projects take place in densely developed urban areas where early cemetery sites were developed for alternative purposes before any cultural and historic preservation laws were enacted. When the properties are subject to modern redevelopment efforts, these cemeteries and burial grounds become subject to archaeological investigation and relocation. In more rural areas, avoidance is a reasonable strategy when known cemeteries fall within the boundaries of proposed development projects, creating a bias in the literature toward urban burial populations (Rothschild and Wall 2014: 163–169). When rural cemeteries are subject to excavation the rates of child mortality and evidence for disease and nutrition are very similar to those found in urban contexts (e.g., Connolly et al. 2010).

A good example of such a project with widely available publications is the Joint Courts Complex project in Tuscon, Arizona (Hall et al. 2008). This project was undertaken by Statistical Research, Inc., and included the excavation of 1083 graves containing 1397 individuals from an urban lot that was redeveloped by Pima County. Two known cemeteries were located on the lot, one military and the other civilian. Both were in operation in the 1860s, and the civilian cemetery closed in 1875 and the military cemetery in 1881. The civilian cemetery likely was used by the Hispanic Catholic population, who were the largest demographic in the city at the time. The site was redeveloped in the 1890s, causing disturbance to some of the more superficial burials, but most interments recovered on the property were intact. The report (Hall et al. 2008) covers the details of this project and is useful for the way it documents a common process involving development, archaeology, and burial sites in the United States.

Children were among the 1397 individuals recovered from the development site and were found in both the military and civilian cemeteries. The children's graves were often easy to identify as the soil discoloration that demarcated the boundaries of a burial corresponded in size to the coffin and therefore the individual interred. A study done on children's burials during a similar type of project in Belleville, Ontario, was designed to assist archaeologists in identifying the presence of children in burial populations when skeletal remains are poorly preserved and records are inadequate or absent (McKillop 1995). The study examined a variety of variables in adult and children's graves from the nineteenth century, including coffin length, the number of handles, the handle motif and size, the presence of glass viewing plates, and the presence/absence of decorative motifs on hardware. The project involved the disinterment of 576 individuals in a context that had many nameplates on coffins, a strong documentary record, and excellent skeletal preservation, offering the necessary controls to definitively link these material variables to adults and/or children. Variables relating to the size of the coffin, such as length, handle size, and number of handles were distinguishing features between adult and child graves, as the smaller size of children's coffins and coffin hardware reflected the smaller stature of the individual being buried. Other features, such as the presence of nameplates, glass viewing plates, or decorative hardware had no differentiation between adults and children, but there were decorative motifs that were reserved for or strongly associated with children. Heather McKillop (1995) compared her findings to catalogues of coffins and coffin hardware that were widely distributed across North America as well as to other reports of excavated nineteenth-century cemeteries and found the identifying features for children's graves in the Belleville study were widespread across the continent.

These insights are useful for burial populations that followed Euro-American norms for burial and commemoration in the nineteenth century, when rural garden cemeteries (see below) were a common feature in North American, as well as many earlier Euro-American, burial traditions. In earlier centuries, however, mortuary treatments varied widely, based on local populations and cultural traditions. A seventeenth-century Narragansett cemetery excavated in North Kingstown, Rhode Island, in the 1980s provided evidence about local Native American burial practices during the contact period. The study of these burials included a focused analysis of children's remains and burial treatments (Rubertone 2001: 132–164). Using skeletal remains and associated burial goods, P. Rubertone identified a distinct age category of children aged three to nine years. The relatively poor preservation of these subadult skeletons meant that the remains could not be sexed, making any analysis of gender impossible. A distinct pattern of burial treatment for all skeletons of this age group regardless of gender was interpreted as marking a particular recognized stage of personal development and accompanying child-rearing practices on the part of parents. This work is an important early example of using archaeology to discern culturally specific definitions of age in the human life cycle rather than imposing normative views of child development in contemporary Western culture onto the past (Baxter 2005; Mays et al. 2017).

These young individuals were interred with the most objects per person of any age or gender category identified in the burial population. These goods included bodily adornments and items placed in graves alongside the bodies. Rubertone connected the variation in grave goods within this age group to different maternal expectations about survival—a deliberate way of thinking differently about children with heavily adorned graves, rather than defaulting to more traditional interpretations of inherited rank or status (see below). Rubertone also noted the prevalence of encircling ornaments, particularly bracelets, necklaces, and headbands being buried with these young children. She interpreted these artifacts as symbolic representations of binding children to earth, to parents, and to social groups. She argued that wearing such objects during one's lifetime, especially bracelets that are easily visible to the wearer as well as to others, was a way to remind children of their connectedness. Burial treatments that included these encircling ornaments were a way of maintaining a symbolic relationship with the children as a continuation of legacy and lineage.

This interpretation has been debated by Christopher Matthews (2010: 43), who suggested that perhaps in the new economy of the fur trade, the wealth of these children's graves was a reflection of the relative success of families as traders. Children's graves may have been a reflection of an achieved status rank of the family as a whole within this competitive economic system driven by culture contact. While this interpretation is more traditional, it also ties achieved rank specifically to success in the contemporary dynamic of competitive fur trade economies, rather than other cultural traditions. Both of these interpretations consider the burial treatment of children as deeply connected to value systems being formed in a moment of significant cultural change and upheaval, and recognize the important roles children played as members of families and communities.

African American cemeteries can be found across the American landscape, but because of America's history of racial segregation these cemeteries have been spatially discrete from burial grounds used for white Americans until relatively recently (Baugher and Veit 2014). Burial grounds for enslaved individuals can still be found on former plantation lands, and churchyards and rural cemeteries specifically for the African American community are common postemancipation landscape features in the American South. Even in northern states where legal strictures maintaining segregation were often laxer, "negro cemeteries" were needed well into the twentieth century, as many cemeteries had charters excluding nonwhites from purchasing burial plots (e.g., Pattison 1955). These policies of segregation included religious as well as municipal burial grounds. The earliest African American cemeteries in northern cities were for enslaved individuals, and the sanctity of these burial spaces was not maintained as cities developed and engulfed lands set aside for interment. As Michael Blakey (1998: 53–54) noted in reference to the African Burial Ground in New York City, "The treatment which the cemetery itself has received over the years might alone fill several chapters on the African-American struggle for human rights."

The African Burial Ground is a cemetery that was in use in colonial New York City from the late 1600s to 1796 and may have originally contained between ten and twenty thousand burials (Barrett and Blakey 2011; Blakey 1998). The burial site was significantly disrupted during its period of active use by grave robbers and adjacent industries, and also in subsequent centuries by urban development projects. In the early 1990s, the lot was again subject to disturbance but this time elected officials intervened, halted development, and initiated a program of scientific research and community consultation to determine how the site would be interpreted as a place of commemoration for the deceased and community heritage for the living. A total of 427 human remains and artifacts were removed from the cemetery prior to the cessation of development, and with community input it was decided that scientific study was the appropriate course of action.

Among the remains exhumed from the site were those of children, and the project's emphasis on understanding the physical quality of life under slavery brought many details to light about their lives. Child and infant mortality rates were extraordinarily high in the African Burial Ground population, and were twice that of the contemporaneous English population in the New York colony (Blakey 1998: 56). Children's remains showed evidence of infectious diseases with 25 percent of children's skeletons having bone lesions associated with generalized infections. Metabolic diseases, such as anemia, were evidenced in the skeletal remains of half the children in the population. Children in the 2- to 12-year-old age category often showed evidence of growth retardation, where dental development lagged approximately two years behind what would be considered typical or normal. Approximately 60 percent of children had defects in dental enamel reflecting bouts of malnutrition and disease (Barrett and Blakey 2011). Evidence for rampant disease and malnutrition was not exclusive to children in the burial population, and both adults and children showed signs of skeletal wear reflecting harsh conditions of labor. Fused vertebrae and strained muscle attachments indicate a population where heavy labor burdens began early in life and continued until death. Yaws, syphilis, and meningitis were among the specific diseases found in the overall population. While these population-wide dynamics provide a definitive picture of the harsh conditions that slavery imposed upon African and African American adults and children, Blakey (1998: 57) highlights a single case of a 6-year-old child that vividly illustrated aspects of a young life lived as an enslaved individual. He wrote:

> It is often said that a society can be judged by the treatment of its most vulnerable members. In this respect, one example from the African Burial Ground is suggestive. The individual known as Burial #39 is a six-year-old child. We do not know whether #39 was a girl or boy. This child has dental developmental defects, showing that he/she was ill at birth, implying maternal ill health as well. The orbits of the eyes show pitting, characteristic of active anemia at the time of death. There are lesions in the outer layers of bone caused by generalized infection. The growth areas (sutures) of the skull have closed

extraordinarily early in development; we are not certain whether this resulted from loadbearing or brain growth retardation due to malnutrition. Burial #39 has lesions at the arm attachments where the brachialis muscles strained, and muscle attachments in the arms are enlarged. The first and second cervical vertebrae (neck bones) are partially fused due to force or heavy load trauma to the top of the head. The only artifacts associated with this burial are the shroud pin stains evincing the care with which the child was interred by members of his or her community.

Comparatively, the rate of disease and malnutrition evidenced in the African Burial Ground is considerably less than in samples from nineteenth-century burial populations of enslaved individuals in the American South (Barrett and Blakey 2011; Blakey 1998). Developmental defects are evidenced in 85 to 90 percent of these populations, compared to the approximately 50 percent of the earlier African Burial Ground population. Researchers suspect this difference may be accounted for by many of the individuals in the earlier population having been raised in Africa where conditions for health, nutrition, and disease were superior to those under slavery in the United States. Stresses evidenced on the skeletons from the African Burial Ground were obviously the result of hard labor, inadequate food and nutrition, and living conditions that would have encouraged the spread of disease and pathogens. These conditions would have begun at the time of capture, continued during transportation to the colonies, and persisted throughout people's lifetimes. Certain populations, particularly children and the elderly, would have been more vulnerable and susceptible to these various challenges and conditions, as they were not considered economically valuable (Mintz 2004) and there was a lack of desire to care for or provide resources to such populations (Barrett and Blakey 2011). Even if slave owners did not wish to invest in the care of enslaved children, burial treatments at the African Burial Ground illustrate a great deal of investment in those interred there as well as a deliberate effort to maintain cultural traditions through symbolic and ritual behavior that were actively discouraged or banned in other settings.

Racial and ethnic background were not the only causes that determined the quality of a child's life or their treatment after death in America's past, as dynamics of social and economic class were also a major factor. During the nineteenth century, the industrial revolution and its many consequences, including urbanization and immigration, resulted in a growing concentration of poor and working-class families in American cities. Another project in New York City, the Five Points Project (chapter 3), involved extensive excavations of nineteenth-century working class tenements. A privy was excavated on one of the lots where a brothel was known to have operated. Among the contents of the privy were the remains of three infants: two were full-term neonates which could have been stillbirths or infanticide, and one was a fetus at 20–22 weeks, which may have been a quickened fetus, miscarriage, or induced abortion (Crist 2005). An analysis of the remains could not determine whether the children were alive or deceased at the time of birth and whether their births were induced or natural. While not a common discovery, there are other documented cases of fetal and infant remains found in privies during archaeological excavations.

The published analysis of these "discarded" children focuses mostly on the limited and often difficult choices for working-class women in the nineteenth century, but the remains also raise questions about children and child-rearing in such precarious situations. Given that prophylactics to prevent pregnancy were widely available, these pregnancies either represent a failure of these contraceptive methods or the desire to have a child. Abortion was contentious but not illegal in the United States during most of the nineteenth century, and would have been a viable option for the women living in Five Points. Women who had abortions were generally pitied as sad and exploited women rather than being scorned or labeled as morally defective. This narrative changes at the end of the nineteenth century, when abortions were seen as a form of depravity and women were blamed for their low circumstances. Such a change in rhetoric points to broader concerns about immigration and growing class divides where women's choices and children's lives hung in the balance.

A final project based in New York City involved the extensive analysis of children buried in the church vaults at a parish associated with political activism around issues of antislavery and abolition (Ellis 2014a, 2014b). This parish was diverse and included both white and African American congregants, immigrants, and native-born families, and working- and middle-class parishioners at a time that New York was transitioning from a rural, agricultural settlement to a dense, urban center. Many of the children who were members of the Spring Street congregation were not necessarily from a group that would have been considered marginal or against the mainstream, but the radical views of the congregation of which they were a part created a distance between their lives and those around them.

The Spring Street Presbyterian Church was built in 1810 and is notable for its involvement with the early nineteenth-century abolitionist movement and its role in the riots of 1834, when the city rose up against abolitionist activities. The charismatic pastors were known for ministering to African and African American members of the community, and their teachings were so outspoken they became targets of the riots and one pastor was burned in effigy in Charleston, South Carolina. The church was closed in 1963 and the site was turned into a parking lot in 1966. The lot was being redeveloped in 2006 when human skeletal remains began to emerge from the excavations and an archaeological team was brought in to investigate. They recovered the skeletal remains of over 200 individuals who were reburied at New York's famous rural garden cemetery, Green Wood, in 2014. Between 2006 and 2014, the individuals who were removed from the Spring Street Church site were held at the Syracuse University Department of Anthropology Bioarchaeology Lab.

Meredith Ellis conducted a dissertation project solely on the children in the burial population at Spring Street Church (Ellis 2014a). The burial population was heavily comingled, making many types of analyses impossible, but nearly half of the population was determined to be children, based on counts of discrete skeletal elements (Ellis 2014b). Her work was multifaceted, but one aspect was identifying the presence of vitamin deficiencies, particularly vitamins C and D, in the children's skeletal remains. Rickets, the manifestation of vitamin D deficiency in the body, was found in over a third of the children in the Spring Street population. Scurvy, or vitamin C deficiency, was a common ailment for children who died at less than two and a half years of age.

Vitamin D deficiency can be the direct result of parenting strategies, labor patterns, clothing, and/or urban air quality that limited children's exposure to sunlight. Scurvy is a more common ailment among children of mothers who had to work, as those children were often weaned earlier than those of upper-class families. Not having access to vitamin C in breast milk, combined with limited dietary choices, often resulted in scurvy in very young children, such as those at Spring Street Church. Ellis's work went beyond health, pathology, and patterns of mortality, however, to consider theories of embodiment or how the body and society are reconciled, focusing not just on how and why these children died but the social reality of their bodies in life. Embodiment theory is a multifaceted approach in contemporary bioarchaeology that addresses how the social becomes biological through embodied practices that are both a product and a producer of the individual and individual reality. Her work combined an analysis of skeletal remains and documentary evidence to illustrate how these diseases may have become manifest in children who came from marginalized communities, participated in a radical religious community, and who would have experienced the world environmentally, economically, and socially on the margins as a result. She noted that, in a religious community with strict guidelines for social and dietary practices, children's bodies would have reflected and become a part of those practices, in some cases to their detriment and demise. Ideas about embodiment are also core to Muller's work on the children termed disabled in the population at the Erie County Poorhouse Complex (chapter 4; Muller 2016).

Children's Headstones and Grave Markers

Access to children's remains is dependent upon how they were buried and how those burials were valued and preserved by subsequent generations. Children of white upper- and middle-class families were buried in cemeteries and graveyards that have been respected by social convention and legal codes for generations. In such instances, archaeological analysis focuses not on the bodily remains of the children themselves but rather the memorials erected for them by families and communities after their deaths. The earliest cemeteries in the United States are church and municipal graveyards in cities along the East Coast, and small family cemeteries where individual families set aside a small parcel of their land to inter members of their family, often over generations (Baugher and Veit 2014). Early colonial graveyards remain in many eastern cities and are now significant tourist sites, such as the Granary Burying Ground on Boston's Freedom Trail. Small family plots can often be seen demarcated by fencing along roadsides or encountered on hikes in now wooded areas that were once the lands of family farms. As in any early burial population, children are commonly interred and memorialized in these spaces.

Most cemeteries in America, however, are not that old and date to the mid-nineteenth century and later when large plots of land outside of cities were designated as burial places for growing urban populations. As cities grew and cemetery populations swelled, concerns over health and sanitation resulted in widespread ordinances to relocate cemeteries outside of cities. These same cities have since grown and enveloped these once rural retreats, but their designs still reveal a great deal about the original intent for these spaces.

Rural garden cemeteries were designed not only to provide a separation between the dead and the living that promoted health and hygiene, but also to offer city residents dedicated spaces to escape into "nature." The landscape of a rural garden cemetery contained key elements including imposing front gates and secure walls around the perimeter. These walls contained planned landscapes with gently curving roadways that invoked the country, peaceful lakes, and carefully planted trees, shrubs, and flowering plants (Baxter 2013). These spaces were designed for active visitation, and there were rules of etiquette for cemetery visiting that allowed people to experience death and mourning while also having a sense of control over death in a time of widespread and rapid cultural change.

One of the major components of this control was the ability to purchase and design family plots within the cemetery. Where one was to be buried, who one's eternal neighbors were to be, and how one's family monument would look were all a part of the carefully orchestrated design of cemeteries. Bohan (1988) argued that this aspect of cemeteries was integral to reinforcing the family as a central organizing principle of American society at a time when social and economic changes were straining traditional American family life. The rural garden cemetery became a place where families would all return home to be together. Elaborate rituals of grief and mourning along with regular visitation were ways of reinforcing the bonds of family for the living.

The commemoration of children in these spaces was often elaborate, and even the humblest of markers erected for children represented an investment in family members and family continuity (figure 5.3). Rural garden cemeteries were one part of what is known as the "beautification of death" movement that was popular in the mid-to-late nineteenth century. This movement included the preservation and decoration of corpses to prolong their lifelike appearance during periods of extended mourning (figure 5.2), the performance of detailed rituals of bereavement and commemoration, and the elaboration of cemetery monuments that denied death euphemistically using terms of sleep and rest (Baxter 2013; figure

Figure 5.3. A particularly elaborate child's headstone from Oak Woods Cemetery in Chicago, dated September 1882 and carved by M & M Peasley. The five-year-old child commemorated by the stone, India Kephart, is depicted in a scallop shell symbolizing her Christian journey through life and her baptism in the church. She is in a position of slumber with a pillow and blanket, as sleep was an integral part of the "beautification" movement that denied death in favor of euphemisms about sleep and rest. She is holding a doll which, in the hands of a child, was a symbol of home and family. Photo by author.

5.3). Being well versed in cemetery visitation etiquette included knowing the complex symbolic system used to convey particular ideas about death, mortality, the afterlife, and grief chosen by the family for one of its members.

Because children were already defined as culturally innocent and pure and in a state that kept them closer to heaven (chapter 2), their role in this symbolic and social system of grief was quite significant. Scholars have argued that the loss of a child afforded particular opportunities for the embellishment of sentiment while denying death and emphasizing the grief of the family. Consolation literature, epitaphs, and mortuary symbolism often prioritized a family's grief for the loss of a child over the concern for that child's departed soul (Smith 1987: 93; Snyder 1992). While very wealthy families could erect elaborate monuments for a particular

Figure 5.4. A small marble pillow reading "Our Darling Walter" from Oak Woods Cemetery in Chicago. This type of commemoration with words of possession and endearment is often interpreted as representing parental attachment, despite the limited text and simple design. The pillow signifies the child at sleep or at rest. Photo by the author.

child (figure 5.3) other families used limited words to convey possession, endearment, and sorrow (figure 5.4). The simple act of referring to a child as "our baby" or "my darling" expressed, in very few words, the place of a child within a family as well as the grieving family's sense of loss (Baxter 2013; Rainville 1999). Similarly, the use of nicknames or pet names in epitaphs alongside given names was an efficient way to convey intimacy and the loss of a particular person.

If children died after the male head of household, their individual graves often matched the chosen style for family members within the family plot. These uniform grave markers, or markers with only a slight variation for adults and children (figure 5.1), symbolically illustrated the continuity of family over time as well as asserting the influence of the family patriarch, sometimes over many generations. A sociological study of American cemeteries by P. J. Frenza (1989) interpreted this phenomenon as the establishment of dynastic family legacies in the cemetery. An individual, generally the male head of household, used their wealth and influence to select the plot location, size, and grave style for their family, and that influence could extend to subsequent generations, thereby conveying a message of the strength of an ideal American family in life and in triumph over death. The prominent inclusion of children was an essential part of projecting the importance of all family members, even if their time on earth with their family had been quite short.

There have been two recent studies specifically of children in America's rural garden cemeteries. Each is comparative but on different scales. The first of these studies was conducted by Jane Baxter (2013, 2015c) who compared the memorial markers for children dating from 1859 to 1906 in two of Chicago's earliest rural garden cemeteries: Oak Woods and Rosehill. These two cemeteries were located to the south and northwest of the city, respectively, and are approximately 20 miles apart from one another. The second study by Eileen Murphy and colleagues (Murphy et al. 2015) compared children's graves dated from 1832 to 1871 in St. Patrick's Catholic Cemetery in Lowell, Massachusetts, to those in Friar's Bush Cemetery in Belfast, County Antrim, Ireland.

These studies identified two significant commonalities among nineteenth-century children's graves in America. First, while it has long been known that lambs were used as symbolic representations of childhood innocence and purity in American cemeteries (McKillop 1995; Rainville 1999; Smith 1987; Snyder 1992), these studies found it to be the only symbol reserved exclusively for children, and a symbol particularly preferred in America (figure 5.5). Second is that unique graves exclusively for children are found predominantly in the earliest years of a cemetery's operation: the 1830s and 1840s in Lowell, and the 1870s in Chicago. These early years when communities were just being established would have been a period when a child's death would likely have occurred before either parent and before the establishment of a family plot. Once family plots or family stones were established, unique graves for individual children become far less common. These studies of children reported results that underscore the symbolic importance of their place in the American family.

The Chicago cemetery research was designed to look at how childhood intersected with other aspects of individual identity, and to explore variation in mortuary practices among geographically distinct communities in the city. The project sought to examine children's headstones through a more complex set of variables than just a symbolic analysis of art and epitaph, to reconcile choices of individual families and broader societal

Figure 5.5. A lamb resting on top of a child's headstone. This particular style and design can be found at rural garden cemeteries across the United States and was reserved exclusively for children, most often those buried alone before a family plot was established. This photo is from Rose Hill Cemetery in Chicago. Photo by the author.

attitudes about children. A total of 238 children's graves was recorded in Oak Woods Cemetery and 192 at Rosehill. Many more graves likely belonging to children were identified but were not included in the study as they were illegible due to significant erosion and weathering. When the number of headstones found in the cemeteries was compared to vital records for the period, it became abundantly clear that simply having a grave marker for an individual child was a relatively rare and exceptional expenditure on the part of families in the city (Baxter 2015c: 11).

Children's headstones were among the smallest found in each cemetery, but they were no smaller than those used for most individual adult interments. Small headstone size was not used to differentiate between child and adult, but rather was an indicator that the stone commemorated a single person rather than multiple members of a family. Graves in each cemetery showed a chronological change from white limestone to gray granite over the course of the study period. The symbolic value of white to reinforce children's innocence and purity may have been made a secondary concern when it became clear that the raw material was not durable against the effects of weather and industrial air pollution (Baxter 2015c). Even within a single city, regional differences were noted. In Rosehill Cemetery, children were much more likely to receive a unique, figural burial marker, while in Oak Woods the majority of graves used a more standard headstone design and formulaic epitaph structure. This more formulaic grave marker was preferred over several decades at Oak Woods, while styles at Rosehill underwent rapid shifts throughout the study period, generally from more elaborate memorials to much more simple commemorations.

Nearly every child was named (98 percent) on their headstone, and epitaphs distinguished between babies/infants and children, suggesting that this was a meaningful cultural distinction, although they did not result in different commemorative practices unless the child was older. Children over the age of ten were a very small proportion of the burial population, but their graves were among the most elaborate in the cemetery for single individuals. Graves were uniquely styled (figure 5.3), combining an array of symbolic imagery and epitaphs to convey a great loss, such as "Oh, what hopes lie buried here." Matthews has argued (2010) that the death of a child in the age of capitalism was not only emotional, but also understood as a loss in the investment of family resources through the prioritization of infant and child care, the deferment of other expenditures to care for a child, and the cost of investing in a child as a family's future. Other common features on children's graves were the presence of nicknames or terms of endearment, terms of possession, and the position of the child (daughter/son) in relationship to the parents. While there were few features distinguishing children's graves from adult graves, with the exception of the exclusive use of the lamb, the predominant emphasis on these graves was to name the child as an individual and to label them as being a part of the family fold.

The Lowell Cemetery project was designed specifically to look at an immigrant Irish Catholic population. This study found that 23 percent of headstones were for children, while 24 percent listed adults and children on the same stone. While there were lambs for many children, most children's graves shared imagery with those of adults, particularly the Latin cross, the willow tree, and the shamrock—symbols that conveyed Catholic identity and Irish ethnicity. Many of the Lowell graves also listed the place of the interred individual's birth, particularly if it was not in the United States but rather somewhere in Ireland.

When compared to the Friar's Bush Cemetery in Belfast there were some notable differences in children's headstones. In St. Patrick's Cemetery, 99 percent of the children's epitaphs named the child buried, compared to only 79 percent in Friar's Bush. The age of an individual at death and epitaphs that conveyed the sentiment that a child died "young" or "early in life" were found on 81 percent of the graves in Saint Patrick's, which was double the percentage of graves containing such features in Friar's Bush. The researchers concluded that the commemoration of an individual child, the details of their life and death, and a statement that they were taken "too soon" were all essential in the immigrant Irish community in Lowell. In Belfast, it was more important to convey that a child was a part of a family, and the personal details of their lives were far less important. They argued that this divergence in burial practices reflected the particular concerns of an immigrant population, where each new child symbolically and practically represented a new start for a family in a new place. Where family continuity was longstanding, children were an important part of a family legacy, but not their survival into the future.

Death as Part of Children's Lives

Children's understandings of their own mortality and the expectations for social performances surrounding grief and mourning were certainly different in earlier eras of American history. The death of siblings, friends, and neighbors of similar ages would not have been an uncommon experience in the life of a child, and funerals for family and community members would have been regular parts of a child's social world. While much of the archaeological evidence for rituals of grief and bereavement and choices in public and private commemoration reflect adult sentiment, it's important to be mindful that children also experienced these rituals and certainly their own emotions when a member of their family or community died. Witnessing the death of age-mates with regularity would have undoubtedly created an understanding that death was a possibility in their own life at any time if illness or injury struck. In the later nineteenth and early twentieth century, there were several ways that children were connected to death through material culture and social practice that are largely absent from contemporary childhood experience.

Certain forms of doll play centered around sickness and death, and were common practices encouraged by magazine articles, children's stories, and toys designed specifically for such play (Carter 2002; Hall 1897). Children could read fictional tales about the ailments, treatments, and cures of sick dolls that paralleled stories of fictional children in other literary genres. Games played with "sick dolls" involved cultivating particular skills associated with care and nurturance considered inherent in women and mothers, and also familiarizing young girls with home-based medical care, which was a growing industry fueled by new medicines and medical devices available on the mass market. When such cures failed, sick dolls died, and a wide variety of funeral play was common.

Some dolls were temporarily buried in a dresser drawer or other hidden space, only to be later resurrected in another incarnation. Other dolls were buried in the ground, and toy coffins were available on the market, although not required for such play. Some girls even had doll cemeteries where friends and siblings were encouraged to inter their deceased dolls alongside those of the cemetery proprietor (Hall 1897). With doll replacement parts widely available and archaeological evidence for intentionally destroyed dolls receiving no ritual burial or memorial (e.g., Wilkie 2000) this type of funeral play was not necessarily tied to dolls actually becoming broken or unusable due to breakage or wear. Being able to bury an intact or easily reparable doll undoubtedly made certain types of funeral play a privilege reserved for children of wealthier families, but these were also likely the same families who could afford burials and memorials for the actual children who died in the household.

Funeral play was designed to cultivate an understanding of and appreciation for rituals of grief and burial that children experienced as an integral part of their lives. Much as home medical care was the purview of the mother, women also were the keepers of mourning rituals and much of this death play was imitative of adult behavior (Carter 2002: 37–41). Play scenarios involving sick and dead dolls were well documented in period sources as being controversial (e.g., Hall 1897). Some adults felt that funeral play particularly was gruesome, morbid, and inappropriate for children. Others approved of the creation of such play scenarios for children so they could better understand funerary ritual and the process of grief and

Figure 5.6. Promotional still from the 1944 film *Meet Me in St. Louis* by Metro-Goldwyn-Mayer. In this scene, where the two sisters lash out in grief over having to leave their home, they discuss the importance of taking *all* the dolls to St. Louis—an act which required disinterring the dolls in the doll cemetery they had made in the yard. Wikimedia.

Figure 5.7. "The William Channing Memorial in Mt. Auburn Cemetery." A mid-nineteenth-century engraving showing family visitation to Mt. Auburn Cemetery, Cambridge, Massachusetts. This image shows an adult taking children to visit the graves in Mt. Auburn and instructing them on some aspect of the commemoration. The disproportionately large crawling child is the focal character of the scene. Wikimedia.

mourning both in public and in private (Carter 2002: 40). This type of play also clearly lingered in American memory, as it was featured in the 1944 film *Meet Me in St. Louis*, which was set in 1903 (figure 5.6). When Esther (Judy Garland) sings the famous "Have Yourself a Merry Little Christmas" to soothe her youngest sister Tootie about the family's impending move from their beloved home, their conversation is one where the young sister expresses concern that she will have to exhume her dead baby dolls so that they can be taken along with the living dolls to St. Louis.

The American rural garden cemetery also was a place for children in life as well as death, and the practice of visiting cemeteries with children was advocated for quite strongly by leading thinkers of the day. For example, Lydia Child in her popular 1831 book, *The Mother's Book,* advised that children should be taken to cemeteries for regular visits to walk in the beautiful surroundings and learn important moral and historical lessons from the monuments and memorials. On their visits, nineteenth-century children would have seen a large number of monuments erected for other children as well as adults and families.

Figure 5.8. Marbles excavated at the Haymarket Martyrs' Memorial, Forest Home Cemetery, Forest Park, Illinois. Photo courtesy of Rebecca Graff.

In the famous etching of William Channing's memorial at Mount Auburn Cemetery in Cambridge, Massachusetts (circa 1844), the dominant figure in the image is a disproportionately large child apparently crawling willfully toward the gates of the carefully landscaped memorial (figure 5.7). A second, older child is being instructed and directed by an adult to approach the memorial and perhaps leave an offering in the form of a plant frond. The adult figure has one hand outstretched toward the memorial as if teaching and explaining, and the other gently guiding the child forward, encouraging interaction.

Recent excavations at Forest Home Cemetery in Forest Park, Illinois, provided evidence for children's visitation to the famous Haymarket Martyrs Memorial (Graff, Scarlett, and Baxter 2016). The memorial is still an important place of visitation for anarchists, labor activists, and others who sympathize with the popular labor movements of the late nineteenth and early twentieth century. It is a very potent site of American labor history.

Excavations at the memorial were sponsored by the Illinois Labor History Society and were designed to search for and potentially exhume a time capsule reportedly buried at the site in 1892, the year before the monument was erected to commemorate the martyrs, and five years after their execution. While the time capsule was not located despite GPR survey and excavation at the site, artifacts relating to the practice of cemetery visitation were recovered from around the monument. Among the fragments of nineteenth-century dishware and other personal items were two marbles, a clay marble and an "aggie" (figure 5.8). These artifacts suggest that children as well as adults came to pay tribute to the martyrs in the months and years after their interment at the cemetery, and spent time at the site engaged in leisure and recreation while doing so. Such artifacts are also a potent reminder that the labor struggles of the nineteenth century were not just about men and women working, but the families they were working to support. Children were not only part of working-class communities taking part in collective action (chapter 3) but were socialized by their families into the labor movement through visitation and commemoration of labor leaders lost as part of the movement.

Some Thoughts

Long before the archaeology of childhood became a field of study in its own right (chapter 1), children were often included in archaeological studies of mortuary populations. The presence or absence of enriched children's grave assemblages was considered the primary way to distinguish whether a prehistoric society assigned rank and status on the basis of achievement or inheritance, and children were viewed as significant indicators of environmental and economic stress in a population as revealed through their health and nutrition (Baxter 2013). On the one hand, these studies were often problematic because they applied Western assumptions about a biologically universal childhood uncritically onto the past. This approach missed the cultural nuances of how human life cycles are interpreted in various ways and become uniquely meaningful in different societies. Simultaneously, however, these studies acknowledged the importance of children in human social groups and saw them as a special (if not marginal) subset of any human community. Now, some 25 years after the archaeology of childhood began as a field of study, there are myriad sources illustrating the importance of studying children through the mortuary record as well as the diversity of what one can learn through such study (Baxter 2008; Mays et al. 2017).

Mortuary studies of children in the American past have combined a rich documentary record with either skeletal or material analysis to illuminate the lives and deaths of children in particular communities, but there are not enough such studies to provide us with broad comparative overviews of children across the country or over the course of its history. What these studies do offer are glimpses into the diverse ways that communities chose to commemorate their children. Rituals have a performative and public element that can offer insights into how children were idealized as individuals and as members of a community. These rituals can often illustrate the symbolic value of children within families and communities as they coped with a death that was outside the natural order. These idealizations of children and the rituals around burial are often deeply informed by shared senses of worldview, eschatology, and cultural heritage.

Particular to this sample of available studies is the way they simultaneously show the equality and disparities of life in America's past. On the one hand, it is clear that infant and child mortality spared no population in America's history. Native Americans, African Americans, poor and working-class whites, and upper- and middle-class families all had to cope with a staggering rate of loss of the youngest members of their family and community. In Graceland Cemetery in Chicago, it is potent to go to the family plot of the great commercial mercantile baron Marshall Fields, and see the row of headstones simply marked "baby" for each of his children lost in infancy. All the wealth in the world could not offer a different fate for his children. Certainly, while some populations had higher rates of infant and child mortality than others, the frequent loss of children and infants was a great equalizer among otherwise disparate populations in the nation.

On the other hand, there are few sources of evidence that can more vividly highlight the diversity of childhood experiences in America than the study of children's bodies and the commemoration of children. Contemporary bioarchaeology emphasizes understanding aspects of children's lived experiences, rather than being preoccupied with concerns about their deaths. The extreme muscle development and skeletal trauma due to labor revealed on the skeletons of very young enslaved children, or the vitamin deficiencies that plagued children living in a radical activist Christian community, remind us how children were never innocent or separated from the realities of the adult world—they were very much a part of those experiences, which were often unfair, strenuous, and in these cases fatal. While all children who died young had unfortunate experiences of illness, accidents, or nutrition, the disparities in resources, the implications of cultural practices, and the divisions that shaped American society emerge in the diversity of lifestyles evidenced in these remains.

The burial practices in these studies also show a care and concern on the part of the living community for these deceased children. A simple shroud pinned around the body of a six-year-old child at the African Burial Ground, or the construction of an elaborate monument in a local cemetery, are both gestures of care for an individual. This care may have reflected a profound sense of loss and bereavement for who a child was in life, but also may have represented ongoing concerns for what awaited them in the hereafter. While burial rituals can tell us much about the culturally prescribed ways to demonstrate bereavement, it is unlikely that we can know of the actual sentiments of those carrying out such rituals. In private, the children found in the privy at Five Points may have been grieved and missed much more than the child with the most elaborate of graves in a rural garden cemetery. Children's bodies and lives were integral parts of public and private discourse, only some of which is revealed through their treatment in death.

~ 6 ~

The Archaeology and Material Culture of Contemporary Childhood

Contemporary childhood is of considerable social and material importance in most families, communities, and America as a whole. Concerns about how children are raised, how they are being provided for by families and institutions, and their physical, social, emotional, and material well-being are all topics of media scrutiny, political debate, and interpersonal conversation. A casual walk through nearly any community provides encounters with schools, day care facilities, playgrounds, parks, sports fields, and organizations that cater to children (Kamp 2015). Signage warning of children's presence, and admonishing passersby of certain laws and regulations to protect children, are posted in public view. All types of stores, including the corner convenience mart, chain grocery and drug stores, and specialty shops sell toys, accessories, and clothing for children. Collectively, it is easily seen that American adults spend a great deal of time, money, and energy on children. Simultaneously, children are more autonomous than they ever have been in history. They have their own spaces in the home, their own media, their own institutions, and their own purchasing power as independent consumers (Mintz 2004). These dynamics are all at work not only in how children are perceived, but how relationships to children and to childhood are created using material culture.

All scholarship on childhood in the past is situated in the present, infused with present-day ideas and information, and reflective of the concerns and interests of the contemporary world. Archaeologists studying childhood have long called for a critical, disciplinary self-examination of how and why childhood has been a neglected, marginalized, and overlooked topic of study, and have correlated the relegation of childhood to the unknowable or uninteresting with contemporary Western ideas about childhood (Baxter 2005; Lillehammer 1989; Sofaer 2000; chapter 1). It is also easy to argue that emergent interdisciplinary interests on childhood in the past stem largely from the contemporary popular discourse, media attention, and expenditure of capital on children that permeates twenty-first-century life (Baxter et al. 2017). Devoting a chapter to contemporary childhoods is more than an exercise in scholarly self-reflection, however, and given the structure of the book it is also not a culmination of a causal narrative of "how we got here," like many of the historical works used in this study (e.g., Chudacoff 2007; Fass 2016; Mintz 2004).

While these may be inevitable byproducts of such a chapter, the real reason for its inclusion is to bring the burgeoning field of contemporary archaeology into the fold (Graves-Brown et al. 2013) and a small sampling of the extensive work on recent childhoods conducted by historians of material culture. Contemporary archaeology offers a vehicle not only to examine current attitudes toward childhood, but also to look at the material, spatial, and social consequences of such attitudes using data from the present day or the very recent past. Scholarship from explicitly archaeological perspectives is buttressed by several excellent studies by historians looking at dynamics of social space and material culture in contemporary America. An important element of this literature is the dematerializing of children's worlds into the digital domain, where activities and relationships traditionally carried out in the material world are now being conducted online and in purely digital spaces.

The contemporary discourse surrounding childhood in America is a very complicated one that requires a bit of unpacking (chapters 1 and 2). Traditional values of American child-rearing emphasize making children independent of their parents by giving them the tools to do so (Fass 2016). The nature of these tools and the timing of their implementation are often critiqued from multiple angles in popular discourse, particularly if we acknowledge that childhood is a relational category and often understood in terms of exclusion (Buckingham 2000: 74). Policing the boundaries of childhood and adulthood is an essential part of how these values are exercised. When should independence be obtained? In which spheres? In what increments? What differentiates such conversations about childhood today, according to Fass (2016), is a shift in rhetoric from concern to crisis. There is a lack of optimism and hope in such rhetoric, with the invocation of a perception that the boundaries of childhood are shifting in irrevocably inappropriate ways.

On the one hand, there is a sense that contemporary childhood is hurried. Children are exposed too early to deleterious influences, such as sex and violence, which should remain in the domain of adults. There is a fear of premature adulthood among young people and a pervasive notion that childhood as an age of innocence is being altogether lost. Media is often the named culprit in concerns about exposure to adult themes, anxieties, and vices. Media strips away the appropriate pacing of child development, leads to a breakdown of family and adult authority, and relatively empowers children through peer cultures that have looser standards about sex and violence than previous generations (Buckingham 2000). Simultaneously, there is a rhetoric that childhood and adolescence are becoming increasingly prolonged in American culture. "Helicopter parents" help college students pick their classes. The Affordable Care Act allowed "children" as old as 26 to remain on their parents' health insurance. If childhood as a period of innocence is being eroded by the media and peer interactions, it is also being unreasonably extended as a period of dependence by institutional and familial structures. If one is to believe all the hype, Americans today are creating overly dependent children and ineffective adults.

Many of these laments about children are comparative, harkening back to the American postwar era of the mid-twentieth century as an idyllic time of childhood characterized by harmonious nuclear families living in suburban homes situated in safe, clean neighborhoods and swept up in the delights of new technologies and consumer products (figure 2.9). This ideal is far from reality, as nearly one-third of America's children grew up at or near the poverty line during this time, and systematic social divides of class and race insured unequal access to this vision of American idyll (Mintz 2004). These divisions, exclusions, and differences in opportunity and prosperity created tensions around the country and in local communities.

What did occur during this period was a surge in birthrates because so many Americans postponed "starting families" due to the Great Depression and the Second World War. Popular discourse engrained ideas like families "starting" only once children were born. Children gave couples and family meaning, and childless couples were pitied and often felt ashamed. The famous "baby boom" accelerated many trends in twentieth-century childhood and adolescence already in place (chapter 2), spawned a whole new economy around children and childhood, and helped delineate the suburbs as a family place. This is also the period when most children stopped contributing to family economies and simply became a source of adult spending, changing the dynamics and priorities of household budgets (Fass 2016). This postwar period set the stage for many of the more recent developments in how childhood and adolescence are constructed in American culture beyond acting as a nostalgic foil for today's "impoverished," "lost," and "diminished" childhood.

The Cult of the Child and Consumer Culture

Anthropologist Daniel Miller, in his work *A Theory of Shopping* (1998: 123–5), argued that children, particularly infants, have replaced fathers as the central devotional subjects of families. Where families once functioned as a patriarchy and orbited around the needs, wants, and priorities of the male head of household (figure 2.9), the material, emotional, and social needs of infants and children have become the driving organizational force of modern families (May 2013; Miller 1998). While these authors are focused primarily on British families and children, there are clear parallels for understanding American childhood, as similar cultural movements are occurring in both places.

The changing status of children in the family from devotees of fathers to devotional subjects themselves is connected to several trends in twenty-first-century family life (Buckingham 2000: 63). Decreasing family size has continued in the twenty-first century, meaning that parents can focus their attention and energies on fewer children, and individual children have more opportunities for direct parental engagement than at any time in American history. Despite this opportunity for attention, increasing divorce rates and the frequent need for both parents to be in the workforce have divided parental considerations between work, home, and their own needs for recreation and self-care. Contemporary parents don't like to be uncomfortable or inconvenienced in their parental roles, and parenting is a balancing act as a result (Fass 2016). The shrinking of families also means children have fewer siblings for peer socialization, play, and recreational partnering, and there are no longer child care options within the family. Children spend more time alone, and in the absence of parental attention and siblings to play with are engaged with technology and social media as caretakers and companions. These dynamics have amplified the influence of peer socialization, empowering child- and adolescent-generated culture as significant influences that extend beyond children and adolescents themselves (Cross 2004). It has also heightened popular concerns about media influence in the lives of American children.

The primacy of such external influences in children's lives has served to increase parental guilt around not spending time with children (Chudacoff 2007: 163; Cross 1997). Parents have sought to assuage their guilt by relying on structured activities that they can schedule. Scheduling children's activities makes them feel involved in their children's lives, but their own engagement is limited to spectating, which is a time that can be used for other tasks as well. Parents also use material culture to ease their guilt of being away from their children, and ironically as a means to entertain children in ways that don't require their own time and energy. Children get an abundance of things from their parents but not necessarily their time (Chudacoff 2007, Cross 1997).

This influx of material culture into the lives of children, and into families in the service, care, and entertainment of children has been the source of considerable scholarship. Supporting Daniel Miller's (1998) assertion that children have become the devotional subject of families are data for how households prioritize the perceived needs of children in their spending. In America in 2004, mass marketers spent 15 billion dollars on advertising consumer goods to children, tweens, and teens. Children and adolescents spend approximately 100 billion dollars each year in the consumer marketplace independent of adults. This purchasing is funded through their own earnings, cash gifts and gift cards, and allowances received from parents. Children and adolescents further influence an estimated 300 billion dollars in annual spending by their families (Jacobson 2008b). Children are no longer a marginal or growing force in the consumer marketplace, but are instead arguably one of the most significant consumer forces in contemporary America.

Contemporary archaeologists Victor Buchli and Gavin Lucas (2000) investigated abandoned council flats in England and closely examined evidence for how modern families prioritize children and their perceived wants and needs in household spending. Their study focused on a home that was previously occupied by a 25-year-old mother and her two children, a four-year-old boy and a six-year-old girl. The home had been abandoned for reasons unknown to the authorities, but what remained was a snapshot of a contemporary household left without disturbance since the tenants' departure.

The evaluation of the household assemblage indicated that the amount of goods that could be identified as being exclusively for adults or for children was similar (22.8 percent for children and 21.2 percent for adults), but the quality of those goods was much lower in the adult assemblage than in the children's, ostensibly to allow for higher-quality items to be purchased for the children. This parental sacrifice in financial and material terms is a central part of children's roles as the devotional subjects of households and is one that has clear material implications. The children's clothing, for example, was of much higher quality and relative cost than that of the mother's, despite the fact that the children would rapidly outgrow their clothing and the mother could invest in a stable size.

The distribution of objects in the home also showed that the dominant emphasis was on the children in household organization and activity. The children had their own room with highly specific furnishings and décor, and a significant amount of their material goods were found there. Other rooms were more spartanly and generically furnished, but children's artifacts were found in every single room of the house. While children had an exclusive domain within the home that was embellished and personalized, there was no parallel space for the adult in the household. Parental sacrifice, relatively significant expenditure on ultimately disposable children's items, and a prioritization of space for children's amusement and happiness were all archaeological signatures of contemporary childhood in this particular household (Buchli and Lucas 2000). Brands, specific media characters, and other connections to advertising and popular culture also were indicative of children's direct and indirect connections to consumer culture at a very young age.

The complete immersion of children and adolescents into consumer culture is a particular tension in the devotional status of children in contemporary homes, and a major area of concern for adults worried about managing the boundaries of where childhood ends and where adulthood begins. Historian of children's material culture Gary Cross (2004) has examined these contemporary boundaries and parsed out some of the complexities that exist in this categorical borderland. He argued that contemporary American adults prize and delight in children's sense of innocence and wonder at the world around them. Unlike adults, children are not jaded, cynical, or apathetic, but neither are they obsessed with the material things and real-world problems that consume adult lives. Children and the objects that surround them are considered, "cute," a term which can be used to describe something's sweet and charming nature, but also to simultaneously diminish its importance. This characterization by adults allows them to feel superior to children through an enhanced sense of knowing what the world is "really about," to act as a protector of children as they approach boundaries with adulthood for which they are not prepared, and to experience a sense of discomfort and fear of children who do not fit idealized images of innocence (figure 6.1). This characterization, Cross argues, puts adults in a particular bind around objects and experiences. Adults cannot experience a child's wonder and delight without providing new and fresh stimuli. Providing a child with a new toy or a novel experience elicits the desired response, but also is another step in breaking down that child's innocence by exposing them to an overcommercialized and materialistic society that cultivates longing for what is new and next.

Once children cross that threshold, their material culture is no longer cute but instead becomes "cool" (Cross 2004). The cute objects adults used to demarcate childhood are replaced by a desire for things that are cool as defined by peers. When a child begins to reject the offerings of adults and instead desires things that are cool, it's a sign that adults have lost or are losing control. Material trends and trends in popular culture rarely originate with adults, and instead adults are in a position where they need to "keep up" with the newest, latest, and coolest trends in the worlds of children and teens. Advertisers are aware of this dynamic and employ strategies to target the "key boy or girl" who can become a trendsetter in a peer-dominated youth culture (Jacobson 2008a). In the world of contemporary America, young people hold the power to determine "coolness," not adults.

The power young people wield in contemporary consumerism and the concomitant sense that adults are not in control of how and where their money is spent are intertwined with concerns about media, social media, and advertising having disproportionate power in the lives of young people, imparting messages that carry more weight and sway than those coming from parents. Popular discourse suggests that advertising and media influence children particularly because they have yet to develop

Figure 6.1. The iconic character of Veruca Salt with her signature line, "I want it now," from the 1971 film *Willy Wonka and the Chocolate Factory*, serves as an enduring cautionary tale against children who are spoiled and indulged with an excess of material things. The Oompa Loompa song calls out such children for being brats, but also the parents for not managing their children's engagement with and desires for material things. Her covetous and demanding nature is not only that of a spoiled child, but also decidedly unchildlike.

the necessary skills to think critically about media messages. However, David Buckingham's work on advertising with children aged 8–12 years old suggests that they are already very savvy consumers at the age when their agency and power in the marketplace is only just beginning (2008b: 153). The children in his study mock advertising, actively question choices made by advertisers, and can spot advertisers' manipulation of identity and culture. In short, they "get" what ads are trying to do. Buckingham minimizes the overarching concern of whether or not children can resist advertising as an indicator of their vulnerability—after all, adults cannot resist advertising either.

Contemporary archaeologist Sarah May (2013) also has explored the dynamics of childhood consumerism by looking at how children are characterized by their "divinity" within the family, and how they are considered to be "desiring subjects" whose inherent material needs and wants should be prioritized and uniquely indulged by families. Children are not born into the world inherently wanting any material object in particular. Their relationships to objects are in large part determined by the social reactions they get from adults and peers when they engage with them.

Children often do not desire trendy goods inspired by movies and television until they go to school and encounter a peer culture that values and prizes those objects over all others. As trends change, so do the objects of desire. This idea of children desiring goods does not begin when they leave the home, however. Contemporary parents actively shape their children's relationships with the material world beginning in infancy, by characterizing them as desirous beings and imbuing their material culture with unique senses of meaning reflecting a child's special, "divine" status in the household (May 2013; Miller 1998). Objects in this way become an active part in how adults construct their sense of their children, and how children come to understand their own relationships to other people as well as the material world.

Sarah May conducted a project of autoarchaeology by observing the world through and with her own child (2013). She argues that young children in Britain have nothing to do with the production, exchange, disposal, and repair or maintenance of material culture, and she suggests that ideas of acquisition and consumption are often conflated. Her study resulted in four vignettes of children's material culture, which demonstrate their "divine" status within contemporary families, and particular relational constructs among children, adults, and material culture. I would argue these vignettes are relevant for understanding contemporary American childhood as well.

First, May looks at children's production of material culture, an area from which she argues they have been largely excluded in the contemporary world. In certain realms, such as children's play, production took the form of imagination that transformed ordinary objects, such as sticks, into meaningful, valuable objects that served as integral parts of peer interaction. While the sticks weren't modified in any physical way, imagining them into other objects that connected them to real interactions gave children the power of production in a culture that generally does not grant them such power. When children do produce things they are generally gifts for adults. These homespun objects do not meet otherwise established cultural criteria for functionality or aesthetic pleasure, but become elevated as prized possessions in the world of adults on whom the gifts are bestowed. Children's creations are displayed proudly in the home and workplace, and are given a distinct level of interest and delight by observers. Such objects, if made by adults, would be considered poorly rendered and discarded. Children's early production, then, occupies a special place of prominence in contemporary culture.

May also examines how objects are used by children in their own lives and worlds. First, she observes how objects allow children to function in a "transitional manner" connecting them to significant social relationships in a time of absence. Contemporary parenting involves periods of absence as children are at day care, school, or after-school activities while parents work outside the home. May recounted particular dialogues she had with her child about time spent at day care, which revealed how particular objects retained and transplanted meaning for children between the worlds of home and day care. These portable objects in the lives of children offered a way to maintain a symbolic tie to people during the course of the day, reminding them of care, comfort, and values as they confronted the world independently from their parents. This idea could easily be extended further into how gifts from distant, infrequently visiting family members are used to cultivate a sense of relationship between a child and those people who are not a part of their daily lives.

May also observed her child at play and detailed the disjoin between how adults contemplate material objects, and how they are perceived by children. Adults generally categorize objects as inanimate, and even in archaeological and material culture discussions of materiality, the agentive nature of objects is rarely perceived as imaginative or deliberately articulated by adult actors. May noted that children do not make such a distinction. Objects are genuinely animated for children, and there is no separation between the thing and the created personality, backstory, and narrative for that object. Objects are often referred to by children in the second person as a direct partner in action and interaction. In the world of children, objects are regularly imbued with liveliness, personality, and life. These roles of objects in the sphere of contemporary children demonstrate how material culture is deeply social, symbolic, and imaginative in the daily lives of children.

A final observation made by May relates to discard, specifically the preferential curation of children's material culture by adults over other types of things. She relates a story about finding singular pieces of children's footwear that had been lost presumably while children were out with their families. Other adults who encountered these lost items carefully placed them in highly visible positions so they could be recovered by the child or their parents. The idea that children's material culture deserved special care, held special meaning, and needed to have its potential recovery by the owner prioritized was revelatory about how adults perceive children's relationships to the material world. Children's items are special and require a different kind of care and oversight than the personal goods of adults.

These four vignettes (May 2013) and Cross's (2004) discussion of "cute and cool" are revealing about how adults in the contemporary world view children and their material culture. Characterizing children as "desiring," and exalting their innocence and wonder in part because of how they interact with the material world, leads to particular patterns of consumption, spending, engagement, and care around children and their personal objects. The emphasis on providing for children materially has an impact on the financial and material worlds of adults, and affects the ways adults interact not only with children themselves but with the objects they create, consume, and discard.

Nostalgia

Casting children as divine and devotional subjects in contemporary families speaks to the power they have in determining the choices adults make in terms of what to buy and how much to spend on their care and contentment. Adults obviously negotiate these decisions and also have a large amount of control over what is purchased, particularly for younger children who have yet to develop tastes and influences outside the family fold. Often, the choices adults make are related to a sense of nostalgia for their own childhoods. Phillippe Ariès (1962), in his seminal work on childhood, noted that historical fashion trends in children's clothing reflect an adult nostalgia for times past. Recent work by Jane Baxter (2016) used the concept of nostalgia in contemporary culture to explore alternative ways of thinking about children's material culture in the past, but also to illustrate how this dynamic relates to furnishing children with material things in twenty-first-century households.

The contemporary colloquial use of the term "nostalgia" is overly broad and inappropriately refers to any displaced sense of longing for the past. Nostalgia, in actuality, is not like other forms of temporal displacement where one believes a particular moment in the past was somehow ideal, but rather it is directly connected to past personal experience and individual memories, however distorted and inaccurate such recollections may be. This distinction is significant because the emotional effect of a personal memory is different than those evoked by a general sense that things were better in a time long ago. Nostalgia involves longing for a real or imagined past and evoking it in a way that affects an individual's sense of self in the present, particularly a present that is believed to be impoverished, problematic, or deficient in some way (Baxter 2016). Childhood is often a focus of adult nostalgia because it is a time in life that is finished and irretrievable and has a narrative from beginning to end. Not only does nostalgia for childhood offer individuals a sense of self-continuity at times of crisis and change, but it also serves to idealize memories of childhood in ways that feed into anxieties about social and economic changes in the present.

Nostalgia is also an integral part of how people experience the material world. Objects are often the focus of nostalgia or the trigger of a nostalgic episode. For adults, nostalgia-invoking objects serve as souvenirs for authentic experiences in the past that can no longer be directly possessed (Baxter 2016: 4). Perhaps unsurprisingly, in late capitalism marketers aggressively use nostalgia as an advertising technique, particularly for children's toys. Such advertising may emphasize physical aspects of objects considered lacking in contemporary toys, such as quality manufacture, the ability to stimulate imagination, and enhanced learning and developmental opportunities. Perhaps the most influential aspect of nostalgic advertising is the promise of meaningful bonding across generations through shared experiences facilitated by a particular object. Baxter's (2016) work focused on two objects available in the contemporary marketplace, the Fisher-Price Chatter Telephone and Mickey Mouse Ears (figure 2.12). The first is a functional object and the second is a symbol of belonging, and both illustrate how nostalgia results in a type of conservatism in the material culture available for children in the twenty-first-century marketplace.

The Chatter Telephone was introduced in 1961 by the Fisher-Price Company as the "Talk Back Phone" for children one to three years in age. The Chatter Telephone is a pull toy with moving eyes and it makes a ringing noise when the dial is manipulated. The toy was designed to be a learning tool, and it is still marketed as such. The young user of the toy can develop the manual dexterity needed to manipulate a rotary dial telephone, lift and appropriately hold the receiver, and pull the phone across the floor. The toy also introduces children to the numbers one through nine, and through imitation and instruction can be used as a tool to teach children proper telephone etiquette. This toy phone is also a powerful vehicle for adult nostalgia.

The Chatter Telephone was the top-selling product for Fisher-Price in the 1970s and continued interest in the product helped revive the company from near closure in the 1980s. In the early years of the twenty-first century, the company tried to update the phone by replacing the rotary dial with light-up push buttons more consistent with contemporary technology, but there was an incredible consumer backlash and the rotary dial was brought back. Annual sales of the Chatter Telephone are more than 250,000 units. What makes the continued popularity of this decades-old toy fascinating is that it has lost any meaningful connection to contemporary adult material culture. Less than half of American homes have landlines, and estimates suggest that only about 10 percent of those phones are still rotary dial. These phones are owned by elderly people living in rural areas. There are YouTube videos designed as entertainment targeting young people that demonstrate how to use rotary dial phones as a rare and outdated form of technology. While the Chatter Telephone offers developmental opportunities for young children, it has no direct purpose as a learning tool in the twenty-first century. It is incredibly unlikely that a child today will ever use or observe a working rotary dial phone. Most children will learn to make calls on tablets or smartphones, or on touch keypads, and there are toy versions of all these objects in the marketplace as well. Yet the Fisher-Price rotary phone persists unchanged due to consumer demand and sells at an extraordinary rate. Fisher-Price actually has a host of nostalgic objects in their toy catalogue, including a camera with rotating flash cube, a TV that plays nursery rhymes using VHF and UHF knobs, and record players.

The second case Baxter (2016) used was Mickey Mouse Ears, which are a traditional symbol of belonging to a particular fan club, and now are a highly visible way to advertise one's recent visit to a Disney theme park. The Mickey Mouse Club began in the 1930s in live theaters in the United States, Canada, and eventually England, and children could join by responding to ads in the back of magazines. Their club membership included a mouse mask and a membership card that allowed the bearer to attend club meetings at a local theater where film reels of cartoons, news stories, and special features geared toward children and young teens were shown. The club migrated to television as a daily afternoon event, and had a famous run on the ABC network from 1955 to 1959. The Mickey Mouse Club was designed for children aged 3–14, but mimicked many of the variety shows that were common in the nascent world of adult television. The Mouseketeers and their adult cohosts all wore Mickey Mouse Ears and matching turtlenecks with their names emblazoned across their chests, giving their appearance the cohesion of a unified group but clearly labeling distinct television personas (figure 2.12). Fans of the club were encouraged to purchase their own mouse ears to demonstrate their club affiliation for all to see. The content of the show focused on themes of particular interest to its age demographic and created a national sense of what it meant to be a child on the brink of adolescence in modern America. Despite brief revivals of a Mickey Mouse Club show in 1977 and 1996, mouse ears have never been a part of any club uniform since the 1950s television run. Yet over 80 million pairs of official Mickey Mouse Ears have been sold at Disneyland since 1955, and over 500,000 pairs were sold in 2016 at all Disney Parks combined. There are over 75 Etsy shops selling off-brand versions of these ears as well.

Children watching the Disney television channel today can see a total of one hour and thirty-five minutes of Mickey Mouse programming per week. Mickey Mouse is not a dominant character associated with Disney in the twenty-first century, and the people who experienced Mickey Mouse Ears as being emblematic of a particular American childhood experience are the grandparents and great-grandparents of today's children. Clearly, the meaning of Mickey Mouse Ears has become lost to younger generations, but the powerful symbol of belonging that was cultivated in the mid-twentieth century persists even in the absence of the cultural contexts that once rendered it meaningful.

These two cases present different versions of how adult nostalgia creates a strain of conservatism in children's material culture. The first is a toy form of an obsolete technology and the second an outdated version of group membership, and both survive and in fact thrive in a marketplace filled with more current technologies and symbols of belonging. The persistence of these toys is not because of an innate childhood desire for them, but because adults are purchasing them to help create a concrete sense of their own past and also to assert control by shaping children's experiences through providing the object and influencing the narrative and context of play that accompanies it (Baxter 2016). The purchasing of nostalgic toys for children can also be seen as powerful acts of love (Baxter, forthcoming[b]). Sharing something remembered as pleasurable, or correcting an omission from one's childhood (the denial of a desired object) that was imagined would bring pleasure are in a sense controlling, but also are acts of love and care for a child's happiness and well-being.

The material effect of these processes is the lingering of objects in the toy marketplace long after they are necessary or relevant in contemporaneous or future contexts. Beyond understanding this dynamic of nostalgia and conservatism in children's material culture in the contemporary world, these insights are useful for archaeological studies of childhood and play in general. Most scholarship emphasizes the ways children's play prepares them for the roles they later will assume in their adult lives. This characterization of play draws parallels between the adaptive nature of play observed in young animals and the role of play in the physical and cognitive development of young children. The material culture of children's play is analyzed for parallels to objects known to be used by adults, and suggests that children's toys should emulate the latest technology found in the world of adults (Baxter 2005, 2008). Play in childhood is consistently believed to be somehow closely connected to later life (Pursell 2015), when in actuality some aspects of children's play may be a "second chance" at childhood for the adults around them.

Gender and Material Culture

The dominant discourse around play emphasizes its preparatory nature, and in contemporary America current rhetoric situates play and material culture as central to reinforcing appropriate sex-role behavior, making it a locus of stress in this cultural discourse (Chudacoff 2007: 203). Toys are often gendered and for a child to use the wrong toy is seen as subversive or aberrant, with traditional labels like "tomboy" and "sissy" persisting for children who show tendencies toward play cultures and toys designed for members of the opposite gender (Pursell 2015). Shopping has been made easier for parents and children by segregating toys into gender-specific aisles, floors, or shop areas, and toys and packages are color coded, with bright pink and purple packaging for girls and darker colors for boys. Baby toys are offered in clean white packaging, and educational toys shared by both genders are wrapped in primary colors (Kamp 2015; Pursell 2015).

Young children themselves are color coded in a society deeply concerned with gender and gender ambiguities, with little girls being clothed in pink and little boys in blue (Paoletti 2012). Jo Paoletti's research (2012) was an exploration of the contemporary fixation with pink and blue as a way of efficiently determining the gender of American children encountered in public places. She found that gendered clothing for children has operated historically in a cyclical pattern that can be understood as manifestation of Barthes' fashion system, where preferences for gender-neutral clothing or highly gendered clothing are juxtaposed as different signaling strategies over time. Children in the nineteenth century were presented in gender-neutral clothing to set them apart from adults and to deny their sexuality (chapter 2), but in the early twentieth century the cycle shifted to highly gendered clothing with different traits changing at different speeds. Paoletti (2012) argues that this early twentieth-century move toward gendered clothing was a response to growing independence in teen and youth cultures (chapter 2) and a greater public awareness about homosexuality in males particularly, making it essential to clearly define and delineate the feminine.

As the twentieth century progressed, science offered parents the ability to sex babies before birth and prepare for their arrival. This knowledge allowed essentialized language, views, and material culture of masculine or feminine to surround a child even before their birth and persist long after. This fixation with predetermination and preparation continues into the twenty-first century, although with the greater acceptance of transgendered and nonbinary categories of identity, clothing for children is beginning to include an increasing number of gender-neutral options.

Clothing and toys do not always cycle together in the demarcation of gender. Colonial children played with the same toys while wearing highly gendered clothing and children in the later nineteenth century were expected to wear the same outfits and play in completely different ways with gender-specific objects.

The highly gendered nature of toys in today's marketplace is a far greater concern to American parents than clothing if popular discourse is any indication, particularly because it is believed limiting toy and play options limits understandings of possibilities for future selves. Trying to break down the complexity of contemporary concerns over gender, toys, and play efficiently is not possible in any comprehensive manner at this

Figure 6.2. Barbie doll mother and child. Photo by Alexas Foros on Pixabay (CCBy).

scale. It is useful, however, to consider a particular enduring case of toys and gender socialization: the Barbie doll (figure 6.2). Dolls are a particularly potent lens for understanding the complexities around gender socialization and the material culture of children, as dolls are miniaturized versions of the human form and force users and scholars to address issues of gender, race, and class in an embodied manner rather than as an abstraction (Mumma and Baxter 2018). Barbie became a topic of scholarly and popular concern almost as soon as she emerged in the marketplace in 1959, and has been a popular topic in recent years in material culture studies and contemporary archaeology (Forman-Brunell 2009; Mergen 1992; Pearson and Mullins 1999; Phillips 2002; Rand 1995; Rogers 1999).

In her "Object Lesson" in the *Journal of the History of Childhood and Youth*, Miriam Forman-Brunell looked at Barbie on the occasion of her 50th birthday (2009) by looking back at a special spread of Barbie's historical wardrobe in *Life Magazine* in 1979 when Barbie turned twenty-one. Barbie is the bestselling doll in the history of America, and her entire life has been one embroiled in heated debates about her meanings. Is Barbie a healthful or harmful ideal for girls? Is she a symbol of American femininity, female liberation, or a plastic agent of female oppression? Miriam Forman-Brunell (2009) explored the multivocality of Barbie through the inherent tension embodied in a doll that simultaneously personifies changing feminine ideals while perpetuating traditional notions of gender. At times, Barbie is living an adventurous life and exploring a variety of careers, but she is just as often shackled in haute couture ensembles that restrict her movement and make her seem more of a spectator than a participant in her own adventures. Any gains Barbie makes as a symbol of empowerment are curtailed and balanced by her stated self-interests in modeling and shopping and acquiring a fantastic wardrobe for all of her adventures. There are clear parallels between Barbie as a creation and her creator Ruth Handler (Forman-Brunell 2009). Handler was an unconventional businesswoman, who hired staff to care for her home and children (named Barbara and Ken) so she could attain success in the business world. Yet she, like Barbie herself, maintained a highly feminized persona through fashion and decorum. Handler, in her day, displayed a greater array of gendered characteristics than the average American woman, and Barbie, as her creation, embodies similar traits and tensions.

This interpretation of Barbie echoes another study that focused on her wardrobe and accessories over time through the lens of company documents and statements about the product (Pearson and Mullins 1999). Rather than being a tabula rasa for young girls' imaginations, as the company suggested, the authors argue that Barbie consistently engaged dominant social currents throughout her history, but only offered select possibilities for imaginary play at any given historical moment. Barbie began as a career girl fashion model who wore a high-end, high-fashion wardrobe and vacationed at resorts and on cruises. Alternative careers that were offered to Barbie by her creators were female-gendered, and while options expanded considerably in the 1960s one of the dominant areas of expansion was new options for doing housework, as well as more creative career options including astronaut and ballerina, thus spanning the likely (housewife) and the highly unlikely (astronaut) for a young woman at the time. Contemporary Barbie's careers have shifted to include doctor, vet, and soldier, but the emphasis is always on fashion and nurturance. Explorer Barbie may be ready for adventure, but only adventures that can be reasonably accommodated in wedge-heeled shoes. The authors conclude that Barbie is not an ideal for aspiration as she imitates a constellation of feminine attributes that have never existed in the first place (Pearson and Mullins 1999: 258).

Other authors have embraced the advertised claim that Barbie is a neutral character who could be transformed into nearly anything through a young girl's imagination. These authors argue that Barbie can be endlessly refilled and readapted to whatever external contexts are created for her, and the ability to outfit her in a variety of ways leads to infinite possibilities to reconstruct her appearance and create scenarios for her life (Phillips 2002; Rand 1995). There is a kind of metaphor in her material composition in plastic (Lord 1994) and this plastic sense of creation and reinvention of her character. The design of plastic Barbie has been reinvented over her life to make her look more like a wholesome adolescent and less like a vampish adult, and she also literally became more mobile with the addition of moving joints (Forman-Brunell 2009). These studies emphasize the fluidity of a fixed plastic Barbie, endlessly adapting and improvising performances to fit external scenarios: a feature which some scholars have emphasized as one of the ways she became embattled and liberated as a kind of metaphor for female social performances (Rogers 1999). This kind of plasticity is only vaguely different from how women often see themselves in the contemporary world as being necessarily shaped by surgery, injections, exercise, body treatments, and makeup (Phillips 2002).

Barbie also has been analyzed in contrast to action figures for boys as a way of thinking about how ostensibly the same type of material culture, a doll, can have such different meanings when placed in gendered contexts. As historian Bernard Mergen quips,

> Tools that provide amusement, possessions that are prized, sticks that can be transformed by the imagination all enter into a child's definition of toys and playthings. As with all words (and objects) the meaning changes according to context. When is GI Joe an "action figure"? When is he a toy soldier? When is it a doll? Why is Barbie a doll and not an action figure when she is so clearly looking for action? (1992: 88)

Kendall Phillips (2002) juxtaposed Barbie as a doll with Batman as an action figure, as enduring symbols of American feminine and masculine ideas. He argued that Barbie is plastic and is read as such, while Batman is textual.

Barbie's plastic quality comes from her being untethered to any sophisticated, preexisting narrative that allows users to engage her with the possibility of creating imaginative scenarios for her life. In contrast, Batman—and, one could argue, other male action figures—exists primarily in textual form as a character in comic books and television shows, which became merchandized and spun into plastic products for interactive play later in the character's history. Action figures like Batman have backstories, developed characters, established networks of friends and foes, and known adventures that can be replicated in play or used as baselines from which children can extrapolate new imaginative scenarios. Masculine role models embodied in action figures are established icons of cultural dominance both in terms of physical prowess and cunning, and their place in the social order is fixed by narrative and far less malleable. Barbie does not have her own narrative, and she is unfixed from explicit agency or subjectivity. As a result, such categories can be filled by the person playing with Barbie.

These multiple interpretations of Barbie express an incredible interest and concern in how gendered toys relate to the worlds of children. No one reading of Barbie is necessarily correct, but the abundance of scholarship and concern for the implications of a popular doll that embodies many contradictory messages about femininity and gendered possibility are indicative of much wider arenas of discourse. How children are codified through clothing, and the way that objects are selected and introduced to them for play, bring material culture into much broader conversation about how children are identified and identify themselves in contemporary America.

Changes in Children's Spaces

Archaeological research is not confined to concerns of material culture, but extends to the use of space, and several scholars have considered how contemporary American culture contains and confines children within culturally prescribed spaces to a greater extent than any previous period in American history. In earlier eras, many childhoods were characterized by a relatively free exploration of space, but this period of a "free-range" childhood was actually quite short-lived (chapter 2). Children's activities that were self-directed, integrated into the natural world, and transpiring parallel to the world of adult activity were curtailed in both urban and rural settings, albeit differently, with the introduction of reform movements in the nineteenth century. The introduction of formal organizations to structure children's time and play along with the creation of specialized spaces to separate children's play from the world of adults are now seen as early interventions by adults into the worlds of children to reduce risk and increase safety (Buckingham 2008; Chudacoff 2007; Fass 2016; Riney-Kehrberg 2014). This interventionism was and is coupled with a rhetoric of fear about the many potential dangers to children who are left unsupervised outside the home or who take part in outdoor activities away from a suitable, adult-structured space.

The nature of "the danger" to children has shifted significantly over time. In the nineteenth century, concerns were environmental, with issues of crowding and sanitation being used to push for reform (chapter 3). The twentieth century ushered in new technologies, especially speeding automobiles, which were thought to make streets unsafe for children. Today, the idea of "stranger danger" and the fear of malevolent and deviant adults who seek to harm children is the most pervasive form of rhetoric used to keep children inside and supervised. While these concerns have transformed gradually and often overlapped, historians have noted that the contemporary fear of adults with bad intentions can be traced to the 1979 introduction of photos of missing children on milk cartons, bringing images of missing and exploited children into every American home. This intimate confrontation with missing children at mealtime was followed by television shows such as *America's Most Wanted* that profiled cases of missing children from across the country in people's living rooms. Now, Amber Alerts interrupt broadcasts, flash on the screens of smartphones, and scroll on digital highway signs. All of these mediums present problems as they exist on a national scale in a way that makes them seem very local and nearby, heightening the sense that people predating on children is a common, ubiquitous occurrence. Dangers to adolescents include those directed at children but also include the possibilities of unsupervised teens engaging in behaviors such as drinking, drugs, and sex, that are considered to be premature forays into adulthood.

The need to keep children safe has brought them indoors, and the twenty-first century has been characterized as the age of the indoor child. Separate recreation rooms for children have been present in middle-class American homes since the twentieth century, and whether called dens or rumpus rooms or playrooms have created dedicated spaces for children's play within the home. For families who can only afford less space, children's bedrooms offer places of privacy for recreation and self-entertainment. The quality of play offered by digital technology makes indoor spaces pleasurable and desirable for children (see below). The ability to have full mental stimulation through digital experiences and

Figure 6.3. McDonald's restaurant with prominent kids' Playland in Panorama City, California. 2010 photo by J. G. Klein. Wikimedia.

rich interactive and social engagement through gaming platforms makes indoor play feel like a complete experience even if it exists outside the sensorium (Riney-Kherberg 2014: 206). Another significant trend noted by Riney-Kherberg (2014: 165–168) has been the rise of the shopping mall as a place of recreation for children, as well as play spaces within fast food restaurants, zoos, and museums (figure 6.3). These types of spaces allow for a kind of controlled socialization where parents can supervise children engaged in active play within the boundaries of an interior space. These spaces offer both climate control for year-round use, and a sense of predictability. A play space within a McDonald's will offer the same smooth, rounded plastic playground designs at every location so parents can be assured of a relatively safe and pleasurable outing with their children, where they can supervise but not necessarily participate in their play activities (figure 6.3). Of course, even the gentlest of equipment does not compensate for poor parental supervision, but cases of liability tend to focus on equipment quality and the safety of recreational spaces in ways that affect their design and maintenance rather than adult responsibility.

The cultural expectation of supervised and structured outdoor play for children developed in the 1950s in response to fears of children moving between spaces safely. Fears of motorized vehicles, kidnapping, or accidents from unsupervised play have significantly curtailed the out-of-doors as a place for children. The pervasive idea that children's outdoor play needs to be supervised has significantly limited children's outdoor time, as it is now tied to the availability of adult time for supervision (Riney-Kherberg 2014:

162–63). Adults have to give up their own free time to supervise children in their own yards, and/or set up play dates, to enable supervision for children of multiple families. This type of surveillance of children's outdoor play and the scheduling of outdoor recreation with friends are now associated with being good parents. Caring parents supervise constantly and good kids are products of constant supervision. A by-product of all this adult intervention is that being outside has become boring and undesirable for many children, and children have come to prefer the comfort and independence of indoor play as a result (Riney-Kehrberg 2014: 180). Other outdoor activities, such as the simple act of walking to school, have all but been eliminated due to concerns of risk, and children who are forced to make their way through public spaces alone due to circumstance are seen as particularly endangered.

In her recent keynote address at the Society for the Study of Childhood in the Past annual conference, archaeologist Kathryn Kamp (2015) used contemporary childhood to illustrate the pervasiveness of children in our everyday worlds, and to demonstrate what we can learn by stepping into consciousness around the spaces and objects for children that we take for granted. She noted that the most common theme in children's material culture was an overwhelming concern for child safety, particularly in the way children's spaces and objects are constructed. Underneath all playground equipment are soft, cushioned surfaces, and metal has been replaced by plastic. Bright, primary colors are not only considered stimulating, but help make obstacles in play spaces obvious to busy children so they will avoid accidental contact. Toys and play equipment are segregated by size so children of different ages can play separately, removing the danger of using equipment either too small or too large for safe play. Age-segregated play also eliminates concerns of encountering vastly different-sized bodies that could result in unintentional harm to younger children.

Much of this demand for safety is tied to litigation and concerns for lawsuits being brought against the owners and operators of playgrounds and toy manufacturers. One of the earliest such lawsuits was in 1915, when parents sued the school board of Tacoma, Washington, on behalf of their son, who had been injured falling off a swing (Riney-Kherberg 2014: 167). The Consumer Product Safety Commission (CPSC) was formed in response to continuous litigation over children's play spaces and objects.

Their work has included advocating for soft, contained play equipment, conducting and publishing rigorous studies on safety, and enforcing standards through prosecuting manufacturers of children's toys and play devices deemed dangerous and defective. They also have provided educational literature for children and parents on playground safety and issue product warnings.

In this environment of highly regulated outdoor play and a strong preference for contained indoor play, children and adolescents who engage in unstructured, outdoor play are characterized as being nonconformist and even deviant in popular discourse (Aitken 2001). Children who are seen outside doing what they want to do are up to no good and are labeled as the products of poor parenting (Riney-Kehrberg 2014: 162). Archaeologist Bob Muckle (2016) has become involved in a collaborative project with one such community: skateboarders. Skateboarders are seen as transgressive youth who (mis)appropriate public spaces for their recreation. In 1977, a skateboard park was constructed in West Vancouver known as the "West Van Skate Park." It was among the oldest of such skate parks in the world and one of the first in North America. The space is legendary in the skater community, and they have initiated a project that combines heritage, preservation, and art around the park. There has been a sincere desire to include a public and community archaeology component to this project that hopefully would unbury the park and perhaps return it to some kind of use. At the very least, it is felt that archaeological investigation would help to give the space the public recognition it deserves for its place in the history of an enduringly popular adolescent pastime.

The skate park was buried in 1984 after it became labeled as a "teenage wasteland" of bonfires and unsanctioned beer drinking. Members of the skating community and those sympathetic to their efforts consider the space significant as a locus of adolescent activities both around a sport and around important spheres of independent teen activity in an age of surveillance and intervention. The site is now on the grounds of a school in a white, conservative neighborhood and the landowners have chosen to deny access for any archaeological research without an explanation. Muckle (2016) has interpreted this rejection of an archaeological investigation and other heritage and preservation efforts as a silencing of alternative youth activities and histories reflecting contemporary characterizations of the skater community.

The Turn to Digital "Material Culture"

Perhaps one of the most significant trends that characterizes twenty-first-century childhood and adolescence is the migration of social worlds from the material to the digital. The spaces and objects of childhood and adolescence are no longer primarily in the material world and instead are being heavily augmented or replaced by a largely intangible, digital one. Many of these digital spaces are seen as benign, such as movies being streamed online rather than being sold and rented as VHS tapes, DVDs, or Blu-ray disks. The streaming of music is not considered a particularly dangerous activity or cause for concern, although it might offend those who prefer the purity of vinyl. Not all aspects of the move to digital culture are met with such acceptance, however.

Today's children and adolescents are often called the digital generation, a concept that combines technology with ideas about childhood and youth, particularly around current hopes and fears held by adults concerning social change (Buckingham 2008: 13). Indeed, the migration of children's worlds from the material to the digital is often characterized as a threat to if not the destruction of childhood. Online spaces are considered quite dangerous because of exposure to pornography, violence, and pedophiles, and spending time in these spaces is associated with significant negative physical and psychological consequences for children. These consequences include unhealthy lifestyles related to obesity and inactivity, as well as exposure to inconsequential violence in digital contexts that results in the desensitization to actual violence in the world (Anderson, Gentile, and Buckley 2007). In a time when children's lives are structured by adult supervision, containment, and surveillance, online activity has become a highly independent space for children. Children and adolescents often outpace their parents in understanding and navigating digital worlds, and parents recognize that their relative ignorance makes it difficult if not impossible to intervene effectively in children's online activities. A major concern of contemporary parenting is how does one supervise children in digital spaces? Interestingly, and erroneously, this rhetoric has led to claims that today's children have some kind of innate digital knowledge and literacy that is denied to adults, resulting in concepts like "digital native" (Buckingham 2008: 41).

Scholars outside the parental fold are far less alarmist over this transition from physical forms of entertainment to digital ones. As Carroll

Pursell (2015: 51) noted, media is the plural form of medium and digital media can be likened to any other technological change in the history of children's play and social interaction. As with many other technologies in the past, digital forms of entertainment are designed for certain types of play and interaction, but children still are active agents in creating and recreating digital media. It is still an imaginative and innovative space for children that is responsive to their needs and interests and also, through outlets like coding and game making, can become a highly creative space as well. Online, digital interactions allow for the creation of new identities and enable children and adolescents to situationally "try on" different persona as ways of interacting with others online (Buckingham 2008). The same types of social disparities that existed in the past around the ability of a family to purchase the right toy or experience or outfit for a child persist in the age of the digital. Not all families can afford the type of internet access or digital platforms their children desire so they can participate in spaces of virtual play and interaction.

One of the reasons that raising the digital generation has become so expensive is that the technology that enables access to digital worlds is either designed for individual use, or has been culturally structured to be used independently by American consumers. American homes now have multiple televisions, computers, and game systems so that individual family members can simultaneously be connected to digital worlds of their choosing without inconveniencing one another. A family all sitting on the couch together watching the same television like the Simpsons is a relic of the twentieth century. Smartphones, personal gaming platforms, and virtual reality devices are designed as single person interfaces. There is an intertextuality and interactivity among such platforms, technologies, and medias, and children and adolescents can shift among them at will (Buckingham 2008: 88). Howard Chudacoff (2007: 202) has aptly characterized the internet as a space of "parallel play," which is a form of play commonly associated with very young children playing in the same space with the same objects but without direct communication. While some games are certainly interactive and collaborative, others allow for completely independent experiences in the company of others. Parallel play has been coopted and extended from preschool play mats to children and adolescents in virtual worlds.

The implications of a migration from the material to the intangible in children's play is highly consequential for archaeology, and archaeologists have not been unresponsive to this shift. It is worth thinking about how entire categories of children's objects now exist almost exclusively on digital platforms, such as movies, music, and games. Instead of an abundance of material objects to contemplate, archaeologists are left with a handful of technological interfaces as the material conduit to complex digital worlds. Contemporary archaeology is providing a rich platform for studying digital technology as an archaeological subject. While the archaeology of contemporary media is not concerned with childhood in particular, the insights provided by such scholarship are a useful way of thinking about how we might envision an archaeology of twenty-first-century digital childhoods.

It has been argued that archaeological interests in contemporary and digital media are no different than the enduring fascination the discipline has with technology in general. Digital media is just another innovation in human technology (Perry and Morgan 2015; Pursell 2015). Media and digital archaeologies are intersected with the material world, and are focused on human/nonhuman interactions like many forms of archaeological inquiry (Piccini 2015). In this way, media archaeology is material as it looks at cultural layers of technology and the tensions that occur when technology migrates and has to be accommodated by human actors. Some aspects of media archaeology are quite literal and focus on the documentation of how obsolete but recent technologies are discarded (Bailey 2015) while others involve the archaeological excavation of relatively recent forms of media, such as the famously terrible "E.T. the Extra-terrestrial" game intentionally destroyed by Atari (Reinhard 2015). Such studies have helped shed light on how technologies of media change in an era of rapid replacement due to technological innovation and market demands. These insights are incredibly relevant for thinking about children and adolescents as consumers and agents in the digital marketplace.

Perhaps the most germane aspect of media and digital archaeologies for an archaeology of childhood is the emerging field of archaeogaming, which is gaining a great deal of traction as an area of scholarly interest. Morgan (2016: 9–10) outlined the broad scope of the archaeology of gaming as a study of the history and materiality of games as an artifact that can include critiquing content, creating and developing games, literally excavating gaming material culture, using gaming strategies to query past landscapes, and examining deep communities of practice. Within this area of study are those who seek to illuminate the material culture of the immaterial by creating "archaeological" methods for "excavation" across platforms as a way of examining virtual material worlds (Reinhard 2016: 19–22). Understanding these virtual material worlds can help illuminate the social experiences of those who enter into them.

Shawn Graham (2016: 16–18) has explained that archaeological explorations of games are multifaceted and include examining the cultural rules that structure games and game play, the possibilities for action and nonaction in games, and the study of narrative, particularly analyzing the story that emerges as the result of an individual's choices or within which game action takes place. He argued that it is also possible to study games typologically, not in terms of genre or marketing category, but typologies that try to distill essential features of game experiences in order to understand how games differ and coalesce to create narrative genres. Archaeological analyses of games can also involve investigating dimensions of space, such as how games treat perspective, topography, the environment, and relationships of time and space. Taking an archaeological lens toward video games offers a particular way of exploring how games can enable or demand particular kinds of thinking on the part of the designer or the user. This approach illustrates how archaeological concerns of materiality, and dimensions of time and space, can be transferred to studying new digital media for children's play and entertainment. In this light, digital "material culture" is simply a new genre of technology to be explored using many of the same ideas, techniques, and approaches that archaeologists use in the material world.

Some Thoughts

This chapter was designed to showcase research in contemporary archaeology and material culture studies beyond the archaeological fold that offered new insights into childhood in America today. The idea of becoming conscious of what we take for granted exposes unarticulated ideas about children not only in the present, but in the American past as well. When beginning this chapter, I thought it would be a really interesting and current addition to the book, but at its completion I realize this chapter is much more important than that. For decades, archaeologists have critiqued their own discipline for unquestioningly relying on their own personal understandings of childhood and projecting those ideas unthinkingly into the past. Such projections resulted in a lack of interest in children as archaeological subjects. Dismissing children as economically dependent and unproductive, as individuals uninvolved in decision-making, as students and learners of how to be an adult, and as people irrelevant as cultural influencers have all been called out as derivative of contemporary constructions of childhood. The same scholars who levied these critiques addressed these disciplinary failings by turning to to the ethnographic record to demonstrate diversity in cross-cultural childhood experiences and constructions, and to offer alternative models for thinking about childhood in the past.

What has not been undertaken is a deeper, richer exploration of the biases and understandings of childhood we hold as American archaeologists looking into the past. I think this chapter is a strong move in this direction. This chapter used the tactics and scholarship of our own discipline to call into consciousness the dynamics of childhood we witness every day. While archaeology and history cannot illuminate all aspects of contemporary childhood, this kind of examination creates a parity between how we view and experience children and adolescents in our daily lives in contemporary America and how we might wish to understand childhood and adolescence in the American past. Interestingly, the research in this chapter does not reveal children who are disempowered, irrelevant, and without influence, but rather demonstrates that in contemporary America children determine how adults structure their time and prioritize spending, and illustrates how complex and nuanced children's lives are in America today.

REFERENCES CITED

Aitken, Stuart C.
2001   *Geographies of Young People*. Routledge, New York.
Anderson, Craig A., Douglas A. Gentile, and Katherine E. Buckley
2007   *Violent Video Game Effects on Children and Adolescents: Theory, Research, and Public Policy*. Oxford University Press, Oxford.
Ariès, Philippe
1962   *Centuries of Childhood: A Social History of Family Life*. Vintage Books, New York.
Ashby, LeRoy
1997   *Endangered Children, Dependency, Neglect, and Abuse in American History*. Twayne Publishing, New York.
Bailey, Greg
2015   Symmetrical Media Archaeology: Boundary and Context. *Journal of Contemporary Archaeology* 21(1): 41–52.
Barile, Kerri S., and Jamie C. Brandon
2004   *Theorizing the Domestic Sphere in Historical Archaeology*. University of Alabama Press, Tuscaloosa.
Barrett, Autumn R., and Michael L. Blakey
2011   Life Histories of Enslaved Africans in Colonial New York: A Bioarchaeological Study of the New York African Burial Ground. In *Social Bioarchaeology*, edited by Sabrina C. Agarwal and Bonnie A. Glencross, pp. 212–251. Blackwell Studies in Global Archaeology 14. Wiley-Blackwell, Chichester, UK.
Barton, C. P., and K. Somerville
2012   Play Things: Children's Racialized Mechanical Banks and Toys, 1870–1930. *International Journal of Historical Archaeology* 16: 47–85.
2016   *Historical Racialized Toys in the United States*. Routledge, New York.
Bassett, Everett
1994   "We Took Care of Each Other Like Families Were Meant To": Gender, Social Organization, and Wage Labor among the Apache at Roosevelt. In *Those of Little Note: Gender, Race, and Class in Historical Archaeology*, edited by E. Scott, pp. 55–80. University of Arizona Press, Tucson.
Baugher, S.
2001   Visible Charity: The Archaeology, Material Culture, and Landscape Design of New York City's Municipal Almshouse Complex, 1736–1797. *International Journal of Historical Archaeology* 5(2): 175–202.
2009   Historical Overview of the Archaeology of Institutional Life. In *The Archaeol-*

ogy of Institutional Life, edited by April M. Beisaw and James G. Gibb, pp. 5–16. University of Alabama Press, Tuscaloosa.

Baugher, S., and R. F. Veit

2014 *The Archaeology of American Cemeteries and Gravemarkers*. University Press of Florida, Gainesville.

Baxter, Jane Eva

2000 An Archaeology of Childhood: Children and Material Culture in Nineteenth-Century America. PhD dissertation, Department of Anthropology, University of Michigan, Ann Arbor.

2005 *The Archaeology of Childhood: Children, Gender, and Material Culture*. AltaMira Press, Lanham, Maryland.

2008 The Archaeology of Childhood. *Annual Review of Anthropology* 37: 159–175.

2013 Status, Sentimentality, and Structuration: An Examination of "Intellectual Spaces" for Children in the Study of America's Historic Cemeteries. *Childhood in the Past* 6(2): 106–122.

2015a The Devil's Advocate or Our Worst Case Scenario: The Archaeology of Childhood without Any Children. In *The Archaeology of Childhood: Interdisciplinary Perspectives on an Archaeological Enigma*, edited by G. Coskunu, pp. 19–36. State University of New York Press, Albany.

2015b The Archaeological Study of Children. Electronic document, http://allegralaboratory.net/the-archaeological-study-of-children/, accessed December 7, 2016.

2015c "'Oh, What Hopes Lie Buried Here!': Nineteenth-Century Children's Headstones in Chicago's Garden Cemeteries." In *Lebenswelten von Kindern und Frauen in der Vormoderne: Archäologische und Anthropologische Forschungen in memoriam Brigtte Lohrke*. PaläowissenschaftlicheStudien, Vol. 4, edited by R. Kory, pp. 1–16. Curach Bhan Publications, Berlin.

2016 Adult Nostalgia and Children's Toys Past and Present. *International Journal of Play* 5(3):230–243.

2017 Archaeology of Childhood. In *Oxford Bibliographies in Anthropology*, edited by John Jackson. Oxford University Press, New York.

forthcoming[a] *The Archaeology of Childhood: Children, Gender, and Material Culture*. Expanded 2nd edition, in press. Rowman and Littlefield, Lanham, Maryland.

forthcoming[b] (anticipated 2019) Emotional Practice and Perspectives on Emotion in the Archaeology of Childhood. In *Archaeologies of Heart and Emotion*, edited by Kisha Supernant, Jane Eva Baxter, Natasha Lyons, and Sonya Atalay. Springer, New York.

Baxter, Jane Eva, and Meredith A. B. Ellis

2018 Introduction: Nineteenth-Century Childhoods in Interdisciplinary and International Perspectives. In *Nineteenth-Century Childhoods in Interdisciplinary and International Perspectives*, edited by Jane Eva Baxter and Meredith A. B. Ellis, pp. 1–8. Society for the Study of Childhood in the Past Monograph Series, Vol. 6, in press. Oxbow Press, Oxford.

Baxter, Jane Eva, Shauna Vey, Erin Halstad McGuire, Suzanne Conway, and Deborah E. Blom
2017   Reflections on Interdisciplinarity in the Study of Childhood in the Past. *Childhood in the Past* 10(1): 1–15.

Beales, Ross
1975   In Search of the Historical Child: Miniature Adulthood and Youth in Colonial New England. *American Quarterly* 27(4): 379–398.

Beaudry, Mary C.
2009   Bodkin Biographies. In *The Materiality of Individuality: Archaeological Studies of Individual Lives*, edited by C. L. White, pp. 95–108. Springer, New York.

Beaudry, Mary C., K. J. Goldstein, and C. Chartier
2003   Archaeology of the Plymouth Colony in Massachusetts. In *The English in America, 1497–1696*, edited by S. A. Tuck and B. Gaulton, pp. 155–185. Avalon Chronicles, Vol. 8. Memorial University, St. John's, Newfoundland.

Beaumont, Lesley A.
2012   *Childhood in Ancient Athens: Iconography and Social History*. Routledge, New York.

Beecher, Catherine E.
1841   *Treatise on Domestic Economy*. Harper and Brothers, New York.

Beisaw, April
2009   Constructing Institution-Specific Site Formation Models. In *The Archaeology of Institutional Life*, edited by April M. Beisaw and James G. Gibb, pp. 49–68. University of Alabama Press, Tuscaloosa.

Beisaw, April, and James Gibb
2004   Beyond Slate Pencils: Schoolhouse Artifacts and Community History. Paper presented at the Annual Meeting of the Society for Historical Archaeology, St. Louis, Missouri.

Beisaw, April, and Jane Eva Baxter
2017   America's One-Room Schools: Sites of Regional Authority and Symbols of Local Resistance. *International Journal of Historical Archaeology* 21: 1–21.

Benes, Peter, and Jane Montague Benes
2002   Introduction. In *The Worlds of Children, 1620–1920*, edited by P. Benes, pp. 5–8. The Dublin Seminar for New England Folklife Annual Proceedings, Vol. 27. Boston University Scholarly Publications, Boston.

Bernstein, Robin
2011   *Racial Innocence: Performing American Childhood from Slavery to Civil Rights*. New York University Press, New York.

Berrol, Selma C.
1992   Immigrant Children at School, 1880–1940. In *Small Worlds: Children and Adolecents in America 1850–1950*, edited by E. West and P. Petrik, pp. 41–60. University of Kansas Press, Lawrence.
1995   *Growing Up American: Immigrant Children in America Then and Now*. Twayne, New York.

Blakey, Michael L.
1998 The New York African Burial Ground Project: An Examination of Enslaved Lives, a Construction of Ancestral Ties. *Transforming Anthropology* 7(1): 53–58.

Bohan, R.
1988 A Home Away from Home: Bellefontaine Cemetery, St. Louis and the Rural Cemetery Movement. *Prospects* 13: 135–79.

Boydston, Jeanne
1990 *Home and Work: Housework, Wages, and the Ideology of Labor in the Early Republic.* Oxford University Press, New York.

Brandon, Jamie
2004 Reconstructing Domesticity and Segregating Households: The Intersections of Gender and Race in the Postbellum South. In *Theorizing the Domestic Sphere in Historical Archaeology*, edited by Kerri S. Barile and Jamie C. Brandon, pp. 197–209. University of Alabama Press, Tuscaloosa.
2013 Bear Grease in the Bear State and the Power of Artifacts in Context. Electronic document, https://fartheralong.wordpress.com/2013/07/10/bear-grease-in-the-bear-state-the-power-of-artifacts-in-context/, accessed July 20, 2013.

Brighton, S. A.
2001 Prices that Suit the Times: Shopping for Ceramics at Five Points. *Historical Archaeology* 35(3): 16–30.
2008 Degrees of Alienation: The Material Evidence of the Irish and Irish American Experience, 1850–1910. *Historical Archaeology* 42(4): 132–153.

Buchli, Victor, and Gavin Lucas
2000 Children, Gender, and the Material Culture of Domestic Abandonment in the Late Twentieth Century. In *Children and Material Culture*, edited by J. Sofaer Derevenski, pp. 131–138. Routledge, New York.

Buckingham, David
2000 *After the Death of Childhood: Growing Up in the Age of Electronic Media.* Polity Press, Malden, Massachusetts.
2008a Introducing Identity. In *Youth Identity and Digital Media*, edited by David Buckingham, pp. 1–23. MIT Press, Cambridge, Massachusetts.

Buckingham, David (editor)
2008b *Youth, Identity, and Digital Media.* MIT Press, Cambridge, Massachusetts.

Bunow, Miriam Jennie
2009 The Archaeology of Childhood: Toys in Nineteenth-Century Upstate New York. Master's thesis, Department of Anthropology, State University of New York at Binghamton.

Cable, Mary
1975 *The Little Darlings: A History of Child-Rearing in America.* Thames and Hudson, New York.

Calvert, Karin
1992 *Children in the House: The Material Culture of Early Childhood, 1600–1900.* Northeastern University Press, Boston.

Camp, Stacey Lynn
2013   *The Archaeology of Citizenship*. University Press of Florida, Gainesville.
2016   Landscapes of Japanese American Internment. *Historical Archaeology* 50(1): 169–186.

Carter, Sarah Anne
2002   Sickness and Death in Doll Play, 1850–1897. In *The Worlds of Children, 1620–1920*, edited by P. Benes, pp. 24–41. The Dublin Seminar for New England Folklife Annual Proceedings, Vol. 27. Boston University Scholarly Publications, Boston.

Casella, Eleanor Conlin
2007   *The Archaeology of Institutional Confinement*. University Press of Florida, Gainesville.
2009   On the Enigma of Incarceration: Philosophical Approaches to Confinement in the Modern Era. In *The Archaeology of Institutional Life*, edited by April M. Beisaw and James G. Gibb, pp. 17–32. University of Alabama Press, Tuscaloosa.
2011   Playthings: Archaeology and the Material Ambiguities of Childhood. In *Children in Culture, Revisited*, edited by K. Lesnik-Oberstein, pp. 35–54. Palgrave Macmillan, London.

Catts, Wade P., and Kevin W. Cunningham
1986   Archaeological Investigations at the Welsh Tract School. *Bulletin of the Archaeological Society of Delaware* 20: 43–57.

Child, Lydia
1829   *The American Frugal Housewife*. Carter and Hendee, Boston.
1831   *The Mother's Book*. Carter and Hendee, Boston.

Chudacoff, Howard P.
2007   *Children at Play: An American History*. New York University Press, New York.

Clark, Bonnie J., and Laurie A. Wilkie
2007   The Prism of Self: Gender and Personhood. In *Identity and Subsistence: Gender Strategies for Archaeology*, edited by Sarah Nelson, pp. 1–32. AltaMira Press, Lanham, Maryland.

Clement, Priscilla Ferguson
1997   *Growing Pains: Children in the Industrial Age, 1850–1920*. Twayne, New York.

Clements, J.
1993   The Cultural Creation of Feminine Gender: An Example from Nineteenth-Century Military Households at Fort Independence, Boston. *Historical Archaeology* 27(4): 39–64.

Cohen, Ronald D.
1985   Child-Saving and Progressivism, 1885-1915. In *American Childhood: A Research Guide and Historical Handbook*, edited by J. Hawes and N.R. Hiner. Greenwood Press, Westport Connecticut.

Cohn, Michael
1983   Evidence for Children at Revolutionary War Sites. *Northeast Historical Archaeology* 12(1): 40–43.

Connolly, Thomas J., Christopher L. Ruiz, Jeanne McLaughlin, Guy L. Tasa, and Elizabeth Kallenbach
2010   The Archaeology of a Pioneer Family Cemetery in Western Oregon, 1854–1879. *Historical Archaeology* 44(4): 28–45.

Cook, Daniel
2004   *The Commodification of Childhood: The Children's Clothing Industry and the Rise of the Child Consumer*. Duke University Press.

Cott, Nancy F.
1978   Notes toward an Interpretation of Antebellum Childrearing. *Psychohistory Review* 6(4): 4–20.

Cowan, Ruth Schwartz
1983   *More Work for Mother: The Ironies of Household Technology from the Open Hearth to the Microwave*. Basic Books, New York.

Craig, Lee A.
1993   *To Sow One Acre More: Childbearing and Farm Productivity in the Antebellum North*. Johns Hopkins University Press, Baltimore, Maryland.

Crawford, Sally
1991   "When Do Anglo-Saxon Children Count?" *Journal of Theoretical Archaeology* 2: 17–24.
2009   The Archaeology of Play Things: Theorizing a Toy Stage in the "Biography" of Objects. *Childhood in the Past* 2: 56–71.

Crist, Thomas A.
2005   Babies in the Privy: Prostitution, Infanticide, and Abortion in New York City's Five Points District. *Historical Archaeology* 39(1): 19–46.

Cross, Gary
1997   *Kid's Stuff: Toys and the Changing World of American Childhood*. Harvard University Press, Cambridge, Massachusetts.
2004   *The Cute and the Cool: Wondrous Innocence and Modern American Children's Culture*. Oxford University Press, Oxford.

Dale, Emily
2015   Households of the Overseas Chinese in Aurora, Nevada. In *Beyond the Walls: New Perspectives on the Archaeology of Historical Households,* edited by Kevin Fogle, James Nyman, and Mary C. Beaudry, pp. 144–160. University Press of Florida, Gainesville.

Danforth, Marie Elaine
2004   African American Men, Women, and Children in Nineteenth-Century Natchez, Mississippi: An Analysis of the City Cemetery Sexton's Records. In *Engendering African American Archaeology: A Southern Perspective*, edited by Jillian E. Galle and Amy L. Young, pp. 237–263. University of Tennessee Press, Knoxville.

Darnall, M.
1983   The American Cemetery as Picturesque Landscape: The Bellefontaine Cemetery, St. Louis. *Winterthur Portfolio* 18: 249–269.

Dawson, M.
2003 The Miniaturizing of Girlhood: Nineteenth-Century Playtime and Gendered Theories of Development. In *The American Child: A Cultural Studies Reader*, edited by C. F. Levander and C. J. Singley, pp. 63–84. Rutgers University Press, New Brunswick, New Jersey.

De Cunzo, Lu Ann
1995 Reform, Respite, Ritual: An Archaeology of the Magdalen Society of Philadelphia, 1800–1850. *Historical Archaeology* 29(3): 1–68.
2001 On Reforming the "Fallen" and Beyond: Transforming Continuity at the Magdalen Society of Philadelphia, 1845–1916. *International Journal of Historical Archaeology* 5(1): 19–43.
2004 *A Historical Archaeology of Delaware: People, Contexts, and the Cultures of Agriculture*. University of Tennessee Press, Knoxville.
2006 Exploring the Institution: Reform, Confinement, Social Change. In *Historical Archaeology*, edited by M. Hall and S. W. Silliman, pp. 167–189. Blackwell, Malden, Massachusetts.

Deetz, James
1977 *In Small Things Forgotten: The Archaeology of Early American Life*. Anchor Books, New York.

de Melo, Andrea
2011 Civil War Attitudes as Seen in Children's Media and Toys. *Journal of Interdisciplinary Undergraduate Research* 3: 1–17.

Devine, Jamie
2012 Bringing Joy and Laughter to Camp: A Study of Children Living in Military Forts. Bachelor's thesis, Department of Anthropology, University of Colorado at Colorado Springs.
2014 *Toying with Americanization: The Impact of Corporate Paternalism on Immigrant Children in Early Twentieth-Century Colorado Coal Mining Communities*. Master's thesis, Department of Anthropology, University of Denver.

Douglas, A.
1975 Heaven Our Home: Consolation Literature in the Northern United States, 1830–1880. In *Death in America*, edited by D. E. Stannard, pp. 49–68. University of Pennsylvania Press, Philadelphia.

Dozier, Crystal A.
2016 Finding Children without Toys: The Archaeology of Children at Shabbona Grove, Illinois. *Childhood in the Past* 9(1): 58–74.

Edwards-Ingram, Ywone
2001 African American Medicine and the Social Relations of Slavery. In *Race and the Archaeology of Identity*, edited by C. Orser, pp. 34–53. University of Utah Press, Salt Lake City.

Elia, Ricardo J., and Al B. Wesolowsky (editors)
1991 *Archaeological Excavations at the Uxbridge Almshouse Burial Ground in Uxbridge, Massachusetts*. British Archaeological Reports Series No. 563. Tempus Repartum, Oxford.

Ellis, Meredith
2014a *The Children of Spring Street: The Bioarchaeology of Children at New York's Spring Street Presbyterian Church.* PhD dissertation, Maxwell School of Graduate Studies, Department of Anthropology, Syracuse University, Syracuse, New York.
2014b A Disciplined Childhood: A Social Bioarchaeology of the Subadults at the Spring Street Presbyterian Church. In *Tracing Childhood: Bioarchaeological Investigations of Early Lives in Antiquity*, edited by Jennifer L. Thompson, Marta P. Alfonso-Durruty, and John J. Crandall, pp. 139–158. University Press of Florida, Gainesville.

Erikson, Erik H.
1968 *Identity, Youth, and Crisis.* W. W. Norton, New York.

Ewen, Elizabeth
1985 *Immigrant Women in the Land of Dollars: Life and Culture on the Lower East Side, 1880–1925.* New York University Press, New York.

Fass, Paula
2016 *The End of American Childhood: A History of Parenting from Life on the Frontier to the Managed Child.* Princeton University Press, Princeton, New Jersey.

Feister, Lois
2009 The Orphanage at Schuyler Mansion. In *The Archaeology of Institutional Life*, edited by April M. Beisaw and James G. Gibb, pp. 105–116. University of Alabama Press, Tuscaloosa.

Field, M. J., and R. E. Behrman (editors)
2003 *When Children Die: Improving Palliative and End-of-Life Care for Children and Their Families.* National Academies Press, Washington, D.C.

Finkelstein, Barbara, and Kathy Vandell
1984 The Schooling of American Childhood: The Emergence of Learning Communities. In *A Century of Childhood, 1820–1920*, pp. 65–96. Margaret Woodbury Strong Museum, Rochester, New York.

Fitts, R.
1999 The Archaeology of Middle-Class Domesticity and Gentility in Victorian Brooklyn. *Historical Archaeology* 33(1): 39–62.
2001 The Rhetoric of Reform: The Five Points Missions and the Cult of Domesticity. *Historical Archaeology* 35(3): 115–132.

Fogle, Kevin R., James A. Nyman, and Mary C. Beaudry (editors)
2015 *Beyond the Walls: New Perspectives on the Archaeology of Historical Households.* University Press of Florida, Gainesville.

Forman-Brunell, Miriam
1998 *Made to Play House: Dolls and the Commercialization of American Girlhood, 1830–1930.* Johns Hopkins University Press, Baltimore, Maryland.
2009 Barbie in "Life": The Life of Barbie. *Journal of the History of Childhood and Youth* 3: 303–311.

Forman-Brunell, Miriam, and Jennifer Dawn Whitney
2015 *Dolls Studies: The Many Meanings of Girls' Toys and Play.* Peter Lang, New York.

Frenza, P. J.
1989   Communities of the Dead: Tombstones as a Reflection of Social Organization. *Markers* 6: 137–158.

Gibb, James, and April Beisaw
2000   Learning Cast Up from the Mire: Archaeological Investigations of Schoolhouses in the Northeastern United States. *Northeastern Historical Archaeology* 29: 107–129.

Graff, Harvey J.
1997   *Conflicting Paths: Growing Up in America*. Harvard University Press, Cambridge, Massachusetts.

Graff, Rebecca, Timothy J. Scarlett, and Jane Eva Baxter
2016   The Last Neighborhood: Archaeological Investigations of the Haymarket Martyrs' Memorial, Forest Home Cemetery. Paper presented at the Midwest Historical Archaeology Conference, Detroit, Michigan.

Graham, Shawn
2016   The Archaeologist Who Studied Video Games and the Things He Learned There. *The SAA Archaeological Record* 16(5): 16–19.

Graves-Brown, P., R. Harrison, and A. Piccini (editors)
2013   *The Oxford Handbook of Archaeology of the Contemporary World*. Oxford University Press, Oxford.

Green, Harvey
1984   Scientific Thought and the Nature of Children in America, 1820–1920. In *A Century of Childhood, 1820–1920*, pp. 121–138. Margaret Woodbury Strong Museum, Rochester, New York.

Griggs, H. J.
1999   GO CUIRE DIA RATH BLATH ORT (God Grant That You Prosper and Flourish): Social and Economic Mobility among the Irish in Nineteenth-Century New York City. *Historical Archaeology* 33(1): 81–101.

Griswold, Robert
1993   *Fatherhood in America: A History*. Basic Books, New York.

Groover, Mark D.
2008   *The Archaeology of North American Farmsteads*. University Press of Florida, Gainesville.

Hall, G. Stanley
1897   *A Study of Dolls*. Kellogg, New York.
1916   *Adolescence*. Appleton, New York.

Hall, John D., Scott O'Mack, Michael P. Heilen, Karen Swope, Joseph T. Hefner, Kristen Sewell, and Marlesa Gray
2008   *End-of-Fieldwork Report for the Joint Courts Complex Archaeological Data Recovery Project*. Prepared for the Pima County Administrator's Office by Statistical Research Inc. Tuscon, Arizona. http://webcms.pima.gov/UserFiles/Servers/Server_6/File/Government/Joint%20Courts%20Archaeological%20Project/General%20Information%20and%20Reports/JCC-EOF-final.pdf.

Hawes, Joseph M., and N. Ray Hiner
1985   *American Childhood: A Research Guide and Historical Handbook*. Greenwood Press, Westport.

Heininger, Mary Lynn Stevens
1984   Children, Childhood, and Change in America, 1820-1920. In *A Century of Childhood, 1820-1920*, edited by Margaret Woodbury Strong Museum, pp. 1-32. Rochester, New York.

Helton, Emily G.
2010   Education and Gender in New Philadelphia. *Historical Archaeology* 44(1): 112–124.

Herndon, Ruth Wallis
2009   *Children Bound to Labor: The Pauper Apprentice System in Early America*. Cornell University Press, Ithaca, New York.

Hicks, Dan, and Mary C. Beaudry
2006   *The Cambridge Companion to Historical Archaeology*. Cambridge University Press, Cambridge, UK.

Hiner, N. Ray, and Joseph M. Hawes
1985   *Growing Up in America: Children in Historical Perspective*. University of Illinois Press, Champaign, Illinois.

Howson, Jean, and Leonard Bianchi
2014   *Covert Larch: Archaeology of a Jersey City Neighborhood. Data Recovery for the Route 1 and 9T (25) St. Paul's Viaduct Replacement Project, Jersey City, Hudson County, New Jersey*. Prepared for New Jersey Department of Transportation by the RBA Group Cultural Resources Division.

Hutson, Scott R.
2006   Children Not at Chuncucmil: A Relational Approach to Young Subjects. In *The Social Experience of Childhood in Ancient Mesoamerica*, edited by Traci Ardren and Scott R. Hutson, pp. 103–133. Mesoamerican Worlds. University Press of Colorado, Boulder.

Jacobson, Lisa
2008a   Advertising, Mass Merchandising, and the Creation of Children's Consumer Culture. In *Children and Consumer Culture in American Society: A Historical Handbook and Guide*, edited by L. Jacobson, pp. 3–26. Praeger, Westport, Connecticut.
2008b   Parents and Children in the Consumer Household: Regulating and Negotiating the Boundaries of Children's Consumer Freedoms and Family Obligations. In *Children and Consumer Culture in American Society: A Historical Handbook and Guide*, edited by L. Jacobson, pp. 63–84. Praeger, Westport, Connecticut.

Kaestle, Carl F.
1983   *Pillars of the Republic: Common Schools and American Society, 1780–1860*. Hill and Wang, New York.

Kamp, Kathryn
2001   Where Have All the Children Gone? The Archaeology of Childhood. *Journal of Archaeological Method and Theory* 8(1): 1–34.

2015   Children are Everywhere: Objects and Spaces of Childhood in Contemporary America. Keynote Address at the Society for the Study of Childhood in the Past Annual Meeting, Chicago, IL.

Kamp-Whittaker, April

2010   *Through the Eyes of a Child: The Archaeology of a WWII Japanese American Internment at Amache*. Master's thesis, Department of Anthropology, University of Denver.

Kerber, Linda, Nancy F. Cott, Robert Gross, Lynn Hunt, Carroll Smith-Rosenberg, and Christine M. Stansell

1989   Beyond Roles, Beyond Spheres: Thinking about Gender in the Early Republic. *William and Mary Quarterly*, 3rd series 46(3): 565–581.

Ketz, Anne K., Elizabeth J. Abel, and Andrew J. Schmidt

2005   Public Image and Private Reality: An Analysis of Differentiation in a Nineteenth-Century St. Paul Bordello. *Historical Archaeology* 39(1): 74–88.

LeeDecker, C.

2009   Preparing for an Afterlife on Earth: The Transformation of Mortuary Behavior in Nineteenth-Century North America. In *International Handbook of Historical Archaeology*, edited by T. Majewsjki and D. Gaimster, pp. 141–57. Springer, New York.

Leone, Mark

2005   *The Archaeology of Liberty in an American Capital: Excavations in Annapolis*. University of California Press, Berkeley.

Lewis, Kenneth E.

2010   Function, Circumstance, and the Archaeological Record: The Elusive Past at Saint's Rest. In *Beneath the Ivory Tower: The Archaeology of Academia*, edited by R. Skowronek and K. Lewis, pp. 9–35. University Press of Florida, Gainesville.

Lightfoot, Kent

1995   Culture Contact Studies: Redefining the Relationship between Prehistoric and Historical Archaeology. *American Antiquity* 60(2): 199–217.

Lillehammer G.

1989   A Child Is Born: The Child's World in an Archaeological Perspective. *Norwegian Archaeological Review* 22(2): 89–105.

Lindauer, O.

1996   *Historical Archaeology of the United States Industrial Indian School at Phoenix: Investigations of a Turn of the Century Trash Dump*. Office of Cultural Resource Management, Department of Anthropology, Arizona State University, Tempe.

2009   Individual Struggles and Institutional Goals: Small Voices from the Phoenix Indian School Tract Site. In *The Archaeology of Institutional Life*, edited by April M. Beisaw and James G. Gibb, pp. 86–102. University of Alabama Press, Tuscaloosa.

Lord, M. G.

1994   *Forever Barbie: The Unauthorized Biography of a Real Doll*. Avon Books, New York.

Loren, Diana DiPaolo, and Mary C. Beaudry
2006   Becoming American: Small Things Remembered. In *Historical Archaeology*, edited by M. Hall and S. W. Silliman, pp. 251–271. Blackwell, Malden, Massachusetts.

Luker, Kristin
2006   Bastardy, Fitness, and the Invention of Adolescence. In *American Families Past and Present: Social Perspectives on Transformations*, edited by Susan Ross, pp. 34–51. Rutgers University Press, New Brunswick, New Jersey.

Marten, James (editor)
2007   *Children in Colonial America*. New York University Press, New York.
2009   *Children and Youth in a New Nation*. New York University Press, New York.
2014   *Children and Youth during the Gilded Age and Progressive Era*. New York University Press, New York.

Matthews, Christopher N.
2010   *The Archaeology of American Capitalism*. University Press of Florida, Gainesville.

May, Sarah
2013   The Contemporary Material Culture of the Cult of the Infant: Constructing Children as Desiring Subjects. In *The Oxford Handbook of Archaeology of the Contemporary World*, edited by P. Graves-Brown, R. Harrison, and A. Piccini, pp. 711–725. Oxford University Press, Oxford.

Mays, Simon, Rebecca Gowland, Siân Halcrow, and Eileen Murphy
2017   Child Bioarchaeology: Perspectives on the Last Ten Years. *Childhood in the Past* 10(1): 38–56.

McBride, W. S.
1994   Civil War Material Culture and Camp Life in Central Kentucky: Archaeological Investigations at Camp Nelson. In *Look to the Earth: Historical Archaeology and the American Civil War*, edited by C. R. Geier Jr. and S. E. Winter, pp. 130–157. University of Tennessee Press, Knoxville.

McCarthy, John P.
2002   Value and Identity in the "Working-Class" Worlds of Late Nineteenth-Century Minneapolis." In *The Archaeology of Urban Landscapes: Explorations in Slumland*, edited by A. Mayne and T. Murray, pp. 145–153. Cambridge University Press, Cambridge, UK.

McGuire, Randall H.
1991   Building power into the Cultural Landscape of Broome County, New York, 1880-1940. In *The Archaeology of Inequality*, edited by R. McGuire and R. Paynter, pp. 102–124. Blackwell Press, Oxford.

McKillop, Heather
1995   Recognizing Children's Graves in Nineteenth-Century Cemeteries: Excavations in St. Thomas Anglican Churchyard, Belleville, Ontario, Canada. *Historical Archaeology* 29(2): 77–99.

McLeod, Anne Scott
1984   The Caddie Woodlawn Syndrome: American Girlhood in the Nineteenth Cen-

tury. In *A Century of Childhood, 1820–1920*, pp. 97–120. Margaret Woodbury Strong Museum, Rochester, New York.

McMurry, Sally Ann
1997 *Families and Farmhouses in Nineteenth-Century America: Vernacular Design and Social Change.* University of Tennessee Press, Knoxville.

Meckel, Richard A.
1982 Educating a Ministry of Mothers: Evangelical Maternal Associations, 1815–1860. *Journal of the Early Republic* 2(4):403–423.

Mergen, Bernard
1992 Made, Bought, and Stolen: Toys and the Culture of Childhood. In *Small Worlds: Children and Adolescents in America, 1850–1950,* edited by Elliot West and Paula Petrik, pp. 86–106. University Press of Kansas, Lawrence.

Miller, Daniel
1998 *A Theory of Shopping.* Polity Press, Cambridge, UK.

Mímisson, Kristján, and Sigurður Gylfi Magnússon
2014 Singularizing the Past: The History and Archaeology of the Small and Ordinary. *Journal of Social Archaeology* 14(2): 131–156.

Mintz, Steven
2004 *Huck's Raft: A History of American Childhood.* Belknap Press, Cambridge, Massachusetts.

Mitchell, Mary Niall
2010 *Raising Freedom's Child: Black Children and Visions of the Future after Slavery.* New York University Press, New York.

Moore, J., and E. Scott (editors)
1997 *Invisible People and Processes: Writing Gender and Childhood into European Archaeology.* Leicester University Press, London/New York.

Moore, Summer
2007 Working Parents and the Material Culture of Victorianism: Children's Toys at the Ludlow Tent Colony. In *The Archaeology of Class War,* edited by Randall McGuire and Karin Larkin, pp. 285–310. University of Colorado Press, Boulder.

Morenon, E. Pierre
2007 Rhode Island State Home and School Project Website. Electronic document, http://www.ric.edu/statehomeandschool/resourcesMorenon.html, accessed January 21, 2017.

Morgan, Colleen
2016 Video Games and Archaeology. *The SAA Archaeological Record* 16(5): 9–10.

Mrozowski, Stephen A.
2006 *The Archaeology of Class in Urban America.* Cambridge University Press, Cambridge, UK.

MSU Campus Archaeology Program Saints Rest Project
2008–2016 Electronic document, http://campusarch.msu.edu/?tag=saints-rest&paged=2, accessed July 23, 2016.

Muckle, Robert
2016 Never Say Last Run: Skateboarders Challenging the Terrain and Becoming In-

volved in Archaeology. Paper presented at the Theoretical Archaeology Group Annual Meetings, Southampton, UK.

2017   Archaeology of an Early Twentieth Century *Nikkei* Camp in the Seymour Valley: A Photo Essay. *BC Studies* 192: 125–148.

Muller, Jennifer L.

2017   Rendered Unfit: "Defective" Children in the Erie County Poorhouse. In *Bioarchaeology of Impairment and Disability: Theoretical, Ethnohistorical, and Methodological Perspectives*, edited by J. F. Byrnes and J. L. Muller, pp. 119–140. Springer, New York.

Mullins, Paul R.

2008   Marketing in a Multicultural Neighborhood: An Archaeology of Corner Stores in the Urban Midwest. *Historical Archaeology* 42(1): 88–96.

Mumma, Katherine, and Jane Eva Baxter

2018   Creating Desire and Little Consumers: Doll Advertising in U.S. Newspapers, 1860–1900. In *Nineteenth-Century Childhoods in Interdisciplinary and International Perspectives*, edited by Jane Eva Baxter and Meredith A. B. Ellis, pp. 107–126. Society for the Study of Childhood in the Past Monograph Series, Vol. 6, in press. Oxbow Press, Oxford.

Murphy, Eileen, Dave McKean, and Lynne McKerr

2015   "The cherub hastened to its native home": Memorials for Irish Immigrant Children in Early Nineteenth-Century Lowell, Massachusetts. Paper presented at the Society for the Study of Childhood in the Past Annual Meeting, Chicago, Illinois.

Napton, L. Kyle, and Elizabeth A. Greathouse

1997   *The Alteville Schoolhouse: Community and State Cooperation in Local Historical Resource Preservation*. California Department of Forestry and Fire Protection Archaeological Reports, No. 19. California Department of Forestry and Fire Protection, Sacramento.

O'Gorman, Jodie A.

2010   More than Bricks and Mortar: A Story of Community Archaeology. In *Beneath the Ivory Tower: The Archaeology of Academia*, edited by R. Skowronek and K. Lewis, pp. 242–260. University Press of Florida, Gainesville.

Onion, Rebecca

2016   *Innocent Experiments, Childhood, and the Culture of Popular Science in the United States*. University of North Carolina Press, Chapel Hill.

Orser, Charles

2007   *The Archaeology of Race and Racialization in Historic America*. University Press of Florida, Gainesville.

Paoletti, Jo B.

2012   *Pink and Blue: Telling the Boys from the Girls in America*. Indiana University Press, Bloomington.

Pattison, William

1955   The Cemeteries of Chicago: A Phase of Land Utilization. *Annals of the Association of American Geographers* 45(3): 245–257.

Pauls, Elizabeth P.
2006   The Place of Space: Architecture, Landscape, and Social Life. In *Historical Archaeology*, edited by M. Hall and S. W. Silliman, pp. 65–83. Blackwell, Malden, Massachusetts.

Pazicky, Diana Loercher
1998   *Cultural Orphans in America*. University of Mississippi Press, Jackson.

Pearson, Marlys, and Paul R. Mullins
1999   Domesticating Barbie: An Archaeology of Barbie Material Culture and Domestic Ideology. *International Journal of Historical Archaeology* 3(4): 225–259.

Peña, Elizabeth S.
1992   Educational Archaeology: Historical Archaeological Investigations at Schoolhouse 12 in the Town of LeRay, Jefferson County. *The Bulletin: Journal of the New York State Archaeological Association* 103: 10–19.

Perry, Sara, and Colleen Morgan
2015   Materializing Media Archaeologies: The MAD-P Hard Drive Excavation. *Journal of Contemporary Archaeology* 2(1): 94–104.

Phillips, Kendall R.
2002   Textual Strategies, Plastic Tactics: Reading Batman and Barbie. *Journal of Material Culture* 7(2): 123–136.

Piccini, Angela
2015   Media Archaeologies: An Invitation. *Journal of Contemporary Archaeology* 2(1): 1–8.

Praetzellis, Adrian, and Mary Praetzellis
1992   Faces and Façades: Victorian Ideology in Early Sacramento. In *The Art and Mystery of Historical Archaeology: Essays in Honor of James Deetz*, edited by Anne E. Yentsch and Mary C. Beaudry, pp. 75–100. CRC Press, Boca Raton, Florida.
2001   Managing Symbols of Gentility in the Wild West: Case Studies in Interpretive Archaeology. *American Anthropologist* 103: 645–654.

Przystupa, Paulina F.
2018   Nineteenth-Century Institutional "Education": A Spatial Approach to Assimilation and Resistance at Hoopa Valley Indian School. In *Nineteenth Century Childhoods in Interdisciplinary and International Perspectives*, edited by Jane Eva Baxter and Meredith A. B. Ellis, pp. 166–180. Society for the Study of Childhood in the Past Monograph Series, Vol. 6, in press. Oxbow Press, Oxford.

Pursell, Carroll
2015   *From Playgrounds to PlayStation: The Interaction of Technology and Play*. Johns Hopkins University Press, Baltimore, Maryland.

Rainville, L.
1999   Hanover Deathscapes: Mortuary Variability in New Hampshire, 1770–1920. *Ethnohistory* 46: 541–597.

Rand, E.
1995   *Barbie's Queer Accessories*. Duke University Press, Durham, North Carolina.

Reinhard, Andrew
2015   Excavating Atari: Where the Media Was the Archaeology. *Journal of Contemporary Archaeology* 2(1): 86–93.
2016   Toward Archaeological Tools and Methods for Excavating Virtual Spaces. *The SAA Archaeological Record* 16(5): 19–22.

Rhodes, Joel
2017   Who Bombed Santa's Workshop?: The Anti-War Toy Movement in the Vietnam Era. Paper presented at the Society for the History of Children and Youth, Camden, New Jersey.

Riney-Kehrberg, Pamela
2014   *The Nature of Childhood: An Environmental History of Growing Up in America since 1865*. University Press of Kansas, Lawrence.

Ringel, Paul
2008   Reforming the Delinquent Child Consumer: Institutional Responses to Children's Consumption from the Late Nineteenth Century to the Present. In *Children and Consumer Culture in American Society: A Historical Handbook and Guide,* edited by L. Jacobson, pp. 43–62. Praeger, Westport, Connecticut.
2015   *Commercializing Childhood: Children's Magazines, Urban Gentility, and the Ideal of the Child Consumer in the United States, 1823–1918*. University of Massachusetts Press, Amherst.

Rogers, Daniel T.
1985   Socializing Middle-Class Children: Institutions, Fables, and Work Values in Nineteenth-Century America. In *Growing Up In America: Children in Historical Perspective*, edited by N. R. Hawes and J. Hiner, pp. 119–132. Green Court Press, Bridgeport, Connecticut.

Rogers, M. F.
1999   *Barbie Culture*. Sage, London.

Rothschild, Nan
2002   Introduction. In *Children in the Prehistoric Puebloan Southwest*, edited by K. Kamp, pp. 1–13. University of Utah Press, Salt Lake City.

Rothschild, Nan, and Diana diZerega Wall
2014   *The Archaeology of American Cities*. University Press of Florida, Gainesville.

Rotman, Deborah
2009   Rural Education and Community Social Relations: Historical Archaeology at the Wea View Schoolhouse No. 8, Wabash Township, Tippecanoe County, Indiana. In *The Archaeology of Institutional Life*, edited by April M. Beisaw and James G. Gibb, pp. 69–85. University of Alabama Press, Tuscaloosa.
2015   *The Archaeology of Gender in Historic America*. University Press of Florida, Gainesville.

Rotman, Deborah L., and R. Berle Clay
2008   Urban Archaeology at the Site of the Argosy Casino: The Materiality of Social Change in the Canal Town of Lawrenceburg, Southern Indiana. *Historical Archaeology* 42(1): 47–69.

Rotundo, Anthony
1993   *American Manhood: Transformations in Masculinity from the Revolution to the Modern Era.* Basic Books, New York.

Roveland B.
2001   Archaeological Approaches to the Study of Prehistoric Children: Past Trends and Future Directions. In *Children and Anthropology: Perspectives for the Twenty-First Century*, edited by H. Schwartzman, pp. 39–56. Bergin and Garvey, Westport, Connecticut.

Rubertone, P.
2001   *Grave Undertakings: An Archaeology of Roger Williams and the Narragansett Indians.* Smithsonian Institution Press, Washington, D.C.

Saitta, Dean J.
2007   *The Archaeology of Collective Action.* University Press of Florida, Gainesville.

Schlegel, Alice, and Herbert Barry III
1991   *Adolescence: An Anthropological Inquiry.* Free Press, New York.

Schmidt, James D.
2010   *Industrial Violence and the Legal Origins of Child Labor.* Cambridge University Press, Cambridge, UK.

Schultz, Jaclyn N.
2018   "He Knows a Good Thing When He Sees It": Advertising to Children in the U.S., 1850–1900. In *Nineteenth-Century Childhoods in Interdisciplinary and International Perspectives*, edited by Jane Eva Baxter and Meredith A. B. Ellis, pp. 91–106. Society for the Study of Childhood in the Past Monograph Series, Vol. 6, in press. Oxbow Press, Oxford.

Scott, Elizabeth (editor)
1994   *Those of Little Note: Gender, Race, and Class in Historical Archaeology.* University of Arizona Press, Tucson.

Shackel, Paul
2009   *The Archaeology of American Labor and Working-Class Life.* University Press of Florida, Gainesville.

Skowronek, R., and K. Lewis
2010   *Beneath the Ivory Tower: The Archaeology of Academia.* University Press of Florida, Gainesville.

Smith, D.
1987   "Safe in the arms of Jesus": Consolation on Delaware Children's Gravestones, 1840–99. *Markers* 4: 85–106.

Snyder, E.
1992   Innocents in a Worldly World: Victorian Children's Gravemarkers. In *Cemeteries and Gravemarkers: Voices of American Culture*, edited by R. Meyer, pp. 11–30. Utah State University Press, Logan.

Sofaer Derevenski, J. (editor)
1994   Perspectives on Children and Childhood. *Archaeological Review from Cambridge* 13.2.

Sofaer Derevenski, J.
2000   Material Culture Shock: Confronting Expectations in the Material Culture of Children. In *Children and Material Culture*, edited by J. Sofaer Derevenski, pp. 3–16. Routledge, New York.
2006   *The Body as Material Culture: A Theoretical Osteoarchaeology*. Cambridge University Press, Cambridge, UK.

Somerville, Kyle
2015   "A Place for Everything and Everything in Its Place": The Cultural Context of Late Victorian Toys. In *The Archaeology of Childhood: Interdisciplinary Perspectives on an Archaeological Enigma*, edited by G. Coskunu, pp. 275–294. State University of New York Press, Albany.

Spencer-Wood, Suzanne M.
1991   Toward an Historical Archaeology of Materialistic Domestic Reform. In *The Archaeology of Inequality*, edited by Randall H. McGuire and Robert Paynter, pp. 231–287. Basil Blackwell, Oxford.
1996   Feminist Historical Archaeology and the Transformation of American Culture by Domestic Reform Movements, 1840–1925. In *Historical Archaeology and the Study of American Culture*, edited by L. De Cunzo and B. Herman, pp. 397–446. University of Tennessee Press, Knoxville.
2014   Archaeology of Childhood. In *Oxford Bibliographies in Childhood Studies*, edited by Heather Montgomery. Oxford University Press, New York.

Stansell, Christine
1986   *City of Women: Sex and Class in New York, 1798–1860*. Knopf, New York.

Starbuck, D.
1994   The Identification of Gender at Northern Military Sites of the Late Eighteenth Century. In *Those of Little Note: Gender, Race, and Class in Historical Archaeology*, edited by E. M. Scott, pp. 115–128. University of Arizona Press, Tucson.

Sterns, Peter N.
1993   Girls, Boys, and Emotions: Redefinitions and Historical Change. *Journal of American History* 8(1): 36–74.

Stewart-Abernathy, L.
2004   Separate Kitchens and Intimate Archaeology: Constructing Urban Slavery on the Antebellum Cotton Frontier in Washington, Arkansas. In *Theorizing the Domestic Sphere in Historical Archaeology*, edited by Kerri S. Barile and Jamie C. Brandon, pp. 51–74. University of Alabama Press, Tuscaloosa.

Struchtemeyer, Dena L.
2008   *Separate But Equal? The Archaeology of an Early Twentieth-Century African American School*. Master's thesis, Department of Geography and Anthropology, Louisiana State University and Agricultural and Mechanical College, Baton Rouge.

Surface-Evans, Sarah L.
2016   A Landscape of Assimilation and Resistance: The Mount Pleasant Indian Industrial Boarding School. *International Journal of Historical Archaeology* 20: 574–588.

Swords, Molly Elizabeth
2008   A Clean Slate: The Archaeology of the Donner Party's Writing Slate Fragments. Master's thesis, Department of Anthropology, University of Montana, Missoula.

Tarlow, Sarah
1999   *Bereavement and Commemoration: An Archaeology of Mortality.* Wiley-Blackwell, Berkeley, California.

Thompson, Jennifer L., Marta P. Alfonso-Durruty, and John Crandall (editors)
2014   *Tracing Childhood: Bioarchaeological Investigations of Early Lives in Antiquity.* University Press of Florida, Gainesville.

Tomaso, Matthew S., Richard F. Veit, Carissa A. DeRooy, and Stanley L. Walling
2006   Social Status and Landscape in a Nineteenth-Century Planned Industrial Alternative Community: Archaeology and Geography of Feltville, New Jersey. *Historical Archaeology* 40(1): 20–36.

Tuttle, William M.
1993   *"Daddy's Gone to War": The Second World War in the Lives of America's Children.* Oxford University Press, New York.

Urbanus, Jason
2014   Childhood Rediscovered. *Archaeology Magazine* 67(4): 22.

Valentine, Deborah
2014   Playing Progressively? Race, Reform, and Playful Pedagogies in the Origins of Philadelphia's Starr Garden Recreation Park, 1857–1904. In *Children and Youth during the Gilded Age and Progressive Era*, edited by J. Marten, pp. 19–41. New York University Press, New York.

Venovcevs, Anatolijs
2016   Playing with Fire: Children at Fort York's Ordinance and Supply Yard. *International Journal of Historical Archaeology* 20(4): 705–719.

Voss, Barbara L.
2006   Engendered Archaeology: Men, Women, and Others. In *Historical Archaeology*, edited by M. Hall and S. W. Silliman, pp. 107–127. Blackwell, Malden, Massachusetts.

Walker, Mark
2008   Aristocracies of Labor: Craft Unionism, Immigration, and Working-Class Households in West Oakland, California. *Historical Archeology* 42(1): 108–132.

Wall, Diana diZerega
1994   *The Archaeology of Gender: Separating the Spheres in Early America.* Plenum, New York.

Wall, Diana diZerega, Nan A. Rothschild, and Cynthia Copeland
2008   Seneca Village and Little Africa: Two African American Communities in Antebellum New York City. *Historical Archaeology* 42(1): 97–107.

West, Elliot
1989   *Growing Up with the Country: Childhood on the Far Western Frontier.* University of New Mexico Press, Albuquerque.

White, Carolyn, and Mary Beaudry
2009   Artifacts and Personal Identity. In *International Handbook of Historical Archaeology*, edited by T. Majewski and D. Gaimster, pp. 209–255. Springer, New York.

Wilkie, Laurie
1994   Children in the Quarters: Playtime at Oakley and Riverlake Plantations. *Louisiana Folklife* 18: 13–20.
2000   Not Merely Child's Play: Creating a Historical Archaeology of Children and Childhood. In *Children and Material Culture,* edited by J. Sofaer Derevenski, pp. 100–114. Routledge, New York.
2003   *The Archaeology of Mothering: An African American Midwife's Tale.* Routledge, New York.
2010   *The Lost Boys of Zeta Psi: A Historical Archaeology of Masculinity at a University Fraternity.* University of California Press, Berkeley.

Wilson, J.
1990   We've Got Thousands of These! What Makes an Historic Farmstead Significant. *Historical Archaeology* 24(2): 23–33.

Wood, Elizabeth
2009   Saving Childhood in Everyday Objects. *Childhood in the Past* 1(2): 151–162.

Yamin, Rebecca
2002   Children's Strikes, Parent's Rights: Paterson and Five Points. *International Journal of Historical Archaeology* 6(2): 113–127.

Yentsch, Anne Elizabeth
1994   *A Chesapeake Family and Their Slaves: A Study in Historical Archaeology.* Cambridge University Press, Cambridge, UK.
2009   Tracing Immigrant Women and Their Household Possessions in Nineteenth-Century San Francisco. In *South of Market: Historical Archaeology of 3 San Francisco Neighborhoods: The San Francisco-Oakland Bay Bridge,* edited by A. Praetzellis and M. Praetzellis, pp. 134–187. Prepared for the California Department of Transportation District 4 by the Anthropological Studies Center, Sonoma State Rohnert Park, California.

Zelizer, Viviana A.
1994   *Pricing the Priceless Child: The Changing Social Value of Children.* Princeton University Press, Princeton, New Jersey.

INDEX

Page numbers in *italics* represent images.

Adolescence, 2, 7, 26, 55, 58–60, 113–16, 154–55, 165
African American children, 25, 50, 56, 74–75, 77–78, 87, 132
Age categories, 2–3, 26, 32–33, 36, 39, 50–51, 55–56, 59, 60, 114, 124, 131
American Indian boarding schools, 9, 19–20, 102–16, 119, 121
Assimilation, 2, 8, 48, 90, 94, 103–4, 107. *See also* American Indian boarding schools; Immigrant families and children

Birthrates, 24, 39, 45, 145; and economic value of children, 126
Boys and boyhood. *See* Gender
Burials, 20, 98, 127, 129–37, 145–47. *See also* Grave markers; Infant and child mortality

Childhood: as a concept/construct, 2–3, 13–14; diversity of, 7–8; in decline, 4–6, 153–55; as natural, 32–33; as a time of innocence, 39, 42–43, 44, 49, 50–51, 60, 118, 141; uniquely American constructs of, 3–12, 22–23, 31–33, 47–48, 55–58, 97, 152–55. *See also* Science/scientific thought
Child labor, 12, 28, 36–38, 39, 45, 47, 48–49, 57, 69, 79–81, *82*; at institutions, 103–5, 107, 118–19; as seen in skeletal remains, 36, 133–34, 136. *See also* Enslaved children and families; Slavery
Children's literature, 23, *40*, 50
Child-specific material culture, 16, 23, 26–27, 29–30, 35, 67, 75. *See also* Dolls; Toys
Child-only spaces, 35, 74–75, 172–73

Class, 23, 31, 41–42, 43–46, 69, 87, 88–89, 127–28, 134–35; as expressed through material culture, 52–53, 70, 74, 83–86, 94
Clothing: as reflections of age and gender categories, 26–27, *27*, 33, *34*, *40*, 50–51, 162, 167; found at archaeological sites, 90, 98, 104, 115, 157
Colonial period, 24–31, 96, 130–31, 132–34, 167
Consumerism and children, 9–10, 60–61, 62, 64, 156–62

Dolls, 51, 54, 64, 74, 76, 87–88, 110, 120, *139*, 145, *146*, 147; Barbie dolls, 168–71. *See also* Child-specific material culture; Toys
Domestic reform movements, 42, 46, 58, 70–71

Education, 25, 35, 38, 45, 47–48, 52, *53*, 58–59, 71, 84, 103, 106–13, 120. *See also* Schools
Enslaved children and families, 28, 36–38, *37*, 76–78, 132–34, 150

Families. *See* Parents/parenting

Gender, 8, 33–34, *34*, 36, 43–44, 98; boys and boyhood, 12, 33–34, *40*, 43–44, 54, 63–64; clothing and, 28, *40*, 50–51, 162, 166–67; education and, 46, 107, 114; labor and, 46, 48, 92, 105–6; material culture and, 23, 30–31, 34, 51–52, 78, 85, 91, 101, 104, 166–71; space and, 11, 71, 73, 79–80, 100–101, 110, 120
Geographic variability, 10–11, 25, 41
Girls and girlhood. *See* Gender
Grave markers, 20, 127–28, 137–44. *See also* Burials

Headstones. *See* Grave markers
Health and sickness: class, race, and, 76, 80–81, 88, 138; environment and, 11, 176; parental concern for, 4, 7, 56, 69; in play, 145; reform and, 47, 55, 58, 72, 80; skeletal remains and, 36, 98, 133–34, 136. *See also* Infant and child mortality

Immigrant families and children, 8, 47–48, 56, 58, 70–71, 79, 107; commemoration in cemeteries and, 141–45; at industrial sites, 89–90; orphanages and, 118, 119–20; in urban neighborhoods, 81–85, 86–87
Indentured servants, 28, 35, 36
Infant and child mortality, 24, 56, 124–25, 129, 133, 150

Literature for parents. *See* Parenting guides

Mothers/mothering, 35, 36, 42–43, 44, 46, 71, 75–76

Native American children, 8–9, 17, 25, 122, 128, 130–32. *See also* American Indian boarding schools

Orphanages, 116–21; defining children as unfit or at risk and, 8, 19, 98, 117–18; as institutions of reform, 49–50; as particularly American, 116–17; result of Civil War, 12

Parents/parenting, 5, 28, 35, 39–40, 41–43, 55–56, 102, 153–54, 155–56; consumerism and, 9–10, 50–51, 60–61, 74, 158, *159*, 162–66; influence of, 6–7, 60, 173–74, 176–77; investment in children by, 69, 84–85, 88, 125–26, *140*, 157
Parenting guides, 22–23, 35, 41, 42, 46, 56, 147

Play: changing views of, 28, 32–33, 34, 43–44, 51–52, 84, 155–56, 166, 172–76, 177; doll play, 35, 54–55, 74, 78, 91, 145–47, 169–70; funeral play, 145–47; independence and, 35, 38, 43, 52, 53–54, 73, 74–75, 101, 155–56; learning and, 38, 51–52, 63–64, 102, 109–10, 120; work and, 45, 47, 71, 73, 78, 80, 84, 85
Playgrounds/playspaces, 79, *80*, 81–82, *83*, 92, 100, 172–73, 174–76

Resistance and rebellion, 23, 35, 54–55, 75, 78, 87–88, 122; against institutions, 99–100, 104–5, 106

Schools: as American institutions, 8–9, 16, 39, 42, 58–59, 95, 106–7; assimilation and, 48, 58, 81, 84, 100, 102; colleges, 113–16; high schools, 58–59, 113; one-room schools, 107–10, 112–13. *See also* American Indian boarding schools; Education
Science/scientific thought, 31–32, 41, 55–56, 59, 167
Slavery, 28, 36–38, *37*, 76–78, 132–34, 150
Small assemblages, 18, 30–31, 67–68, 93
Symbolic value of children, 32, 38, 39, 69–70, 88, 94, 117–18, *139*, 139–40, 144

Toys: archaeological over-reliance on, 16, 67–68, 93; at archaeological sites, *68*, 73–74, 76–78, 82, 84–88, 90–92, 98, 100–101, 104, 108–10, 120, 158, 167, 174; marketing and purchasing of, 9–10, 60–64, 158–59, 163–66; socialization and, 12, 28, 34–35, 51–56, 67, 166–67, 168; as symbols, 16, 53, 94, 163–66, 161, 169–71. *See also* Child-specific material culture; Consumerism and children; Dolls; Play

War, 11–12, 35, 47, 52, 63–64, 79, 90–93, 100–101

JANE EVA BAXTER is associate professor of anthropology at DePaul University in Chicago, Illinois. She has written extensively on the archaeology of childhood, including *The Archaeology of Childhood: Children, Gender, and Material Culture* and two edited volumes, *Children in Action: Perspectives on the Archaeology of Childhood* and *Nineteenth-Century Childhoods in Interdisciplinary and International Perspectives* (coedited with Meredith Ellis).

THE AMERICAN EXPERIENCE IN ARCHAEOLOGICAL PERSPECTIVE

Edited by Michael S. Nassaney

The Archaeology of Collective Action, by Dean J. Saitta (2007)
The Archaeology of Institutional Confinement, by Eleanor Conlin Casella (2007)
The Archaeology of Race and Racialization in Historic America, by Charles E. Orser Jr. (2007)
The Archaeology of North American Farmsteads, by Mark D. Groover (2008)
The Archaeology of Alcohol and Drinking, by Frederick H. Smith (2008)
The Archaeology of American Labor and Working-Class Life, by Paul A. Shackel (2009; first paperback edition, 2011)
The Archaeology of Clothing and Bodily Adornment in Colonial America, by Diana DiPaolo Loren (2010; first paperback edition, 2011)
The Archaeology of American Capitalism, by Christopher N. Matthews (2010; first paperback edition, 2012)
The Archaeology of Forts and Battlefields, by David R. Starbuck (2011; first paperback edition, 2012)
The Archaeology of Consumer Culture, by Paul R. Mullins (2011; first paperback edition, 2012)
The Archaeology of Antislavery Resistance, by Terrance M. Weik (2012; first paperback edition, 2013)
The Archaeology of Citizenship, by Stacey Lynn Camp (2013)
The Archaeology of American Cities, by Nan A. Rothschild and Diana diZerega Wall (2014; first paperback edition, 2015)
The Archaeology of American Cemeteries and Gravemarkers, by Sherene Baugher and Richard F. Veit (2014; first paperback edition, 2015)
The Archaeology of Smoking and Tobacco, by Georgia L. Fox (2015; first paperback edition, 2016)
The Archaeology of Gender in Historic America, by Deborah L. Rotman (2015; first paperback edition, 2018)
The Archaeology of the North American Fur Trade, by Michael S. Nassaney (2015; first paperback edition, 2017)
The Archaeology of the Cold War, by Todd A. Hanson (2016)
The Archaeology of American Mining, by Paul J. White (2017)
The Archaeology of Utopian and Intentional Communities, by Stacy C. Kozakavich (2017)
The Archaeology of American Childhood and Adolescence, by Jane Eva Baxter (2019)

CPSIA information can be obtained
at www.ICGtesting.com
Printed in the USA
LVHW031224070119
602433LV00004B/15/P